Comments from Pat Foran's Consumer Alert viewers:

Your segment provides a very valuable service and information to our community. It's much appreciated by this consumer, and I'm sure many others. Keep up the good work!
— Lorna Lenehan

I am a major fan of *Consumer Alert* on CTV News. I have used many of your tips and think that you have saved me a great deal.
— Cameron Gordon

Consumers such as myself really appreciate what you bring to the table — good or bad, we need to hear it.
— Barbara Best

Thank you for your excellent program, I try never to miss your segment.
— Maureen Hardie

It is greatly appreciated that you and CTV are looking out for the little guy (or girl in my case)! It is a pleasant surprise to say the least.
— Ilijana Culjak

I try to catch your segment every time it is on. I find it interesting, enlightening, and informative.
— Jim Forsyth

Your show is regularly watched. The information provided is insightful. We particularly appreciate how you make the system appear "fair." Thanks for doing a great job!
— Beverly Pinsent

Canadian
CONSUMER
ALERT

101 Ways
to Protect
Yourself
and Your
Money

PAT FORAN

**McGraw-Hill
Ryerson**

Toronto   Montréal   Boston   Burr Ridge, IL   Dubuque, IA   Madison, WI
New York   San Francisco   St. Louis   Bangkok   Bogotá   Caracas   Kuala Lumpur
Lisbon   London   Madrid   Mexico City   Milan   New Delhi   Santiago   Seoul
Singapore   Sydney   Taipei

McGraw-Hill
Ryerson Limited
A Subsidiary of The McGraw-Hill Companies

ISBN: 0-07-088767-5

1234567890 WEB 0987654321

Printed and bound in Canada.

National Library of Canada Cataloguing in Publication Data

Foran, Pat
    Canadian consumer alert: 101 ways to protect yourself and
    your money

Includes index.

ISBN 0-07-088767-5

1. Consumer education. I. Title.

TX335.F67   2001   640'.73   C2001-930785-3

Publisher: **Joan Homewood**
Editorial Co-ordinator: **Catherine Leek**
Production Co-ordinator: **Susanne Penny**
Editor: **Tita Zierer**
Interior Design and Electronic Page Composition: **Heidy Lawrance
    and Associates**
Cover Design: **Sharon Lucas**

ACKNOWLEDGEMENTS

I want to thank all the consumers who shared their stories to help make this book possible. I also want to recognize the experts who selflessly passed on their knowledge and wisdom.

Special thanks to my inspiration, my beautiful wife Carole, for her unwavering support and our precious daughters, Lisa, Vanessa and Sarah. Thanks as well to my steadfast mother, Helen, who raised ten children and taught us to care for others as well as ourselves.

A note of appreciation to the CTV Network and CFTO television for employing me in a job which I truly enjoy and allows me to help the public.

I hope whoever reads this book gets some good out of it.

CONTENTS

KEEPING YOU IN THE DRIVER'S SEAT

HOME SWEET HOME

CAVEAT EMPTOR — LET THE BUYER BEWARE!

MAKING YOUR CASH COUNT

BEYOND THE BARE NECESSITIES

INTRODUCTION

Whether you live in British Columbia or Newfoundland, chances are the problems you face every day as a consumer will not differ greatly from your Canadian neighbours. Grievance lists compiled by consumer agencies across this country indicate that the same areas continue to plague consumers, such as disputes with car dealers, auto repair shops, moving companies, modelling agencies, vacation offers, home renovators, furniture stores and electronic retailers. In our high tech age, increasingly dilemmas involving computers, Internet providers and on-line scams are also showing up as a constant source of irritation for consumers.

When I told a friend about *Canadian Consumer Alert: 101 Ways to Protect Yourself and Your Money*, he mentioned it sounded like it could save people about 10 years of bad experiences they would have had to learn the hard way. I like that assessment. I've also thought about it in terms of the well-travelled "wise uncle," who can tell you the straight goods because he's experienced life's hard knocks first-hand. This book is packed with consumer information from experts, consumer advocates, as well as people who have been ripped off and are willing to share their stories to help others. It is also filled with ways to help save you money on housing, vehicles and investments. Many of the money traps consumers fall into could be avoided with just a little knowledge. Sensibly dealing with situations as they arise and being an effective complainer can pay off over the long term and help protect you and your family. There are entire books on some of the subjects in this guide, and I encourage you to do additional reading on the topics of interest to you.

Canadian Consumer Alert summarizes 101 of the most frequently asked questions I have faced as a consumer advocate. I've been able to obtain refunds of thousands of dollars, have had dubious contracts reversed and ensured that malfunctioning automobiles were replaced. As a consumer reporter for the CTV Network based at Toronto television station CFTO, it became clear early on that the same trouble spots for consumers surface again and again. Often when I would do a report on a modelling scam, for example, I would get calls months later from other victims of a similar scheme. "If only I had known this beforehand" they would say or "Why don't you write a book with all this information." In the past, many people were embarrassed to share their stories as they were too often met with the idiom "buyer beware" — a catch-all phrase used to blame the victim. I also felt that while many people would like to know more about home inspectors, trying to get a better interest rate, or auto leasing, they may not want to buy an entire volume on just one topic. In the following pages, consumers can find out about **101 subjects** in short concise passages. I have used true life stories to introduce each Alert and to summarize the dilemma facing the consumer. The names are fictitious but the problems are real.

I have been fortunate to see life from a range of perspectives. I was born on a farm, raised in town and now live in the city. During more than 15 years in broadcasting, I've reported from some of Canada's smallest communities and now from Canada's largest city. As well as learning from consumer experts, lawyers, government officials and other professionals, I have learned from my own experiences. My parents, Gordon and Helen Foran, certainly had their hands full raising me and my nine brothers and sisters. Later when my mother had to tackle the job on her own, she became a consumer expert searching for deals on food, clothing and life's other necessities. I also learned early to be an effective complainer. When I was 11 years old, I was given a Timex watch that I was very proud of. However, it quit working eight months later and the receipts and one-year warranty that came with it were long gone. I sent it off to Timex with a letter explaining that it quit eight months after I got it and that even though I had no proof to back up my claim, I hoped they would repair it. I was pleasantly surprised when weeks later, I got my watch back from Timex repaired and with a fresh battery! I will always remember that Timex came through for me when I was a young consumer.

A neighbour of mine, an affable Newfoundlander, purchased a nearly new vehicle and decided to pay extra for a warranty in case there was a problem. Shortly after buying the car, it developed a malfunctioning rear shock. He assumed the problem would be repaired under warranty, but because of a technicality the dealer said there would be a charge of $300. My neighbour felt that the problem should be repaired free of charge and said if it wasn't, he would promptly set up a lemonade stand outside the dealership on the sidewalk. He would announce for all to hear that he was selling lemonade made from the lemons being sold at the dealership. At first the car dealer assumed this was a ploy, but when he saw my neighbour's determination, he relented and the shock was fixed for free. I'm not advocating this as a way to deal with problems but in my neighbour's case it worked. Being an effective complainer is an important part of being a savvy consumer. Having said this, no one likes a whiner either. Put yourself in the retailer's shoes to determine if you are being fair and reasonable.

It's not just faulty products that consumers must be aware of. Canadians are trusting people and they must be on guard against fraudulent door-to-door charitable collecting, driveway pavers and unscrupulous energy marketers. There was a time when snake oil salespeople had to go from town to town selling wares to the unsuspecting public, only to ramble off as consumers realized they had been duped. Now in our high tech age, fraud artists can peddle their wares on an unsuspecting public by phone, fax, e-mail, television and any other means of communication. Many thieves have thrown down their balaclavas and turned to white collar crime. Why commit armed robbery and risk 10 years in prison when a sales scam involving fine print and misleading documents can be just as profitable and, in some cases, legal? Fraud artists are able to stay ahead of the law using their knowledge of contracts, loop holes and other legal maneuvers and if they do get caught, the fines and jail terms are usually not much of a deterrent. Consumers are not always swindled by criminals into making bad judgments. Many of us are swayed by slick marketing campaigns, overbearing sales staff and spur of the moment decisions, only to realize later that we should have been more prudent.

I would like to thank the many experts who have selflessly provided their insight for this book, as well as the thousands of CTV viewers who have called and written letters and e-mails to share their stories. Thanks as well to Industry Canada for providing excellent sources and contacts to help consumers, which are in the back of this book. I know first-hand how difficult it can be to save money, especially with our family of five. The knowledge I have gained while preparing *Canadian Consumer Alert* will help my family and hopefully yours too. My vision is that every person buying this book will quickly save the purchase price and more. Over time, the knowledge in these pages could save you hundreds and thousands of dollars.

MONEY
MATTERS

INVESTING FOR THE FUTURE

Cynthia had a relatively good job and earned a respectable salary. She rented an apartment, enjoyed travelling and dining out. As she got older, she was concerned that she was not putting enough money away for her future. She had some savings but she knew little about investing. She was distressed and felt she should be doing more to get her money working for her.

Unless you win the lottery or belong to a wealthy gene pool that will allow you to inherit riches as you grow older, you had better have a good financial plan in place. Investing is more than just hoarding dollars, it's making wise financial decisions that will allow your money to grow through shrewd fiscal management and by taking advantage of the effects of compound interest. Many people are timid when it comes to investing their money, accepting low rates of interest in return for virtually no risk. One should never underestimate the magic of compound interest when investing.

For example, if $1,000 was placed in an account that had an annual rate of return of 6% interest, in 35 years it would be worth $7,686. If that same $1,000 had an annual rate of return of 11% over the same time period, it would be worth $38,575! Those extra interest points really add up and compounding builds wealth. It's like the tale of the King and the suitor who wanted the King's daughter's hand in marriage. The King told the suitor that he could marry the young woman if he could place a penny on a square on a checkerboard and then double the amount of money as he proceeded to each square until he reached the end of the board. No problem, said the man as he added one penny to the first square, two to the next square, four to the next and eight to the next, etc. Of course as the man made his way along the board, the money doubled out of his reach long before he got to the 64th square and the suitor headed to the door a bachelor.

As an investor, practising diversification is the best way to protect your investment. Over time, even investing in the stock market can be safe if you buy quality stocks and mutual funds.

Garth Turner, one of Canada's most recognized personal financial advisors, puts it simply when he says "people who save, will fail. People who invest, will not." Turner says the biggest financial mistake Canadian investors can make is trying to do their own financial planning. "The second mistake flows out of the first because most of us are wimps and we attempt to avoid all risk when it comes to investing. We're overcautious to a fault." There is no doubt that Turner takes an aggressive approach to investing but he says if investors practice diversification, not "putting all your eggs in one basket," he believes that over time the market is a safe place to be as long as investors buy quality stocks and mutual funds. Investing should never be treated as a crapshoot.

Turner has some basic rules to follow. "Hot stocks get cold real fast. By the time newspapers notice a flaming stock, it has already peaked," he advises. Hot tips can also burn. If you do decide to take a chance on a stock that people at the water cooler are calling a sure bet, be cautious. "Never put all your financial resources into one play. Even 5% or 10% of your portfolio will give you a good return if the stock soars. If it doesn't, you won't suffer an irreversible setback." Turner maintains that it's always better to diversify. "Don't invest in one stock, invest in 10. Don't invest in one sector of the economy, but several. More diversity equals less risk."

We all know people who claim to have made a killing on a stock. What they don't tell you about is the one that went into free fall. My own investment advisor told me that over time, mutual funds can offer the same returns as individually picked stocks with a lot less stress and worry. Turner agrees that the easiest way to diversify is with mutual funds, an investment type which is really just a fund made up of many different stocks. Since one fund may contain 10 different stocks, the overall value is usually less volatile. With mutual funds, "you buy less risk along with superior management. Be careful not to diversify too much or you can water down your returns. A maximum of eight or nine funds will get the job done," suggests Turner.

There are many different kinds of investment instruments on the market and they each come with their own level of risk. An investment considered to be safe will mean you are likely to preserve your original investment, but the rate of return will be low. Conversely, other investments may offer higher returns but they will come with a certain amount of risk. Take risks when you are younger, as you will not be able to afford to when you're older. It's up to you to analyze your own adversity to risk, depending on your wealth, goals and stage in life. Most financial institutions will help you determine if you are best suited for high, medium or low risk investments. You will also have to establish how long you are willing to have your money tied up as well as being aware of its liquidity, in case you need it in an emergency.

Generally in your twenties and thirties, you may be concentrating on a young family. You could be dealing with bills, car payments, a mortgage and have little extra money left to invest. However, this is the time when you should consider getting your finances in order. In your thirties and forties you should have more disposable income and begin to focus on short, medium and long term financial goals. You should be trying to maximize your annual RRSP contributions and as well, have other investments in somewhat higher risk investment vehicles such as equity funds, as you have the time to let them grow. In your forties, fifties and early sixties, your big spending days will come to an end as you age. You should be trying to maximize your investments and switch to lower risk products as you head into your retirement years.

You should also re-examine your portfolio regularly. You don't have to read the newspaper or be on the phone on a daily basis checking your stocks or funds, but neither should you stick your head in the sand and assume they are always creeping upward and meeting your goals. Every three months, six months or at least once a year, you should evaluate your holdings and make sure that your fiscal plan is on track. Some funds or stocks may need to be reconsidered and after consulting with your financial advisor, you may want to make changes within your portfolio.

Many investors get cold feet in a volatile stock market. Hasty retreats during a market fluctuation can see some investors who have bought at a high price, selling low. If you are looking for long term gains, you should stay with your financial strategy. Investors should concentrate on the long term and not overreact to market fluctuations. Turner states that "I have absolutely no doubt that North American stock markets will double or even triple in value over the next decade, based on technological advances, demographics, government balance sheets and globalization." Even if you feel that you can't afford to invest, it may be that you can't afford not to.

2

INTEREST RATE WRAP-UP

Gabriel found there was little money left after he paid his bills each month. He sat down and figured out just how much of his monthly paycheque went to interest payments and was shocked at his calculations. There was $600 a month in interest on his mortgage, $70 a month in interest on his car payment, $60 in interest on a consolidation loan and another $50 a month in interest on his credit card. In total, he was paying $780 a month just in interest payments! He wondered if he would ever get ahead.

After taxes paid to the government, for many of us another large chunk of our income goes to financial institutions in the form of interest payments. In a perfect world, we would pay cash for everything and never have the worry of debt hanging over our heads. Most of us do not have this luxury and so we are forced to borrow money from the bank, credit card companies or department stores. These institutions are more than willing to lend us money — at a price. In our credit driven society, there are fewer and fewer people who "pay cash on the barrel," a reference to pickle barrels in old fashioned supply stores from an era long ago. Some people can pay cash for purchases large or small, but the rest of us will have to borrow money at one time or another, so it's wise to make sure you are getting the lowest lending rate possible.

Just as higher rates of interest on investments tend to compound and help your money grow over time, high interest rates on loans and debts cause you to lose large amounts of money. Your hard earned money goes toward interest payments, rather than paying off the principle. According to the Canadian Bankers Association, there are several factors that cause interest rates to fluctuate: global market forces, the supply and demand for money, the current and expected rates of inflation, the length of time the funds are lent or borrowed and monetary policy. The Bank of Canada, Canada's central bank, sets the bank rate or interest rate it charges major financial institutions when they want to borrow money. It is this bank rate that sets the standard for interest rates at all of Canada's major banks and other financial institutions.

Obviously, it is wise to avoid all borrowing where a high interest rate is involved. Credit cards and financial services have lending rates as high as 29%. Credit cards allow you to make minimum payments which basically pay off the interest rate, hardly putting a dent in the principle. Loans at 29% interest are offered over a period of years, so it's possible that borrowers could actually pay back more in interest to the lender than they borrowed in the first place! It's a good idea to avoid these lenders at all costs to avoid getting trapped in a vicious high interest cycle. If you are someone who carries a balance on your credit card, it may be worth your while to pay an annual fee to get a credit card that offers a lower interest rate.

The Canadian Bankers Association says when consumers shop for loans there are many variables that will affect the interest rate when borrowing money: the term of the loan (as rates differ for short and long term loans), the amount you are borrowing and your reason for borrowing. A car loan will give the bank something to repossess if you miss payments while a vacation won't. Your credit rating, other risk factors to the lender, the prevailing interest rates in the economy and marketplace and expected inflation also affect your interest rate.

Now enough of the background, how do you *get a better interest rate!* Many of us are sometimes sheepish when applying for loans but we shouldn't be as banks want our business badly.

As Gabriel found out, he is paying nearly $800 every month just in interest payments. That is money banks don't want to lose. Always keep in mind that the posted interest rate is just a guideline and you can and should ask for a lower rate. The banking industry has become increasingly competitive and banks are eager to get your business.

The best tools you can use when shopping for a loan are the phone, a newspaper and a loan calculator. A loan calculator can be found at most financial Web sites, in financial software or in some books. A mortgage calculator is included at most banking Web sites. Type in the words "mortgage calculator" and the name of any major Canadian bank in a search engine query line to find one.

You should enter a bank already knowing how much you want to borrow, the loan term in months and the interest rate you want to pay. Play hardball. Don't believe the warm and fuzzy commercials. Banks are large institutions that treat clients like numbers. I personally have no problem with being treated like a number by a large institution. It allows business to be business so you can bargain for the lowest interest rate you can get.

> Always keep in mind that the posted interest rate is just a guideline and you can and should ask for a lower rate.

The larger the loan, the more money you can save by trying to knock down the rate. The largest savings realized is on mortgages. For example, if you were to borrow $160,000 to buy a house over 25 years at an interest rate of 8%, you would pay the bank the incredible amount of $221,776 in interest alone. By negotiating an interest rate of 8 1/4 % just 1/4% lower you will pay $214,028 — a savings of $7,748 in interest! Not bad for haggling a quarter percentage point with a loans officer. Shrewd operators know how to deal with banks and there is a degree of bluffing involved to get a better deal. It also depends on your credit history and if you have been a good customer.

Check the newspaper and see who is offering the lowest interest rates in town. Check not just banks, but trust companies, credit unions and other lenders. Ask if they would like your business as they most surely will. When you go to your bank to get a loan, let them know you have been in touch with other institutions and are prepared to move your accounts elsewhere as they are offering lower interest rates on loans and mortgages. In most cases, your bank will match the rate to try and keep your business. They would rather lose a few hundred or thousand dollars in interest payments than lose your entire account. A few thousand dollars is not much to a huge corporation but it is to you! In the end, even if they don't budge and you decide to stay with your bank, there was no harm in trying to get a better deal for yourself because remember, you're just a number anyway.

When you finally have your loan worked out, keep in mind there are still ways to save money after the deal is done. You can double up on payments or make lump sum payments when you have extra money. You can make biweekly or weekly payments to shorten your amortization period. The shorter the length of your loan the less total interest you will pay. A good financial planner will be able to give you the tax advantages of various types of interest payments. For example, interest paid on money to earn business or investment income is tax deductible. If you have a mortgage on a rental income property, the interest payments are also tax deductible. In the United States, interest payments on your home's mortgage is tax deductible, but unfortunately in Canada we do not have that luxury. Just keep in mind, the less interest you pay, the more money you will have left for yourself and your family. Analyze regularly how much of your income goes to pay interest and do everything you can to reduce it.

PAY YOURSELF FIRST — Forced Savings

Douglas had a fairly good income but found it difficult to save money. It seemed after paying the rent, a car loan and other bills and expenses, there was never enough left to stash in a savings account. His friends were able to successfully put money away for a rainy day, but try as he might he could not find a saving method that worked for him.

I and hundreds of thousands of other Canadians can thank David Chilton, author of *The Wealthy Barber*, for his financial advice from a fictional small town barber named Roy. *The Wealthy Barber* is one of the best-selling books in Canadian publishing. The book was given to me as a gift from my brother Bill a decade ago. My only regret is that I let it sit on the shelf for a year before I got around to reading it. What Chilton was able to convey in his common sense tale of personal finance was that by following a few simple rules, one can save for the future and become wealthy in the process.

The heart of the book is simple — pay yourself first. Most of us who have trouble saving money are not necessarily bad money managers. We are able to pay our bills on time. We don't miss the rent or the mortgage payments. We pay our phone, heat, cable and other bills without fail. The main problem is that there never seems to be enough left to stash away for our retirement. The answer is forced savings! We must make a payment to ourselves every bit as important to make on time as a payment to the electric company.

The most money I ever saved in my life was through putting Chilton's philosophy to work. I was renting and had some extra income so I decided to have my bank deduct two hundred dollars from every paycheque as soon as it was deposited into my account. I allocated the money for mutual funds and made it part of my registered retirement savings plan. At first, I felt the financial squeeze and noticed the money missing from my pay, but before long I got used to it. It just seemed like the absent cash was going toward another bill. After a few years, I managed to accumulate tens of thousands of dollars. The savings also grew as the mutual funds increased in value and I received a tax refund from the government as the funds were part of my RRSP. This was the first feeling of financial empowerment I had ever felt.

> The most money I ever saved in my life was through Chilton's philosophy — pay yourself first.

Of course then came love, marriage and a baby carriage. There is no doubt it can be extremely difficult to save money depending on your station in life. While I was unable to keep up my aggressive forced savings plan after buying my first home, I have my plan to pay myself first back on track. Even $50 consistently deducted from your paycheque adds up over time. Some people also use forced savings arrangements to help them save for Christmas, winter vacations or a new car. A bank or investment company will usually be more than happy to help you set up such a plan.

In Chilton's *The Wealthy Barber*, Roy would tell his clients "invest 10% of all you make for long term growth. If you follow that one simple guideline, someday, you'll be very rich." Doing without 10% of your income will not dramatically change your lifestyle, but over time it could lead to a huge increase in your wealth. Whether you pay yourself 10%, 5% or 2% of your salary, it will start you on the road to financial freedom.

RRSPS — Saving for Your Golden Years

Roland was forty-years-old, married with two children. He had paid off a portion of his mortgage, saved some money in a bank account and had a few stocks and bonds. What he did not have was a registered retirement savings plan (RRSP). As he grew older, he realized that he should have put more money into an RRSP when he was younger. He wondered if there was anything he could do to catch up.

A registered retirement savings plan, or RRSP, may be the best way that Canadians can improve their financial situation, yet amazingly about two-thirds of the population doesn't have one! RRSPs were created in 1957 to help Canadians plan for their retirement and allow their savings to grow in a tax-sheltered environment. Garth Turner is recognized as one of Canada's foremost experts in the area of personal finance and RRSPs. Turner says he is not surprised that many people are unaware of the benefits of RRSPs because their benefits are not taught in school and financial companies have been unable to educate the public in a concise straightforward manner. "Canadians should view an RRSP like a large bubble where you can stack your financial assets. The assets are then free to grow and compound within the bubble which shields them from taxes," he explains. Turner, a former federal Finance Minister, believes there is no faster way to build wealth than by doing it within an RRSP.

There are many reasons why investing your money in an RRSP just makes good economic sense. The most lucrative reason is at tax time. "The money put in the plan is deducted from your taxable income so most people will get big tax refund cheques," maintains Turner. Taxable investments can also be put into your RRSP so they can grow in value, tax-free. When you finally do need your money, you can roll your RRSP assets into a Registered Retirement Income Fund (RIFF) which further defers taxes, as long as you take a minimal amount out of the plan each year. Turner says "an RRSP allows you to save a bundle on lifetime taxes. By deferring taxation until later in life and using an RRSP to split income with your less-taxed spouse, you will, in most cases be taxed at a lower rate."

Generally you can contribute 18% of your income to a maximum of $13,500 per year. The more money you make, the bigger tax break you will get. For example, if you contribute $5,000 in one year and are in a 40% tax bracket, you will get an immediate savings of $2,000. If you are in a 54% tax bracket, you will save $2,700. Many people who do contribute to their RRSPs wait until the last minute but finding a large amount of money all at once can be difficult. "Contribute monthly and soon a regular RRSP payment becomes like a car loan — something you forget about," suggests Turner. While many Canadians put their retirement savings into low return GICs or savings bonds, Turner says investments with higher rates of return such as mutual funds, term deposits, Canadian stocks, small business shares and even mortgages can be placed inside an RRSP to grow tax free.

If you don't have money to put in an RRSP, it's wise to get a loan to make a contribution. Usually this will enable you to get a tax refund cheque, which in turn can promptly be used to pay back a portion of the loan right away. You also don't want the bulk of your assets to end up in the name of the person who pays the most tax. Consider contributing to an RRSP plan for the spouse who is the lower income earner. The higher income spouse will get the same tax break and when the money is withdrawn, it will be taxed at a lower rate.

RRSPs are the best tax shelter in North America. There is no faster way to build wealth.

You can also catch up on missed contributions. "The 1997 budget removed a restriction limiting the ability to carry forward missed contributions for only seven years. Now it's unlimited, but the ability to catch up might not be around forever," warns Turner. You cannot over-contribute more than $2,000 to your RRSP or you will be penalized. Turner is adamant that Canadians who have missed making RRSP contributions in the past should do their best to catch up. The problem? Many people don't know how much room they have left in their RRSP. Turner says while a financial advisor should be able to calculate this for you, you can also find out for yourself by checking the blue pages (gray in Manitoba) of your phone book and finding the TIPs (Tax Information Phone Service) number in the Canada Customs and Revenue Agency (formerly Revenue Canada) Tax Services section. Turner says "have your birth date, social insurance number and last year's income tax return ready. When you answer the computer generated questions, the TIPs machine will tell you what your current RRSP contribution limit is, along with the total amount of missed contributions."

Turner says all Canadians should take advantage of what he calls the best tax shelter in North America. Canada's leading expert in personal finance says "contributing just $100 a month can result in a quarter-million dollar RRSP in just 25 years. It's the best leg up on the future you are going to get!"

MANAGING YOUR MORTGAGE

Jack and Tita had fulfilled a lifelong dream of buying their first home. It was a financial squeeze but by amortizing the home over 25 years, they were able to buy the house they wanted. At the end of the first year in their home, they received their annual mortgage statement. They were stunned that despite their hefty monthly payments, they had paid off very little of the principle. They wondered how they would ever get the house paid for.

Whether you already own or are buying a house, townhouse or condominium, becoming an expert on mortgages will save you tens of thousands of dollars in interest payments. For many of us, buying a home is the largest purchase we will make. The generation before us had the luxury of buying houses and seeing them increase dramatically in price. Many economists believe that the real estate cycles that helped our parents' homes double and triple in value will never come around again, so don't buy a home thinking it will be your ticket to retirement. Your home will keep you and your family warm and dry, and hopefully increase marginally in price at the same rate as inflation but it should not be considered an investment vehicle. Because of this, you want to be especially concerned about how much money you are paying in interest.

When I bought my first home I was astounded, shocked really, at the profit the bank would make from me in interest! I believe in many ways that mortgage rates are very misleading. Sure, the mortgage rate may be an annual interest charge of 8%, but is it really 8% when you have to pay the vast majority of interest charges *upfront*? Does the bank pay you your profits upfront on your investments? Of course not. In the United States, homeowners can at least deduct the amount of interest they pay on their home from their income taxes. Why can't Canadian homeowners, who also have to pay huge income and property taxes, get some kind of break as well? While I would like to see some reforms and more fairness in the mortgage sector, don't count on it happening as Canada's major banks are making billions of dollars annually and see no need to share the wealth. I've always felt that banks must love starter homes especially because they hardly ever get paid off. People move in, make bank payments top heavy with interest, move out after a few years and let someone else move in and start the process all over again. It's as if the banks are absentee landlords.

Every home buyer should have their own mortgage calculator or amortization tables either in a book or on a computer. With today's financial software, you can easily plug in the appropriate figures to see how much you will be paying in interest over time. The software available to the public is the same as the banks use, so there is no mystery to the process.

As an example, let's say that Jack and Tita are going to buy a house and need a mortgage from the bank of $185,000. They negotiate an interest rate of 8.5% (see Alert 2 on negotiating a better interest rate) and agree to amortize the mortgage over 25 years.

$185,000 mortgage at 8.5% interest rate over 300 months
= monthly payments of $1,471.
Total amount of interest paid to the bank over the term
of the mortgage = $256,429.

If Jack and Tita made an effort to pay the money back in 20 years, they would save considerably.

> $185,000 mortgage at 8.5% interest rate over 240 months
>   = monthly payments of $1,588.
> Total amount of interest paid to the bank over the term
>   of the mortgage = $196,199.

Jack and Tita's monthly payment would go up only $117 dollars a month, but they would save $60,230 in interest payments and be done with their mortgage five years sooner!

If they tried to pay it back in 15 years, they would save even more.

> $185,000 mortgage at 8.5% interest rate over 180 months
>   = monthly payments of $1,806.
> Total amount of interest paid to the bank over the term
>   of the mortgage = $140,061.

If they paid their mortgage off in ten years, the amount of interest they would pay would be only 35% of what they would have had to pay if it were amortized over 25 years.

> $185,000 mortgage at 8.5% interest rate over 120 months
>   = monthly payments of $2,279.
> Total amount of interest paid to the bank over the term
>   of the mortgage = $88,510.

When I did these calculations while buying my first home at 28-years-old, I was determined not to give the bank any more in interest payments than I had to. My wife and I agreed to try and pay back our mortgage over 15 years. We stuck to that schedule for three years, however when along came babies, diapers, strollers and other expenses in our growing family, it became difficult to maintain that pace of repayment. An older, wiser colleague at work told me, "Pat, sure you want to pay your house off as quickly as possible, but if you don't have money left over for other expenses and to have some fun, you'll end up getting divorced." My wife and I agreed to scale it back through the baby years.

It is difficult to try and put extra money toward a mortgage, but many homeowners do not realize how much interest they end up paying the banks over the long term. Often when you go in for a mortgage the bank automatically qualifies you for the 25-year term and makes little effort to inform you of other options. Why? They want you locked in as long as possible to get the most money out of you.

You can cut down on the interest paid by making lump sum payments whenever you can, doubling up payments or paying on a weekly or biweekly basis.

If you have no choice but to settle for a long amortization period, you can still make lump sum payments, double up payments or pay weekly or biweekly. Matching biweekly mortgage payments to your paycheque is helpful so you don't end up scrambling for funds at the beginning of each month. Make 26 payments a year instead of 24 and resist the temptation to skip a payment when the offer is made by your bank. It's pitched as a way to give you more spending money around the holidays, but it's just another way that banks can get more interest in the long run.

SAVING FOR YOUR CHILD'S EDUCATION

Rosie had two young children and was concerned about the rising cost of post-secondary education. She wanted them to be able to attend university eventually but was aware that with skyrocketing education costs, she may not have enough money for their tuition and other expenses. She wanted information on the best way to plan for her children's future.

Parents want the best for their children so it's not surprising that many people are now more concerned than ever about what kind of education their children will get and how they will pay for it. It is estimated that two-thirds of new jobs will require education beyond high school and to receive a college diploma or university degree is now an extremely expensive endeavor. Tuition fees have risen sharply and are expected to continue to rise. Full-time tuition fees can top $3,000 or $4,000 a year and professional degrees for doctors, lawyers and dentists can cost as much as $12,000 annually. In addition to tuition, students must pay for books, supplies, transportation, rent and other living expenses.

Of course if you don't set aside money for your child's education, they can obtain government or private loans to attend school which is what many students have to do. Upon finishing college or university, many students have loans in excess of $30,000. Paying off these loans while searching for employment, getting a place to live and possibly buying a car can be discouraging which is why many parents want to start saving early for their children's education. The Canadian Bankers Association estimates that in 15 to 20 years, four years of education for a student living away from home could cost as much as $75,000 to $100,000! No wonder concerned parents are looking for savings vehicles for their children's education fund.

The federal government understands that parents are going to have to foot more of the bills for their child's post secondary schooling, so it has created the Registered Education Savings Plan (RESP). RESPs allow savings you set aside for your children to grow tax-free until your child is ready to go to college, university or any other eligible post secondary institution. For every dollar you save in an RESP, the federal government will contribute 20% up to $400 per child, per year. For example, if you contributed $25 every two weeks into a RESP for a total of $650 a year, the federal government would kick in an additional grant of $130.

The person putting money into an RESP does not get a tax deduction similar to that of an RRSP, but the money is allowed to grow tax-free until the funds are used to educate your child. RESPs are offered at many financial institutions and anyone can contribute; you don't have to be a family member. The maximum amount that can be contributed is $4,000 per child, per year to a lifetime limit of $42,000. Since there was no tax benefit when the contribution was made, it can be withdrawn tax-free but any interest, dividend or capital gains income earned on the money is taxable. Of course many students are essentially broke, so they would effectively pay little or no tax on money taken from an RESP fund.

If your child does not go on to a post-secondary education, you will have to repay the 20% grant to the federal government, or you can use the money for another child's education, or donate the earnings from the plan to a post-secondary institution of your choice. You can also create other savings programs in your child's name such as an informal trust. This is a regular non-registered investment account set up for the purpose of investing funds for a child. The money is held in trust for the child until he or she reaches the age of majority.

Parents are already pressured to pay bills, mortgage payments, loans and also save money in RRSPs and other invest-ments. It can be extremely difficult to also set aside money in an education fund. By starting early, taking advantage of the magic of compound interest and using contributing dollars from the federal gov-ernment, you can start a nest egg for your child's education. The Canadian Bankers Association explains that a monthly savings plan of $100 per month can grow up to $33,978 by the end of 15 years, assuming an 8% annual return rate. As education costs continue to rise, planning ahead could give you peace of mind and help your family avert a financial crisis down the road when those big education bills start rolling in.

An RESP savings plan of $100 a month can grow to $33,978 after 15 years, assuming an 8% annual return rate. And the federal government will kick in too.

ALERT
7

YOUR FINANCIAL WORTH

Stan was poorly organized. His finances were never in order at tax time. He had trouble keeping track of his debts and bills and important documents were scattered throughout the house. He always managed to get everything paid on time, but his records were in a constant state of disarray.

One of the best investments you can make is a filing cabinet. One of the worst mistakes you can make is not keeping a close and constant eye on your financial situation. Keeping haphazard records is not only a bad habit but it will also affect your long term wealth as being unsure of your financial position is not helping it flourish. Know exactly how much money is coming in and out of your life, or it will be impossible to plan for the future. Also, your investments, tax returns, bank accounts, credit card debts, loans, safety deposit box information and other important documents should be in order and easily accessible in case you were to die or become seriously ill. Your will, life insurance policy and contact information for your financial advisor should be kept in a safe place where your family can find it.

A crucial part of your monetary planning which should be performed often, at least once a year, is determining your financial worth. If you had to sell everything you owned and pay off every debt you had, what would you be left with? It is easy to figure out. Simply subtract your assets (what you own) from your liabilities (what you owe) to determine your net worth. The following chart is a guide.

Assets		Liabilities	
Savings Account	$2,500	Mortgage (balance	
Chequing Account	$1,000	owing)	$118,000
Investments	$8,000	Car Loans	$14,000
– mutual funds	$2,000	Other loans	$8,000
– stocks	$800	Credit Cards	$2,500
– bonds	—	Property Taxes	$2,700
– GICs	—	Income Taxes	$500
– term deposits	—	Bills owing	$1,600
Value of home	$150,000	Other debts	$700
Value of		**Total**	**$148,000**
automobiles	$20,000		
Value of other property			
or big ticket items	—		
RSPs	—		
RRSPs	$14,000		
Pension holdings	$12,000		
Other holdings	—		
Total	**$210,300**		

> Assets – Liabilities = Net Financial Worth
> $210,300 – $148,000 = $62,300

Sounds simple enough, but many people fail to do this calculation. It's one you should do regularly to ensure your net worth is rising. When you take control of your affairs, you will know exactly where you stand financially and gain confidence that your situation will improve under your scrutiny.

WHEN THE BANK MAKES ERRORS

Olivia went to the bank to withdraw money from her account and found there was no money left. Apparently her live-in nanny withdrew $15,000 over a three-month period by forging cheques and using her debit card. The nanny had since been fired and was nowhere to be found. Olivia was furious with her bank, but the bank manager said she should have noticed the activity sooner. They refused to reimburse her and Olivia felt helpless.

There may be times when you feel that you have been treated unfairly by a bank and have nowhere to turn. However, the Canadian Banking Ombudsman Inc. is an independent body which investigates complaints from small businesses and individuals about banking services. The organization's aim is to be fair, impartial and to seek resolution of problems in the banking sector. Olivia took her case to the Canadian Banking Ombudsman and won! On investigation, the Ombudsman concluded that the bank should have noticed the uncustomary activity in Olivia's account and the poor forgeries. The Ombudsman recommended that the bank reimburse Olivia the $15,000 and the bank complied.

Michael Lauber, currently the Canadian Banking Ombudsman, says "the advantage of an ombudsman process is that it will investigate and provide a decision based on fairness in the circumstances, rather than on strict legal principles." The Ombudsman can help with problems related to bank products and services such as insurance, investments and transactions that may be in dispute. There are areas that the Ombudsman cannot investigate such as the setting of interest rates, service charges, credit card charges, the credit granting policies of banks or issues that have been before the courts. "It's a free service. This is advantageous to customers who may otherwise not be able to afford to argue their case in court," explained Lauber. Service provided is in English and French but Lauber says an effort will be made to help anyone in any language.

The aim of the Canadian Banking Ombudsman is to be fair, impartial and to seek restitution.

The Canadian Banking Ombudsman has investigated complaints related to selling practices, privacy and confidentiality issues, account transactions and changed credit terms. In another case, a young couple sold their home to purchase a new one. They applied for a new mortgage at the same bank and asked for the same coverage they had on the previous mortgage, which included life insurance. In the process of obtaining the mortgage, the couple was never presented with an insurance application for completion. A few months after applying for the mortgage but before the housing deal closed, the husband was diagnosed with cancer and subsequently died. The widow tried to collect under the life insurance, but the bank refused payment on the basis that there was no policy in force. Following an investigation by the Ombudsman, it was recommended that the bank treat the case as though the insurance existed. The Ombudsman felt the widow's credibility was important and that there was a good deal of evidence to support her claim. The bank was told to give the widow $120,000 to pay out the mortgage. It did.

The Ombudsman did not rule in favour of a woman who claimed her husband had been stealing money from her bank account. In this case, a woman gave her husband her banking personal identification number (PIN). Over three years, the husband had drained her account of $17,000 using her ABM card and forging her signature on cheques. Upon finding out, the woman wanted the bank to reimburse her for her losses. The Ombudsman felt there was nothing that could be done, as the woman had failed to check her accounts on a monthly basis, the forged signatures occurred over three years and she gave her card and PIN to her husband, which violated the bank's contract that a PIN is not to be shared with anyone.

Neither you nor the banks are bound by the Ombudsman's recommendations. However, the Ombudsman is required to report publicly the name of any bank which does not comply with a recommendation. To date, all of the Ombudsman's recommendations have been implemented. Using the Ombudsman's services does not force you to give up any legal rights and you may still pursue the matter in the courts if you wish. Currently, 12 of Canada's major bank financial groups are members of the Canadian Banking Ombudsman Inc. They are Amex Bank of Canada, Bank of Montreal, Canadian Western Bank, CIBC, Citibank, HSBC Bank, ING Bank of Canada, Laurentian Bank, National Bank, Royal Bank, Scotiabank, and TD Canada Trust. Its Board of Directors is made up of six directors who are prominent Canadians and independent of the banks as well as five directors who are senior bank executives. Once the Ombudsman has made a decision, there is no appeal to the board.

Before contacting the Canadian Banking Ombudsman, you must try to resolve the complaint directly with your own bank and their banking ombudsman. If you do not get satisfaction at that level, you can contact the Canadian Banking Ombudsman at 1-888-451-4519 or check their Web site at www.bankingombudsman.com. You will be asked to put your complaint in writing. The Ombudsman may deal with your case in an informal manner or a detailed investigation may be required. After your complaint has been reviewed, you and your bank will be given the Ombudsman's recommendations and the reasons for it. If you ever believe you have been treated unfairly by a bank, take heart that an independent third party may be able to help you, for free.

CHECK YOUR CREDIT RATING

Hans applied for a car loan and was surprised when he was turned down at the bank because of his poor credit rating. He turned to a credit repair agency that said it could fix his credit problems for $1,000 upfront. The agency said that the fee was for going through his credit file, finding his credit problems and attempting to have them removed from his file. However, in the end, the agency did nothing to help Hans' situation. In fact, he was worse off than before because they kept his $1,000.

Almost all of us rely on some form of credit to make purchases. Paying bills on time is extremely important and ignoring credit card debts or missing loan payments will negatively affect your credit rating. Every time you take out a loan, sign up for a department store charge card or are significantly late paying a bill, it is kept on file at Canada's two major credit reporting agencies — Equifax Canada and Trans Union. Sheila McCraken of Equifax says "credit files contain information on how you pay your bills and credit cards. The information tells us if you pay your debts on time and if you've had any bankruptcies or registered loans." A credit file usually includes identification information such as your date of birth, addresses, employment information, a list of creditors, payment history and any inquiries made about your credit history.

All credit information, bad or good, is kept on file for six years including Hans' failure to pay his credit card bill for several months. If you are denied credit because of a mistake on your file or incorrect information, it can be rectified by contacting the appropriate credit reporting agency. If the negative information is correct, the information cannot be changed and will remain on your file, negatively affecting your credit rating. Trans Union says credit information is removed from a consumer's credit file in six years but that in some provinces, data may be kept on file for as long as seven years.

> If you have had credit problems in the past, be upfront with the lender, as they will find out anyway. Let them know what steps you have taken to remedy the situation.

Hans could have checked his credit rating without charge. Despite paying the credit repair clinic $1,000, the clinic did nothing that he couldn't have done himself. McCraken says consumers should know that if they have a bad credit rating, there is nothing they can do to change it. "If the negative information is accurate and does belong to that consumer, it will stay on file for six years. It doesn't matter how much money you pay to anyone, it won't change that," she explains.

Check your credit rating every year or two to make sure there are no problems that have cropped up. Also, if you're planning to get a loan or make a credit application, you may want to check your credit history first, so you won't have any surprises. If you have had credit problems in the past, it's not the end of the world. Be upfront with a lender since they will find out about it anyway. Let them know that you are working to improve your credit situation and are now paying your bills on time. You may have to pay a slightly higher interest rate or some other penalty until your credit rating is back in good standing.

To check you credit rating free of charge, you can contact Equifax at 1-800-465-7166 or at www.equifax.ca or write them at Equifax Canada Inc., Consumer Relations Department, Box 190 Jean Talon Station, Montreal, Quebec, H1S 2Z2. You can also contact Trans Union at www.tuc.ca or 1-800-663-9980 or write them at 170 Jackson Street East, Hamilton, Ontario, L8N 3K8. It's a good idea to check your credit rating with both agencies.

When sending for your credit file, you should include your name, including any maiden names, daytime and evening phone numbers, your current address and previous address (if needed for a five-year credit history), your date of birth and marital status. You should also include your social insurance number and photocopies of two pieces of identification such as a driver's licence or credit card. Trans Union also requires a photocopy of a utility bill. If the credit information is for your spouse as well, then you should include his or her name, social insurance number and identification as well. It will take 10 to 15 days before you get your credit rating in the mail.

If there is an error on your credit report, you have the right to contact the credit reporting centre and request a change. You may have to get in touch with the original creditor directly and request documentation of the debt. If you can provide materials or paperwork to prove your case, the negative information on your credit file should be removed from your credit history.

CREDIT CARDS — Taking It to the Limit

Phoenix signed up for her first credit card in college. After graduating, her credit card was maxed out to the credit limit, but she was still able to make the minimum monthly payments. When she got her first job, she needed new clothes and signed up for another charge card and she soon ran that card up to its credit limit as well. Now she was making monthly payments on her school loan, a car, two credit cards as well as trying to pay for food and rent. The majority of her charge card payments went toward paying interest charges and she felt that she would never get them paid off.

What happened to Phoenix happens to tens of thousands of Canadians every year. Recent statistics show that the average Canadian has $3,000 worth of credit card debt. Credit card overspending has reached epidemic proportions as finance companies make credit cards easy to acquire and effortless to use. Many companies charge interest rates that can be as high as 28%! People struggling with other debts can find it hard to pay off the principal amount and are then stuck paying the minimum monthly payments. A large part of this payment goes toward interest and not the principal. There have been calls for credit card reform by some federal politicians to cap interest rates on cards but change has never materialized. You must take it upon yourself to be in control of your finances and be aware of the lure of accessible credit.

Many people who abuse credit cards say that their use just doesn't seem like spending actual money. This can lead consumers to go on spending sprees that they later regret. Many people also buy things on credit that they wouldn't have bought if they had to pay cash. The Credit Counseling Service of Toronto is a free confidential agency that helps people get out of debt. Credit Counsellor Laurie Campbell says that many people use credit cards to the extreme and for impulse purchases. "When you're counting out $10, $20 or $30, you know how much you're spending, but when you use a credit card, for some people it doesn't seem real."

Some credit users must hit rock bottom in their quest for additional credit before they realize they have dug themselves into a serious financial hole.

There are many remedies to try to deal with credit card overspending. I knew of one acquaintance who froze his charge card in a block of ice in the freezer, so he would use it only if it was absolutely necessary. Later he was embarrassed to say that he ended up chipping away at the ice with a hammer and pick to get his next credit fix. Campbell says "some people struggle for years before they make a conscious decision to get rid of the debt they have accumulated. The sooner they do it, the better." Some credit card users must hit "rock bottom" in their quest for additional credit, before they realize they have dug themselves into a serious financial hole.

Some consumers deal with credit card debt by consolidating charge card balances into bank loans so they can make "one easy payment." This is a good move for someone serious about getting rid of the debt they have accumulated. One payment at a lower interest rate over a longer period of time can allow a person to get back on their feet financially. However, many consumers fail to cancel their credit cards at the same time, or take out new ones. A purchase at a time of true need or crisis can be legitimate, but to simply run up the bills once again along with new credit card debts is irresponsible.

Many municipalities offer credit counselling services. Get advice through your local municipal offices or by asking your local elected representative. If smaller communities do not offer counselling, it may be worth the trip to a nearby larger centre to seek help with your financial situation. The counselling is discreet and coming to terms with your debt is your first step toward getting out of it. If you are serious about paying off the bills you have accumulated, financial companies may agree to stop interest from accumulating on your account. This happens only after intervention from the counselling service and will be noted in your financial history. It will allow you to pay your bills, and allow the lender to get back the principal amount that is owed. It also can prevent a consumer from declaring personal bankruptcy.

Budgeting may sound boring, but it can prevent many financial problems. A simple philosophy can help most people deal with their debt situation. Is it a want or a need? If it's a need, you need it. If it's a want, it can wait until you can afford it. Of course, sometimes waiting is the hard part and that's what distinguishes people who are good with credit and those who aren't.

11

DAY TRADING — The Lure & Dangers

Daniel was having some success buying and selling commodities on the stock market and was interested in the practice of day trading. He heard that some professional traders were able to make large amounts of money during the volatility of the market by buying stocks and holding them for short periods of time before selling them. Some traders claimed to make a living day trading and Daniel was curious to learn if he could turn his investments into a fortune.

It's been said that the stock market is the biggest casino in the world and there is no faster way to make or *lose* money than in the volatile world of day trading. Fortunes are won and lost on the markets each day as investors attempt to make money on a stock as it moves. Day traders will buy stocks and keep them for only a matter of minutes before deciding to cash out, hoping to take with them gains, not losses. Most agree that the risks are great and some investors are gambling with money they can't afford to lose.

Peter Beck is President of Swift Trade Securities Inc., an Ontario-based securities dealer. His company has opened offices across Canada to provide state of the art electronic day trading and training facilities. Beck's company provides high speed access to U.S. markets and offers two training programs to teach investors how to read the momentum of the markets. One is a two-week theory course for $2,500. The other is a four-week practical course which is $1,500. There is more information at the company's Web site at www.swifttrade.com or by phoning 416-351-0000.

Beck believes that "if you know what you are doing, it is not gambling." He says an educated investor can be taught to skim profits off stocks on the rise. Many investors will pool their savings to have an investment portfolio they can use to buy and sell stock. Beck maintains that profiting only 50¢ a share within an hour can add up fast. "A half a point may not sound like much, but when you do that with 1,000 shares and earn $500 three or four times a day, that's not bad for a day's work."

> There are many true stories of people who have made a killing on the stock market. But there are many more where investors have lost money — they just don't talk about it with the same enthusiasm.

There are people from all walks of life attempting day trading. The reasons? According to Swift Trade, it's because there is no boss, no clients, no suppliers, no inventory, no weekend work and you only have to work market hours (9:00 a.m. to 4:30 p.m. EST). Day trading involves considerable uncertainty and Beck says that traders should never put funds at risk if they cannot afford to lose the whole amount. While it may be easy for some to make money day trading, it's just as easy to lose it. Also, whether you end the day with a profit or a loss, the day trading firm you used will still receive commissions on every trade you made. The total daily commissions will add to losses and reduce earnings. Some investors may feel they have what it takes to be a day trader, but make no mistake, it is a risky business.

Don Holmes is the former Practice Director with Ernst and Young Chartered Accountants in Toronto. He says while older investors are more inclined to hold stocks over time, many younger capitalists may hold stocks for only a few hours, days or a week. "Everybody wants a bargain and what seems to trigger it more than anything is the rumour mill." The problem is that by the time many of us in the working world hear a stock tip, it's already old news to the movers and shakers on Bay and Wall streets. Often investment gossip at the water cooler has been around a lot longer than we think. Of course there are true stories of people who have made a killing on a hot stock tip. But there are many more where investors have lost money — they just don't talk about it with the same enthusiasm.

Holmes observes, "many people are investing huge sums of money into a stock without really doing their homework. People get caught up in the hype of making easy money. Investors must be on guard against false or misleading information as there are those who are intent on deceiving you and taking your money for their worthless stock." It's true that some investors enjoy the exhilaration of the marketplace. Still, every decision should be based on facts. Know exactly why you are buying a stock and when you intend to sell it. Is there value in the investment and what are the risks? You should never trade with money you cannot afford to lose. Keep in mind that you may have better luck at a blackjack table than gambling on the stock market.

12

LOAN BROKERS — Why "Anyone" Qualifies

Carlos needed a loan but his bank refused to lend him money because of his credit history. He noticed ads in the classified section of the newspaper that guaranteed loans for people with credit problems. Carlos called and was pleased to find out that he would be accepted for a loan, although he would have to pay $500 upfront to secure financing. He paid the money and waited for the loan to be arranged. After a week had passed the loan broker not only failed to secure financing, he refused to return Carlos' calls and kept his $500.

The vast majority of consumers are able to get loans through banks, credit unions and other financial institutions. However, if you have a poor credit history, these institutions may refuse to qualify you for a loan. That's when desperate consumers turn to loan brokers who charge advance fees to arrange financing. Many companies or individuals who broker loans advertise in newspapers and magazines. They often say they will guarantee they can find anyone a loan regardless of their credit history. Loan brokers may seem like a good alternative for someone who has nowhere else to turn for financing, but one should be aware that this practice is often nothing more than a scam. Even when consumers do get loans, they are often charged sign-up fees, exorbitant interest rates and annual surcharges.

There are no guarantees in the money lending business. If a bank won't take the risk of lending you money, you should be wary of a broker who promises you that he or she can. You are usually better off dealing with a reputable finance company, even if it is one that will charge you a higher interest rate. Some consumers may find themselves in the unenviable position of having no alternative but to deal with a loan broker for money. If this is the case, take precautions so that you don't get ripped off. Also, make every effort to maintain a good credit rating in the future, so that you can deal with other more mainstream money lenders.

> Beware of any broker who wants non-refundable service fees upfront, or who tells you that you qualify on the basis of a phone conversation.

Beware of any broker who wants you to commit to non-refundable service fees. If someone is asking you to pay an upfront fee to arrange a loan, this could be a signal that the loan may never materialize and you will lose your deposit. Don't be coerced into sending money immediately even when a broker claims it's necessary to "lock you into the loan." Be suspicious if you "automatically qualify" just by telling a broker your financial situation over the phone or by faxing them your credit history.

If you do want to do business with a loan broker, spend a lot of time going over the contract and fine print as there are often additional fees and service charges that will add to the cost of the loan. Some loan brokers work on behalf of private individuals who lend out their money at interest rates significantly higher than what banks charge. There may also be "signing bonuses" which are just another charge to benefit the lender.

Many provinces including Ontario make it illegal for loan brokers to charge advance fees to arrange a loan. The *Ontario Loan Brokers Act* also requires a full refund of any fees that may have been prepaid, within five days at the consumer's request. As well, the Act, gives consumers the mechanism for seeking damages greater than the fee in civil court. The Ontario Ministry of Consumer and Commercial Relations has laid more than 700 charges under the Act to stop unscrupulous loan brokers from taking advantage of consumers. Some loan brokers convicted in illegal loan scams have been forced to pay fines of up to $50,000. Check with your provincial consumer ministry regarding laws and advance fee loans. You can also check with the Better Business Bureau to see if there are complaints against a broker you are considering. Lastly, regardless of how bleak your current credit situation may seem, taking steps to turn it around will help put you back on the road to a better credit rating in the future. This will allow you to benefit from lower interest rates and fewer hassles when you need to borrow money.

ALERT

13

WILLS AND ESTATES — Anticipating the Inevitable

Chantel was an organized person who had her finances in order. She paid meticulous attention to her home and business affairs. Despite this, she had still not made out her will. She knew she should to protect her children, assets and savings. Still, she could not find the time or the resolve to get a will made. She thought that she would get around to it eventually. She just never did.

A will is one of the most important documents we will ever prepare, yet about half of all Canadians don't have one. Whether it's because we must face our own immortality, the fact there is no sense of urgency or just because we are simply lazy, many people haven't taken the time to plan their last will and testament. It seems that the most difficult part of making a will is getting around to doing it. Of course, there is also the expense of having a lawyer draw up a proper will, but it's money well-spent for the loved ones you will leave behind.

Michael Reilly, of Reilly, D'Heureux, Lanzia, a Toronto law firm, recommends that everyone have a will. In the event of a death, a will can stave off huge legal bills, bureaucratic red tape and prevent family feuds when dividing up assets. "If people want to make their own decisions and not leave it up to some-one else, they should have a will," he advises. If you die and you don't have a will in place, you could end up leaving a financial mess for your family. If the upright piano is to be left to Susan and the power tools to John, why not put it in a will to save confusion, stress and hurt feelings later. Reilly says that when there is a will in place, things go more smoothly for everyone when someone dies. He adds, "it's also more expensive to administer an estate if someone dies intestate (without a will)."

Review your will after major life events such as marriage, the birth of a child, divorce or the death of a spouse.

When you finally get around to hav-ing a will done, you should try to update it periodically. "Review your will especially after major life events, such as marriage, the birth of a child, a divorce or the death of a spouse."

There are also Will Kits on the market, but the Canadian Bar Association (CBA) doesn't recommend them. Of course this cheaper, alternative is also competition for lawyers. If the will kit is filled out correctly, it will be recognized in court.

Lawyers will tell you that kits and self-drawn wills could lead to complications after you're gone. According to CBA officials, the major concerns with will kits are that people make mistakes filling them out; they can't offer advice; and that they are a one-size-fits-all tool which does not take into account unique family situations. The CBA says you are paying a lawyer not just to fill in the blanks, but for advice on the best way to deal with your estate. Certainly anyone with significant assets should have a will drawn up by a professional.

Of course, if you wanted to, you could also write your will for nothing on the back of a napkin. This is known as a holo-graph will. It would only be recognized under very strict and unusual conditions. For example, the court may choose to recog-nize a holograph will written by an adventurer to the North Pole who wrote it while dying, trapped in a cabin by an avalanche. However, under normal circumstances, a will written on a scrap of paper would not likely stand up in court.

A standard will can be drawn up by a lawyer for about $200, but this price will vary depending on the lawyer you choose. It is now recommended that you also have Powers of Attorney for your property and personal care. Reilly says that "these extremely important documents give authority to others to look after your affairs if you're in a coma or for medical reasons become unable to make decisions for yourself." A Power of Attorney for your property will allow you to name someone to look after your financial situation, while a Power of Attorney for your personal care can put someone in charge of your medical care if necessary. Some provinces combine property and personal care matters in the same document. The Powers of Attorney are now recognized as an important part of estate planning and a lawyer in your area can guide you as to what documents are needed to properly address your financial and medical concerns. Law firms often will try to sell you a will package. This may include a will and powers of attorney for you and your spouse for about $500.

You may also want to consider a living will. A living will spells out your wishes as to the kind of care you want to receive after an accident, illness or when you are unable to speak for yourself and your condition is terminal. Some also refer to this as the document where you must decide whether or not you want to "pull the plug," in other words, not be kept alive artificially. For more information on living wills there is a Web site sponsored by The University of Toronto Joint Centre for Bioethics. They offer samples of living wills and instructional booklets on their site which is at www.utoronto.ca/jcb. Their phone number is 416-978-2709.

If you would like more information on preparing a will, you can check The Canadian Bar Association's Web site at www.cba.org. November is Make a Will month and during this time, some lawyers offer information sessions or free consultations regarding wills. At the very least, they may have a brochure to pass on and you can find out their fee for drawing up a will. An excellent book entitled *The Canadian Guide to Will and Estate Planning* (Douglas Gray and John Budd, McGraw-Hill Ryerson) also has the answers to most questions dealing with wills in Canada.

DECLARING BANKRUPTCY — a Last Resort

Mohammed was facing a financial crisis. He was divorced, paying child support and living from paycheque to paycheque. He had made some bad investments and had outstanding loans and credit card debt. He could see no end in sight to his financial problems. He felt he had no option but to declare bankruptcy but he was unsure how to go about it or if this was really something he should consider.

Bankruptcy is a legal undertaking which allows people to get a new lease on life by freeing them from a financial burden they may otherwise never be able to recover from. However, for a business or corporation, bankruptcy means the end of its financial life. Declaring bankruptcy is a common occurrence for both businesses and consumers. In 1999, there were 83,023 bankruptcies in Canada. Of those, 72,997 were consumers declaring bankruptcy while 10,026 were businesses closing their doors. The record high for Canadian bankruptcies was in 1997 when there were 97,497 bankruptcies.

All bankruptcies and insolvencies (to be unable to meet demands of creditors) must be dealt with in a fair and orderly manner and if a person or company files for bankruptcy, all information about the file is available for public scrutiny. The Office of the Superintendent of Bankruptcy has a database in Ottawa of all bankruptcies filed in Canada from 1978 to date. For a fee, usually about $8, the department will launch a search on your behalf to find information on an individual's or business's bankruptcy status. You can find out more about the database through Industry Canada in the blue pages of your telephone book or by checking their Web site at www.ic.gc.ca/.

Declaring bankruptcy will eliminate most of your debts and provide immediate relief from legal actions by creditors. Once you file for bankruptcy, an automatic stay of proceedings goes into force against your creditors so that all legal actions against you (such as wage garnishees) will cease. You will have to sign over most of your personal property to a Licensed Trustee in Bankruptcy who will sell your assets and use the money to pay off as much debt as possible. Any remaining debt with certain exceptions such as court fines, alimonies or child support, is then legally eliminated. The process does allow you to retain certain property, such as clothing, furniture and tools required for your occupation. Laws regarding what you can keep and what you must sell vary from province to province. To qualify for bankruptcy, you must owe at least $1,000 and be unable to make regular payments on time or owe more than the resale value of what you own.

Pat Robinson, President of Pat Robinson Inc. Trustee in Bankruptcy, says that before declaring bankruptcy, consumers and businesses should consider all other options. They should contact creditors and explain their situation, consider a consolidation loan or seek help from an outside party. However, if you absolutely have no other options available to you, bankruptcy may be your only way out. "A financial crisis may be the final result of poor management over time, insufficient income and inappropriate spending patterns," explains Robinson. The person may or may not be to blame for their misfortune. "A major debt load may be as a result of unexpected or external events or because of mismanagement, lack of self-discipline or ignorance."

When bankruptcy becomes inevitable, the trustee will notify all creditors of your bankruptcy and ensure that they no longer seek payment outside of the bankruptcy process. There are two required sessions of financial counselling in order for the debtors to acquire budgeting and money management skills. "Normally you will be in bankruptcy for about nine months and during that time, you will be required to submit monthly statements of your income and expenses," says Robinson.

If you do not have complicated financial affairs and owe less than $75,000 excluding the mortgage on your residence, you can make a Division Two Proposal to creditors, known as a Consumer Proposal, to try to avoid bankruptcy. A proposal may seek an extension of time for payment, reductions in interest rates and repayment of less than 100 cents on the dollar. If those who are owed money agree to a proposal, bankruptcy can be avoided. If they don't, bankruptcy may be your next option. Someone owing in excess of $75,000 files what is known as a Division One Proposal, but in the event that it is refused, it leads to automatic bankruptcy.

> Declaring bankruptcy will eliminate most of your debts, however, it will be kept on your credit file for seven years.

Many people facing bankruptcy are concerned about their long term credit rating. However Robinson says, "if their debts have become so unmanageable, their credit rating may already be in a terrible state." Like the status of your bank accounts, credit card statements and other lending information, filing for bankruptcy will also be kept on your credit file for seven years. The bankruptcy information will come off your credit rating after seven years, unless the consumer has been bankrupt more than once. "While a lender will know that you have filed for bankruptcy, they will consider other factors such as your current financial situation, your employment income and whether there is collateral for the loan," she advises. You may have a difficult time getting a credit card initially after a bankruptcy, so you may need to apply for a secured card. A secured card is backed up or secured by funds you have deposited with a bank or credit union and will have a limit depending on how much secures the card.

To declare personal bankruptcy, the general fee is around $1,300. Fees for a corporate bankruptcy will depend on the complexity of the file. The trustee receives its fees from the realization of the assets from a bankrupt estate, as set out in the *Bankruptcy and Insolvency Act*. The bankruptcy process is designed to rehabilitate the debtor and create a fair environment for creditors. It may be an offense to fraudulently dispose of assets or give false information before or after a bankruptcy. Also, a decision to declare bankruptcy should not be taken lightly, as it is something you do not want to do, as it will affect your credit rating for the next seven years. However, if your financial situation is so dire that you see no other way out, you should speak to a trustee in bankruptcy about your circumstances. You should also work to improve your financial situation by budgeting, exercising restraint and realizing why you got into financial trouble in the first place.

ALERT

15

BANK MACHINE MALFUNCTION

Jeff needed cash and while in a corner store, he noticed an automatic money machine. He decided to take out $260. He was shocked when the machine gave him only $60 but spit out a receipt saying he had been given the entire amount! He complained to the cashier behind the counter, but she said the store had nothing to do with the machine. Jeff wasn't sure what to do. He wondered who would his bank believe — him or the machine?

Every day in Canada, millions of dollars flow through bank machines without a hitch. But problems do happen and chances are at some point, you will be shortchanged by an automated teller. Depending on the institution that owns the machine you are using, the mistake can be fixed within an hour or take months to rectify.

Most machines, regardless of who owns them, will usually have a toll-free help number to phone if you don't receive the proper amount of money when making a withdrawal. In the event you are shortchanged, *don't panic*! When you call the help line, you will realize bank machine errors are common enough that there is a procedure in place to deal with them. In most cases, you will be told to take the receipt to your own bank where officials will start a trace to see what went wrong. If the error takes place in the lobby of your local bank, the problem could be corrected in minutes. If the malfunction happens at a private banking machine at a convenience store, it could take two to six weeks for your funds to be returned. Either way, it's frustrating trying to get your own money back.

Most automated tellers are owned by Canada's big banks and are easily recognizable by their prominently displayed logos. There are private companies that also offer banking machine services, but they charge an additional fee, about a dollar, on top of the fees you already pay your bank to withdraw cash. Frank Helt is the president of ABM Direct Incorporated, a company that provides private banking machine services. He says that if a bank machine makes a mistake, there is an electronic trail that can be traced to correct it. "The bank machines have electronic journals that record everything that happens within them," says Helt. "When there is a problem with a bank machine, usually it will be something as simple as a bill jamming."

If you get short-changed by an automatic money machine, call the toll-free help line and save your receipt.

Bank machines can hold between $80,000 and $120,000 depending on the denomination of bills placed in the cash dispenser cartridges. Paper money is constantly recirculating so it's no surprise that a battered bill could cause problems during a mechanical process involving small moving parts. Of course, there are times when a customer is given more money than they should be, although they may be less likely to complain. When someone doesn't get their proper withdrawal, it can take time for the person to be credited their money because there must be an audit conducted. Surprisingly, this is because of false claims. There are many occasions when customers say they have been ripped off by a bank machine, when they haven't.

If you do get shortchanged by an automatic bank machine, keep your receipt (if you don't have it, your transaction can still be traced electronically), call the toll-free number on the machine and follow the instructions if you get a recorded message. If you have truly been shortchanged by a bank machine you will, in almost all cases, have the amount credited back to your account. It will just be a matter of time.

CO-SIGNING LOANS — Think Before You Sign!

Brenda's friend, Wayne, was having financial difficulties. When Wayne told Brenda that he had been refused a car loan which could jeopardize his getting to work and therefore his job, Brenda agreed to help him out by co-signing a bank loan. A year after co-signing, Wayne lost his job and when he started missing payments, the bank immediately demanded money from Brenda. Brenda was now also strapped for cash and would have to undergo tremendous financial pressures to pay Wayne's loan as well as her own bills.

By co-signing a loan, we are telling a lender that we will pay back the money if our child, spouse, relative or friend cannot. You are agreeing to take on a risk that the bank or other lending institution won't. What many people do not know is that co-signers are often required to pay loans that go into default. Be very cautious before agreeing to help someone out by guaranteeing their debt. Before signing, consider if you can afford to pay the loan back if you have to. You may also be liable for additional interest charges, late fees and collection costs.

The creditor can use the same methods of collection against you that they would against the borrower. So you could find yourself being sued, having your wages garnisheed and your credit rating adversely affected. If you do co-sign for a loan, this may also affect your ability to seek new credit for yourself. Do not pledge property as collateral for a loan because if the borrower defaults, you could lose it! You could ask that the contract include a statement which would say "The co-signer will be responsible for the principle balance of the loan at the time of default." Ask that the lender notify you in writing if the borrower misses a payment. This could ward off a more serious problem if you were able to help the borrower make a payment or two, rather than have the bank come after you immediately for the money.

A creditor can use the same methods of collection against you as the co-signer as they would against the borrower. Can you afford to make payments if the borrower defaults?

If a family member or friend asks you to co-sign a loan, understand exactly what your obligations will be before agreeing to it. While there may be emotional considerations which cloud the issue, don't be pressured into a situation that you will regret later. How trustworthy is the borrower? Why can't they get a loan on their own? Can you afford to make the payments if they default? Will co-signing a loan cause complications for your own credit limit and mean you could be turned down for a loan? Is there another option available to the borrower that does not involve you, such as a loan at another institution that charges a higher interest rate? Coming to the aid of a relative or friend is a noble thing. Just don't let it come back to haunt you later.

FINANCIAL ADVISORS

Rita was left alone to deal with her finances after her husband passed away. She had $180,000 in savings but no idea how to manage her money — her husband had always done this. She contacted a broker who told her not to worry, he could manage her account. She trusted the broker completely and gave him special access to her funds. He provided her with handwritten reports, detailing her account transactions. Within two years, the broker left town and Rita was shocked to see that her account had dwindled to less than $15,000.

The vast majority of financial advisors are professional money managers who have their clients' best interests at heart. There are however, many cases of customers being defrauded, mislead or at the very least, poorly served by someone offering financial guidance. Stan Buell is the President of the Small Investor Protection Association (SIPA), a group he formed in 1998 after having his own bad experiences with the investment industry. "I went from a position of not needing a job to needing a job to survive. It was very difficult to cope with that. When you lose a large amount of money, you can't believe it has happened," says Buell. His volunteer group has a three-part mission: to make people more aware of how the investment industry operates, to provide financial guidance, and to fight for improved regulations, audit and enforcement to benefit investors.

In a survey of its 300 members, SIPA found that 80% of the respondents suffered an average loss of $83,000.

Sadly there are too many cases of money managers who have churned accounts (buying and selling funds to make commissions), gambled with investors' money hoping to make profits for themselves and who have moved investments from solid to risky holdings. Buell says, "I've seen people who are in a terrible state. People feel guilty and embarrassed. Some people say clients wouldn't lose their investments if they weren't greedy, but that's not true. It's a matter of trust and you have to be able to trust the people looking after your money." Buell's group has heard from many people who have lost large amounts of money. "More than 90% of brokers are good and no more than 10% are bad. The problem is if you meet up with a bad broker, it can destroy your life savings and in some cases, ruin your life." He warns that you must know what is going on with your accounts and never give your broker special access to your funds. Ask for monthly evaluation showing the value of your account. You should get it each month and if your broker can't provide that, then don't deal with them. Buell recommends making sure that the report is produced as a company standard, and not a handwritten or typed report. All correspondence, good, bad or indifferent, should be put in writing. "Often when problems arise between investors and their financial advisors, much of the correspondence is verbal which can create problems later." Written correspondence will establish a paper trail of your transactions.

"There are good financial advisors out there who provide their services for a fee and that is the best kind of financial advisor you can have," says Buell. Money managers may sell themselves as financial advisors, leading clients to believe that they are getting objective advice. "People selling financial products are financial products salespersons and not financial advisors," advises Buell. Clients should be careful not to be mislead. "When you buy insurance, you buy from an insurance salesperson, so someone representing a limited number of mutual funds or trust units should not be able to pass themselves off as a financial advisor." Buell says that consumers must realize that the people they are buying products from may be commission-motivated and could receive higher commission rates on some financial products than on others, which could affect their objectivity. Investors must also make themselves aware of how much of their investment is going to pay management fees. For example, mutual funds are extremely popular and all mutual funds charge fees for managing your investments. In addition to management fees, you may have to pay commissions when you buy a fund (a front-end load) or when you sell a fund (a back-end load). There may be one-time fees for setting up accounts, switching or transferring funds or redemption fees as well as annual trust fees for registered plans such as RRSPs and RRIFs. The various fees and charges will reduce the fund's return and these expenses are deducted regardless of the fund's performance.

Clients should never give power of attorney to an investment advisor as this will give the advisor full and complete access to accounts to trade, buy, and sell at will. Giving a money manager that kind of access can lead to serious problems. Never assume that your money is always in good hands just because it is in the care of a financial advisor. Ask questions, monitor your accounts and don't be satisfied with the "trust me, everything is fine" mentality. Play an active role in watching your accounts and in decisions involving your money. Always have a good balance with any investments and do not invest too heavily in any area. "We are trying to make people understand how some firms sell worthless penny stocks and how some firms sell limited partnerships, where the chances of investors getting their money back are remote," Buell says.

For more information on the Small Investor Protection Association you can check their Web site at www.sipa.to or telephone at 905-471-2911. There is an annual membership fee of $20 per family, but in some cases it may be waived. For other excellent information on investing check out the following sites:

- The Investor Learning Centre of Canada at www. investorlearning.ca
- Industry Canada's Business and Consumer at www. strategis.gc.ca
- The Investment Funds Institute of Canada at www.ific.ca

LIFE AND DISABILITY INSURANCE

Connor and Vanessa were in their mid-thirties and had two children. They had a mortgage, some savings and a few investments. While Connor had a limited life and disability insurance policy through his workplace, Vanessa did not. They were unsure if they were properly covered, or if they had enough insurance to adequately protect their family.

Life insurance is really death insurance but calling it that makes it a tougher sell. Still, having adequate life insurance for you and your family may be one of the most important decisions you will ever make. Richard Young, sales representative and industry expert with Liberty Mutual Insurance, says life insurance should not be viewed as an economic plan for retirement. "Life insurance is to help provide consumers with a safe and secure lifestyle," says Young. Your exposure is one of the most important factors when deciding how much life insurance you need. To determine how much, use actual scenarios. "If you died tomorrow, will your family be left in a good or bad position? How much will they need to be financially protected and comfortable?" Young says. Conversely if your spouse died, what position would that leave you in? Will there be enough money for your lifestyle, daycare, car payments, vacations, house-cleaning and your children's post-secondary education?

There are basically three kinds of insurance: term, term to 100 and permanent. Term insurance is the most inexpensive life insurance policy you can buy and it's basically pay as you go. Insurance is purchased in "chunks" of five, 10 or 20 year terms. The younger you are, the cheaper the premiums will be, but they will increase as your term runs out and it comes time to renew. You can also buy a term to 100 plan, which is basically unending no frills term insurance. Permanent insurance comes in the form of whole life or universal life protection. Both kinds include an investment component as well as a cash value option. If you agree to give up the death benefit, you can cash in the policy for money that has built up in the plan. Whole and universal plans cover you for your entire life and your premiums won't change. Your payments will be decided on your age, job, health and other risk factors.

Life insurance can be expensive and you should only buy coverage that is right for your situation. "The bottom line is that life insurance has to be affordable. There are people who are oversold insurance and then can't keep up paying premiums of hundreds of dollars a month. They then end up cancelling policies," Young says. You have to be comfortable with your insurance because you don't really want to think about it after getting it. If money is tight because of mortgage, car loans and other financial responsibilities, you may want to start out with basic coverage and increase your benefits when you can afford to. You can also opt for less insurance as you age and your exposure decreases such as when your children leave the nest and your home is paid for.

Someone who is single with no dependants may feel that they do not need life insurance, except to cover their funeral costs. "Everyone should have enough money for their funeral arrangements. Funerals are expensive and may be an unwelcome financial burden on a retired parent on a fixed income," says Young. By signing up for permanent insurance early in life, you will always be insured as long as you keep paying your premiums. Once you have a life insurance policy in place, you can change jobs, careers, remarry or become seriously ill. True life insurance has no restrictions, unless you commit suicide within two years of signing a life insurance policy.

While many people have life insurance through their workplace, there is a potential problem. "If you become unemployed, you become uninsured. This could be a disadvantage for someone who is in their forties with a medical condition. They may find it difficult to get insurance," advises Young. Do you know exactly how much coverage you have through your workplace? Can you buy additional coverage through your workplace if you want to?

Disability insurance is necessary for income replacement in the event of an accident that leaves you alive, but unable to work. Young maintains that "your biggest asset is not your home. Your biggest asset is your ability to work and generate income. If you get injured and can't work, how much money will you need?" Young is adamant that everyone should have some form of disability insurance especially self-employed individuals or workers in high risk jobs. "While homeowners have mortgage insurance, without life or disability insurance the fact that your house is paid for may mean little because without proper funds you or your family won't be able to maintain it." If you are injured in a car accident and have auto insurance, accident benefits will pay your wages, medical bills and other expenses. If you are injured in another kind of accident and are not covered by worker's compensation or disability insurance then you may be exposed to financial hardship.

Different scenarios require different insurance strategies. Estate taxes will be costly for the baby boomer generation. As the family cottage is handed down to the children following a death, there may be tens of thousands of dollars to pay in estate taxes. Parents with large assets may decide to take out a life insurance policy on themselves and have their children pay the premiums. The death benefit will then pay the estate taxes.

If you have a family with a history of disease, you will have to disclose this when you buy life insurance but once you have a life insurance policy and make your payments you're covered. However, if you are diagnosed with a serious medical condition and then try to get life insurance, it may be extremely difficult and expensive. Also, always be extremely honest about your medical condition when applying for any kind of insurance. The last thing you would want to happen is to pay premiums for years, only to find out your policy will be void because you were less than honest on the application form.

If you have a business partner, you may want to take out a life insurance policy on him or her. That way if your partner died, the death benefit would allow you to buy out that portion of the company so that the business could carry on. While mortgage insurance is offered through banks, you can seek coverage elsewhere. Unlike a 20-year term insurance policy which will pay out the same in year one as it will in twenty years, with bank mortgage insurance the payout will be less each year as you pay off your home. In the event of the death of a spouse, you may also decide that having your home paid off is not your first priority.

> Always be extremely honest about your medical condition when applying for life insurance.

Also, beware of advertised life insurance policies that promise low monthly premiums with no medical exam. Of course, in the end there may not be much of a payout either. Do your homework on the various insurance policies, especially permanent life polices which can be complex. Find an insurance company and agent you can trust and are comfortable with. As Liberty Mutual's Richard Young says, "don't get talked into insurance you can't afford, but use common sense to make sure you have adequate coverage to protect the ones you care about."

KEEPING YOU IN THE DRIVER'S SEAT

VEHICLE LEASING — the True Cost

Mario and Avery were looking for a sports utility vehicle and found one they liked. The purchase price was more than they could afford, so they decided to lease the truck. Everything was going fine until Mario took ill. He was so sick, he couldn't work and Avery was at home with their two children. They decided to end the lease and asked the dealership to take the truck back. That's when they were told that they could not get out of the arrangement and would have to make the $550 monthly payments whether they wanted the truck or not.

Leasing is a way that consumers can drive a new car or truck off the lot without actually having to purchase it. What consumers often fail to recognize when entering into leasing agreements is that they are basically signing a long term rental contract. American consumer advocate Ralph Nader says that "consumers are getting gouged far too often. It's more like auto fleecing than leasing." What happened to Mario and Avery takes place often as people sign long term leases and then get divorced, lose their jobs, their eyesight or their lives and still car companies refuse to break the leasing contracts. Consumers must realize that when they sign a contract to lease for three years, it's for three years regardless of what happens in their life. Before leasing, it's also important to do some basic math to realize that long term leasing is far more expensive than buying a vehicle outright.

Car companies have spent a lot of time advertising leasing as a low-cost alternative for those who want that new car smell, but don't have the finances to purchase. It's true that leasing is a way to get into a new car with lower monthly payments than what loan payments would be on the same vehicle. However, when consumers factor in along with their monthly payments, a down payment, interest, additional fees and taxes, it becomes clear that leasing is extremely profitable for car dealers. There are some benefits to leasing and consumers can negotiate to get a better deal, but everyone should weigh the pros and cons before signing a leasing contract.

The least expensive way to acquire a new car is to pay cash for it. Since most of us can't afford to do that, we can take out a loan for a used car, or lease, or borrow money for a new one. Some consumers prefer leasing because they don't mind having perpetual monthly payments as long as it allows them to drive a new car that is under warranty. A motorist who leases can avoid tying up a lot of money in a vehicle and if they have a business, they can write off the leasing payments. At the end of the lease you can decide to buy the vehicle or simply turn it over to the leasing company.

The pitfalls? When you lease a vehicle, you don't own it and never build up equity in it as you would if you had bought the same vehicle. Leasing can be expensive if you decide to keep a car, truck or van for a long period of time. If you miscalculate the number of kilometres you plan to drive, leasing can be costly as well. Even though you don't own the leased vehicle, you are still responsible for maintaining and repairing it. Many of the repairs will be covered under warranty if you are leasing a newer vehicle, but if you are leasing an older one this can become expensive.

There are two kinds of leases: closed and open. In a closed lease, the most popular kind used in the marketplace, there are a set number of payments to be made during a specific time period. After you have fulfilled your obligation, the vehicle is

returned to the leasing company and you have an option to purchase it at the previously-agreed-to buyout price. At this time,
you may have to make additional payments if there is excess
wear and tear on the vehicle and if you have driven a higher
number of kilometres than what you were allotted.

In an open end lease, you also make a set number of payments over a predetermined time frame. When the vehicle is
returned, you may have to make an additional payment to cover
the difference between the actual value of the vehicle and its
residual value. For example, if the vehicle had a residual value
of $11,000 but the leasing company could sell it for only $9,500,
you would have to pay an additional fee of $1,500. If the vehicle
could be sold for more than the residual value, the consumer
should be refunded the difference.

While lower monthly payments may seem attractive, keep
in mind that there are additional costs involved when leasing a
car. Most leasing companies require a down payment of thousands of dollars. This "down payment" does not build up equity
in the vehicle at all but is merely a payment in advance to make
the monthly lease payments appear smaller. You may have to
pay a security deposit, licence and registration fees, acquisition
fees (paperwork charges) and Gap protection insurance (see
Alert 24 on Gap insurance — it may be cheaper through your
insurance company than the dealer). You may not be allowed
to remove your vehicle from the province or territory where you
leased it for an extended period unless you have permission from
the leasing company. You may also want to take out life and
disability insurance on the lease in case something happens and
you can't honour the contract.

Give your full attention to the excess kilometre charge. A
typical lease may allow for 20,000 km to be driven annually for
a total of 60,000 km over three years. If a consumer racks up
78,000 km during this period, this will translate into an excess
kilometre penalty, or overage charge, at the end of the lease.
For example, if the contract calls for a 12¢ a kilometre overage
charge this means that the 18,000 excess kilometres will be
multiplied by 12¢ for an additional payment of $2,160! Excess
wear and tear charges could also be levied against you. This could

include balding or mismatched tires, damage to the car's exterior, missing parts or rips or scratches to the car's interior. Don't get railroaded into being told that there is excess wear and tear on your car if you feel there isn't. Remember your security deposit and try to use it as your last month's payment.

When you sign a lease, under no circumstances are you allowed to walk away from the contract. Most leasing arrangements with car companies are iron clad and make it clear that you will not be allowed to end your lease early unless it is stated in your lease. If you are able to negotiate a right to early termination into your lease, it should contain the formula for calculating the early termination amount. It should also be noted that someone buying a car may try to negotiate the selling price down from $25,000 to $22,000. However, someone leasing this same car usually does not take part in this kind of haggling so they will end up making leasing payments based on the $25,000 selling price.

Along with your monthly leasing payments, factor in a down payment, interest, security deposit, repairs and maintenance, license and registration fees, acquisition fees and Gap insurance.

If you lease a vehicle and need to get out of the contract, be aware that you may have to try and sublease your vehicle to someone else. While a dealer could help you do this, chances are they would rather try to lease another vehicle to another customer rather than help you. If you want out of your lease, you may also have to purchase the vehicle at a buyout price set by the leasing company or make the monthly payments until you have fulfilled your obligation. Avoid leases that are longer than the manufacturer's warranty. Some dealers may try to get you to sign a 39-month lease rather than 36 to make the payments seem lower. However, if the warranty is up, you could be required to make repairs to the vehicle just prior to having to give it back.

Avoid leasing after December 31st as you will then be leasing a car that will be half a model year old. Cars depreciate quickly, so it's best if you strike a leasing deal when new models come out which is usually between September and December.

Shop around to see if the car you want can be leased elsewhere cheaper. Do the math on purchasing the car through a lender to see if buying the car would make better sense. Ask yourself if you would be better off financially to purchase a car that is two years old rather than lease a new one. Don't lease unless you are fairly secure in your job and life situation, as three years is a long time. Could you have children and then need a minivan instead of a sports car? Never sign an agreement that you don't fully understand. Do the math — you may find in some cases that you will pay less in loan interest at a bank than what you will pay in finance charges to a leasing company.

BUYING A NEW VEHICLE

Leo was in the market for a vehicle and after driving used cars for more than a decade, he considered buying a brand-new car. He wasn't sure where to start and was concerned that he might pay too much, that his car would drop in value immediately after he drove it off the lot and that he was being extravagant by buying new. He was looking for information to help him be sure that he was making the right decision.

After buying a home, purchasing a car is usually the second biggest investment a consumer will make so it's wise to take the time to shop before making a commitment. In fact, Dennis DesRosiers, one of Canada's most recognized independent automotive consultants, says it now takes 28.8 weeks of after-tax family earnings to purchase a new vehicle versus 20 weeks only a decade ago. On average, vehicle prices have increased about 6.4% per year over the last 15 years. DesRosiers says "there are three elements to any negotiating process — time, information and money." He believes that if a consumer can stay in the power position on these variables they will be more likely to get a good deal.

A consumer who waits until the last minute to buy a car and places themselves in the hands of a dealer are more likely to pay top price for a car. "Consumers who take their time and shop around, know what they are looking for, are knowledgeable about the vehicle they want and understand the money side of the purchase will generally get a better deal," DesRosiers says. Many dealers will put time limits on sales such as 'only available until the end of the month or this weekend only.' That's to keep the time element on the dealer's side so it's best to start the car buying process early to keep time on your side. "While every incentive has an end date to entice consumers to act quickly, if you let the deal pass it is only a matter of time before another incentive on the same vehicle or a similar one is offered," says DesRosiers. Vehicles are also built better than ever before so there may be no need for consumers to rush into another vehicle when they have one that is working fine.

DesRosiers points out one exception to the time variable — when dealers clear out models, usually from August to November. Dealers will often discount the previous model year to get them off the lot. Choice is limited and you may not have the pick of options as these vehicles are not being produced specifically for you. They may have also been poor sellers during the year. While you may see a savings, DesRosiers says, "by buying late in the model year, the vehicle will lose one year of depreciation very quickly. If you are going to keep the vehicle for a long time, at least seven years, then this doesn't matter. If you plan to trade it in a year or two, keep in mind the resale value will be lower."

If information is power, this is especially true when buying a new vehicle. With the Internet, consumers are now firmly in the driver's seat when it comes to researching new car purchases. Every major manufacturer as well as independent publications and research groups have Web sites crammed with information about pricing, fuel economy, reliability, options, comfort, space, performance and a host of other details. A good source of independent information is the Lemon-Aid series of car guides by author Phil Edmonston. Edmonston has been writing his evaluations of new and used cars for more than 25 years and is a respected consumer advocate who provides unbiased information on the auto industry's best and worst vehicles.

DesRosiers believes the best way to research a car is to test drive it. "By test driving vehicles, consumers can gather information on the physical elements of the vehicle such as design, driving characteristics and handling."

It's also a way to "test drive" the dealership. It's important to have a positive relationship with the dealer and visiting a bricks and mortar site will help you develop a sense of whether the dealer is trustworthy, professional and knowledgeable. "I believe consumers should trust their gut. If deep down they feel uncomfortable with a dealership, then they should go somewhere else," DesRosiers says.

The final element to negotiating a deal is money. Financing a car can be complex and you must be sure to always read the fine print! While the cheapest way to buy a car is cash, most of us will have to use a lender to finance our purchase. Prearranging your financing can make buying a car less stressful if you already know it is something you can afford. The buyer who shops first and worries about financing later could be in for an unpleasant surprise. While DesRosiers says that dealers have become increasingly competitive with banks on financing, it's best to compare before doing any deal. The profit margin at the dealership level varies only between $500 and $5,000 depending on whether the vehicle is a high end Sports Utility Vehicle or a low-cost compact. Keep this is mind when negotiating. Try to get the best deal possible but there will be a limit on how low the dealer will go, as they must profit from the sale as well.

Before buying any car, call your insurance company to see how much it will cost to insure your new car. Premiums vary widely depending on the make and model. Be aware that when the sales representative is closing the deal, he or she may try to sell you rust-proofing, undercoating and other dealer options. You may wish to avoid any add-ons as the dealer usually charges a substantial mark-up on these items to sweeten their profit.

If you are trading in a vehicle, you should have a rough idea of what it is worth by checking used vehicles magazines, classified ads or dealer lots. Keep in mind that the dealer will want to make money by selling your trade-in, so expect $1,500 to $2,000 less than if you sold it yourself. While a thorough cleaning and polishing may help with your car's appearance, a dealer won't be fooled by a car with serious wear and tear or mechanical problems.

BUYING
NEARLY NEW

Britney wanted to buy a new car but knew it wasn't in her budget. She knew about cars sold as nearly new that were only two or three years old. The vehicles were sold certified and with warranties and she wondered if this would be a better way to buy a car. Still, she was concerned that she could end up purchasing someone else's problem.

With the explosion of leasing in the automotive sector, a new concept in vehicle sales has spawned — the nearly new vehicle. Leasing now accounts for about 40% of all new car purchases and since consumers can walk away from vehicles at the end of a lease, and many do, leasing companies have thousands of cars on their hands to get rid of. I personally own two vehicles that were once leased by someone else. I bought a 1992 Ford Taurus sedan in 1994 that had 110,000 km (it now has 280,000 km and is still going strong). Our family later purchased a 1995 Chevrolet Lumina van in 1997 with 100,000 km. At the time I realized there was a degree of risk in buying used vehicles with this much mileage; however in both cases I calculated that it was a reasonable risk as I purchased two-year-old vehicles at about half their original purchase price.

Auto consultant Dennis DesRosiers says, "nearly new vehicles are one to four years old and still have some of the manufacturer's warranty remaining. Because of their age, they also feature the latest designs and technology offered by the industry." The emergence of the nearly new vehicle has radically altered traditional consumer attitudes toward used vehicles. In the past many consumers feared buying a used vehicle as they were concerned that they were buying someone else's problem. This is not the case today. DesRosiers says a vehicle bought new today will now last up to 300,000 km where as 20 years ago they averaged only 150,000 km. Modern vehicles hold up very well over time and a five-year old vehicle is not considered old as it may have been in the past. The adage that vehicles lose half their value when they are driven off the lot is no longer true, according to DesRosiers. "The average depreciation of a new vehicle is about 10 to 12% per year, that's all." That means some of these nearly new vehicles can be worth 60 to 80% of their original price.

You can get a great deal on a nearly-new vehicle if you find one privately that has just come off a lease. Many people would rather buy-out a decent car from a leasing company, rather than turn it over at the end of the lease.

One of the best ways to get a deal on a nearly-new vehicle is to find one privately that has just come off a lease. Often companies or individuals that have leased a vehicle will buy out the lease rather than turn it over to the leasing company so they can try to sell it themselves and make a grand or two (this is how I got mine). Deals like this may be hard to find and consumers will also have to be sure they are not dealing with a curbsider, someone who misrepresents themselves when selling a car (see Alert 25 on curbsiders). "Consumers must really be on guard as 20 to 25% of all private sales are done by curbsiders," says DesRosiers. More likely consumers looking to buy a nearly new vehicle will find them on a car lot where dealers are hoping to sell nearly new vehicles for a profit. To ease the mind of the consumer, dealers are offering things like 100 point vehicle inspections, 12 month/20,000 km warranties, 24 hour roadside assistance and financing. These added reassurances for the consumer also add to the price of the car.

DesRosiers has a formula to help consumers decide the value of a nearly new car. He says as the average vehicle lasts about 300,000 km and costs about $30,000, the capital cost of a new vehicle is about 10¢/km to own over its lifetime. This calculation can be used to determine the value of a nearly new vehicle as well. Divide the price by 300,000 km minus the odometer reading. For example, a three-year old vehicle selling for $30,000 with 100,000 km on the odometer costs about 15¢ per potential kilometre of use [$30,000 divided by 200,000 km (300,000 km − 100,000 km) = 15¢]. Not a great deal for a nearly new vehicle when you consider a new vehicle is only 10¢ per potential kilometre of use. A better deal would be a cost of eight to 10¢ per potential kilometre of use or about $18,000 to $20,000.

DesRosiers points out that his formula only works if you compare identical makes and features of new and used vehicles. If you can't afford to buy new, you can have some confidence when considering nearly new vehicles. There may be some repairs down the road, but if you strike a good deal on a well-priced one- to four-year-old car, truck or van, it should still provide you with tens of thousands of kilometres of worry-free motoring.

BUYING A USED CAR

Rebecca had just finished university and had thousands of dollars in school loans to pay off. Despite her debt, she knew she had a better chance of securing a job if she had transportation to and from work. With her financial situation as it was, she resigned herself to the fact that she would have to buy a used car. Still, she was worried she might get "taken" by a dishonest seller.

As discussed in the previous Alert, the automobile is a lot more reliable than it was 10 or 20 years ago, so you can still expect a used vehicle to provide years of operation. Having said this, it's obvious the older the car and the higher the mileage, the more likely a consumer will have problems down the road. Buying a used car does not only mean a lower purchase price. It also can lead to savings on financing charges and insurance costs. But oh those repairs! That's why researching your used car purchase is every bit as important as when buying a new one. Keeping "time, information and money" on your side is important and planning ahead will improve your chances of getting a car that will serve you well.

Knowing the kind of car you want is an important first step. Once you've established you want a compact economy car over a four-door sedan, compare the different models available in the segment you're interested in. Does the colour matter? What about options? Will you be driving the car long distances? How many kilometres do you reasonably expect to put on the car annually? How much can you afford to spend on a car? Will you have money left over for gas, maintenance, insurance and unforeseen repairs?

Next comes the research. The Internet and reference materials at libraries are good places to start. Pricing is generally arrived at by car pricing guides known as the Red and Blue books. Phil Edmonston, author of the Lemon-Aid Series of car guides, says the Blue books are American guides with U.S. prices. "In Canada, most dealers go by the Canadian Red Book, a monthly publication. It's $85 for a yearly subscription and while there are other regional guides, the Red Book is the one used nationally by most dealers," says Edmonston. You can usually find the Red Book at a library's reference desk, a credit union or local bank. "The Canadian Red Book is privately published and shows the original selling price (MSRP), the wholesale price (what dealers charge dealers) and retail price (what dealers charge walk-ins)," advises Edmonston.

Even if you don't look at the pricing guides, check the prices of at least three to five other cars on the market with similar mileage and options to see what they are selling for. Collect information on a model's track record, reliability, repair history, problems specific to that vehicle (such as faulty turbo chargers or digital dashboards), its likelihood of rusting and anything else to help you find the best value in a used car. A good used car can be a blessing. A bad one can be a curse leading to endless repairs, time off work to get it fixed, rental car expenses when it's in the shop and eventually, you will have to get rid of it and possibly sell the "lemon" to someone else.

It would be great if you had an elderly relative who meticulously cared for his sports car and wanted to sell it to you for a song. More likely, you will have to buy a car from a dealer or through a private sale. Auctions can be risky for the inexperienced buyer. You may get a better deal buying privately but who are you buying the car from? Was it really just driven to work and back for three years? Is the odometer really 90,000 km and not rolled back from 190,000 km? Is it certified? If not, what will the car need to be roadworthy and how much will it cost to ready it for certification? Will it pass an emissions test if required? Has it been in an accident? Is the person who is selling the car the true owner or are they flipping the car (see Alert 25 on Curbsiders) to make a quick profit? If you are well-prepared, you can get a good deal buying a car privately, but some consumers prefer buying from a dealer who may provide some peace of mind with a warranty. Warranties should be examined carefully to determine if they are of any value. Often they provide only limited coverage, so read the fine print and know exactly what kind of protection you are getting. Keep in mind, a warranty is often negotiable so don't pay full price if you can.

Have an independent mechanic check out a used car before you purchase. A thorough inspection could save you thousands of dollars if the car needs major work.

Once you find a model you like, inspect the individual car to try to determine what kind of care it has had. Does the previous owner have maintenance records? If the oil has been changed regularly and a new starter and fuel pump were installed recently, is there paperwork to back this up? There are things to look for that can tell you about the car's past. One way to check if it has been in an accident is to look for mismatched paint on body panels. If shades of colour are different from the fender to the hood, the car may have been in a collision. Are there dents and scratches? Do panels and seams line-up perfectly? After running the car for a while, you should park it in an area with dry pavement to check for leaks. Check the oil to see if it has been changed recently or if it is a dark dirty black colour. The transmission fluid should have a reddish appearance. If it's brownish, this could mean it hasn't been changed in some time or that there could be a transmission problem looming.

The test drive of the car is very important. When it is safe to do so on a level road, it's a good idea to take your hands off the wheel to see if the car tracks straight. If it pulls to the side, this could be a sign that the car was in an accident, needs an alignment or has a suspension or other serious problem. The car shouldn't shake or vibrate. The brakes should work well and also not cause the car to pull to the side when they are applied. Does the vehicle sit level? Bounce each corner of the car. It should bounce back once or twice. Does the car start easily? Does it idle smoothly? Does it stall? Does the automatic transmission shift smoothly? Is the manual shift transmission smooth or does the clutch slip? If the vehicle has four wheel drive, does it engage in and out of four wheel drive without clunking?

Are the tires mismatched? How much life is left in the tires? Is there a spare? Is the jack still with the car? The owner's manual? Spare keys? Is there rust along the wheel wells, door handles, in the trunk or under the hood? How is the appearance of the interior of the car? If the interior has rips, burns and smells, this could be an indication the owner didn't bother taking good care of the vehicle. Do all the options work such as the tape deck, power door locks, windows and seats? Does the air conditioner work? The heater? Blue or black smoke from the exhaust could indicate a badly worn engine while grey smoke could mean there is water leaking into the engine.

You should always try to buy a vehicle in daylight when it can be easily seen. Keep in mind when you buy a car "as is" you have no idea what the car will need to make it pass certification. That is why it is an important step to have a mechanic check it out for you. It may cost you $50 or even more for a thorough inspection but a mechanic's opinion will give you the best indication of what kind of shape the car is in. Of course the mechanic should be independent and not the dealer's employee or seller's friend. Don't be rushed buying a used car. Take time off work if necessary and bring a friend who will be another pair of eyes to help you size up the car and the seller. By being patient and arming yourself with as much information as you can about a vehicle's history and pricing, you should be able to find a car that will suit your needs and budget.

PROTECTING
PRECIOUS ONES

Janice was the proud mother of a new baby boy and took great care in keeping him safe. She bought a new car seat and always kept her baby buckled in tight. She was running errands one day when another car crashed into her. She wasn't hurt but her baby was. The police told her part of the reason her child was injured was because the car seat had been incorrectly installed. Janice was heart broken knowing her child may have escaped the collision unscathed, if only she had put the car seat in properly.

It's hard to believe but there are still some parents who don't bother strapping their children into a car seat. They may think it's unnecessary if they're taking a short trip or if their kids find it uncomfortable. This attitude is not only highly irresponsible, but it's also illegal. More common are the loving parents who mean well and always buckle their children into car seats, but for whatever reason, do it incorrectly.

Children are at greater risk than adults in collisions because they have soft bones, underdeveloped muscles and large, heavy heads. That's why it's extremely important to make sure they're buckled in tight. Sergeant Gordon Garfield, of the Toronto Police Department and a member of the Child Safety Seat Coalition, runs clinics to help parents properly install car seats. Garfield says "I've found that 99% of the time, parents have done something wrong while installing their car seats. Very seldom have I ever found one that's installed perfectly." One might wonder why installing a car seat would be so difficult, but there are common mistakes that many parents make.

One common error is picking the wrong seat for a child. There are three different stages of car seats a child must use before he or she is ready to sit with only a seatbelt. Use the proper model for your baby's height and weight. Never position a car seat in the front seat of a vehicle and certainly nowhere near an air bag. Always read the manufacturer's instructions, as not all car seats are the same.

A child's first car seat should face the rear of a vehicle until they are one-year-old or more than 22 pounds and able to pull themselves to a standing position without help. An infant seat may come with a base that stays belted into the seat so the child can be lifted out in a carrier. If this is the case, a locking clip may be required to secure the base and prevent slippage. The seat should lean back on a 45-degree angle to allow the baby's head to be comfortable and prevent it from falling forward. Some seats now come with automatic levellers. If yours doesn't, Garfield recommends using a section of a pool noodle to prop up the seat to the proper angle.

Soft bones, under-developed muscles and large, heavy heads put children at greater risk than adults in collisions.

No matter what seat your child is in, you must make sure the harness fits tightly. "At the collar bone, only one finger should fit under the harness. If you can get two fingers under it, it's too loose. Tighten it up," says Garfield. The chest clip should be even with the armpits and no closer than three inches to the chin. If a baby is not properly belted in, he could fly out of the seat in a crash. A tight fitting harness will also help evenly dissipate the energy from a crash.

A driver may want to see a baby's face while driving, but Garfield says there is a good reason the child should face the rear of the vehicle until she is 22 pounds or can pull herself up to stand. "Babies must face the rear of the vehicle because their neck muscles are not strong enough to withstand a frontal impact." Also, if your seat has a base, make sure the seat always locks into it securely and that the carry handle is flipped back so it can't hit your baby in the head in the event of an accident. Mirrors that attach to the vehicle's seat behind a baby in a rear-facing model can comfort parents who can see their child's face in the rear view mirror.

The next stage for a child is a forward facing car seat that he will be in until he is about four years old. Once a car seat is used in a forward facing position, it requires a tether strap, which is now the law in Canada. A tether strap will anchor the car seat from behind and prevent it from moving forward in a crash. While a tether is an important safety component of a forward facing car seat, many parents fail to use them. "There are an awful lot of car seats out there that aren't tethered. Many older cars have the tether anchors beneath the car's back shelf and some people don't realize they have to cut through the ledge to get at it," says Garfield. As of 2001, all new cars must come with a ready-to-use tether anchor, saving parents any confusion.

A seat that too often gets skipped over is the booster seat. A booster seat "boosts" the child higher up so that the lap and shoulder belt will provide proper positioning of the seat belt and better protection in an accident. The booster seat ensures that the seat belt goes over a child's pelvic area, which is the strongest part of her body. Children should use booster seats until they are about 80 pounds, meaning some children may need to stay in them until they are eight or nine years old.

Many parents also make the mistake of buying an unsafe second hand seat in the classifieds or a garage sale. You should know the history of a car seat and not use one that is more than 10 years old or one that has already been in an accident. Once your child has outgrown a booster seat, he should remain sitting in the back seat of a vehicle until he is at least 12 years old because it's safer than sitting in the front. If a child is belted into the middle of the back seat of the car, she will be the furthest away from any point of impact.

GAP INSURANCE — A Leasing Must

Peter felt that he could not afford to buy or lease a new car, so he worked out an agreement to lease an older vehicle through a dealer. When he was driving the five-year-old car, he was involved in a serious accident. Luckily he was not badly injured, but the car was a total write-off. After assessing the demolished car, the insurance company paid him $5,000 for it, but the leasing company said according to their calculations, the car was worth $8,000. When Peter complained to the insurance company, he was told he was being paid fair market value for the car. Peter ended up having to reimburse the leasing company the additional $3,000 even though he no longer had their car to drive.

While leasing may seem like an affordable way to get a car, over time it is more expensive than buying one. This is especially true of leasing deals involving older cars, which usually come with high interest rate charges. One should avoid leasing older vehicles for various reasons, but one of the main ones is exactly because of what happened to Peter.

When you sign a car lease, you are agreeing to pay the leasing company monthly payments over a set term. For example, in Peter's case the purchase price at the time he wanted to buy the car was $7,500. He couldn't afford this, so he agreed to pay the leasing company $250 a month over 48 months. (This amount over four years adds up to $12,000, far more than the original price of the car.) When Peter was involved in the accident, he was only partway through his obligation to the leasing company. The insurance company evaluated the car's market value and gave him $5,000 for it. Peter assumed the insurance payout would be enough to satisfy his commitment to the leasing company.

This is where the problem arises. The leasing company is not as concerned about the fair market value of the car, as it is about the additional lease payments it will not receive because the car is no longer useable. The leasing company therefore wants to hold Peter to his 48-month leasing commitment as agreed to in the leasing contract. They want him to pay the buyout figure of the lease — an amount which is *substantially* higher than the car's actual market value. Many Canadians are caught in this difficult situation when the car they are leasing is involved in a serious accident, fire or is stolen. And it's not just a dilemma involving used leased cars, but *new* ones too!

> Some insurance companies offer limited waiver insurance also known as "gap" insurance to cover the difference between what the insurance company is willing to pay, and what the leasing company wants.

When you lease a new or used car, ask the salesperson what your commitment will be if you drive the vehicle off the lot and are then immediately involved in an accident that causes the car to be written off by your insurance company. You will find that the car dealer will be seeking far more from you than the fair market value of the car. Some insurance companies offer limited waiver insurance also know as "gap" insurance to cover the difference between what the insurance company is willing to pay and what the leasing company wants. However, most insurers will offer gap insurance only on new cars, not used ones. What happened to Peter is a wake-up call for anyone who leases. Read the fine print in leasing contacts, particularly those involving used vehicles and high interest rates.

25

BEWARE OF CURBSIDERS

Colleen was looking for a used car and thought she had found a perfect deal through the classified ads. When she called the seller, he said he was planning to be in Colleen's area the next day and could drop by and show her the car. Colleen agreed and the next day, she thought the vehicle appeared to be in good shape and the price seemed fair. After a short test drive, Colleen agreed to purchase the car on the spot. Later that week Colleen started to have concerns about the car. It leaked oil and had mismatched paint that she failed to notice on the day of the sale. When she tried to contact the seller, he didn't return her calls and she had no idea how to find him.

Curbsiders are people who sell damaged or stolen cars through auto magazines and classified ads. While legally they are required to have a dealer's licence if selling cars is their business, many curbsiders will misrepresent themselves and sell hundreds of cars a year. Sellers who operate in this manner may buy cars at auctions and then do minor mechanical or cosmetic repairs before selling the vehicles at a profit. They may also buy cars that have been written off by insurance companies and sell them without revealing the major repairs the car has undergone. Curbsiders are usually masters at concealing a car's problems and flaws may only become apparent after the sale is made. They may tell you that they are selling the family car, when in fact it's a vehicle that has been reconstructed after an accident. As many as 20% of cars sold through classified ads are sold by curbsiders.

Carl Compton is the Director of the Ontario Motor Vehicle Industry Council, a group responsible for administrating the provincial *Motor Vehicle Dealers Act*. OMVIC also reviews public complaints, many of which relate to consumers buying cars sold by unscrupulous individuals known as curbsiders. Compton says "Often these are vehicles that have been stolen or they're rebuilt wrecks, odometer-tampered vehicles and vehicles that have liens on them." Curbsiders are often smooth operators who don't want you to know anything about them. They will try to sell you a car on the side of the street, ask to meet you at a coffee shop or drive right to your house to do the deal. If you buy a car from a curbsider and then find out it's a lemon, usually you are stuck with it. Compton says, "you don't know where they live. You don't know where they work and when it comes right down to it, you don't even know who they are." OMVIC says the most common complaints against curbsiders deal with the odometer being turned back; failure to disclose the car was in an accident; invalid mechanical certification; and false claims as to the car's condition.

Make sure the car you are buying is registered in the name of the seller. If it isn't, ask why? A person selling a car privately and using someone else's name may claim they are selling it for their sister, but this could be a tip-off, he or she is a curbsider. Check to see if the vehicle registration number on the paperwork matches the number stamped on the identification plate on the dash of the car.

You could be worse off if the car you buy is stolen. There are many cases of people buying cars through the classifieds at a price that seemed too good to be true, only to find out later the vehicle had been stolen. When this happens, the car is repossessed and the buyer gets *nothing*! When buying through the classifieds, be leery if the same telephone number appears often and never buy a car from someone unless you're sure you can find them if there is a problem. Most provinces now offer used vehicle information packages through their transportation ministries, which can assist consumers by providing the car's complete history and how many times it has changed hands. When buying a car privately, insist that the seller provide you with this package. Beware if the seller refuses this important paperwork, or if they demand cash or are insistent on closing the deal right away.

Most provincial ministries of transport now offer used vehicle information packages, which provide consumers with the car's complete history, including the names of previous owners.

There are many quality used cars in the classified ads, being sold by honest people. It is not my intent to discourage private sales. By buying privately, you generally do not have to pay the Goods and Services Tax. In most provinces, when buying a used car through a dealer, you will have to pay the GST. Go through all the regular precautions when purchasing a used car (see Alert 22 on Buying a Used Car), including getting it checked by a mechanic who is trained to spot potential problems.

PROTECTING YOUR CAR DEPOSIT

Lionel went looking for a used car and found one that he liked. The salesperson said it would sell quickly, so Lionel put down $300 as a deposit to hold the car. He went to the bank to get a loan and was surprised that because of an unpaid student loan, he was turned down. Dejected, he went back to the dealership to get his deposit money. The car dealer told him that the deposit was non-refundable. Lionel caused a scene and demanded to see the manager about getting a refund, but in the end he left the dealership without his money.

I once had a boss who was a very savvy businessperson and he told me to *never* sign anything. The *never* was for dramatic effect, but his point was to always remember that a signature should never be given out carelessly. By signing your name on a document, you are agreeing to be held responsible and accountable.

Many people assume that if they leave a deposit for a car purchase, they will get the money back if the deal falls through. Leaving a deposit and signing an agreement to purchase means that you are actually signing a contract to buy the car. If you leave a deposit on a vehicle and try to get financing through a bank but are turned down, such as in Lionel's case, the car dealer still wants the deal to go through. The dealer has your signature on a contract saying you have agreed to buy the car. He or she may then offer you financing for the car to make the deal happen — but at a much higher interest rate. Some lending rates can be as high as 28%. You, as the car buyer, may then find yourself in a bind. You can say no to the financing, but then you lose your deposit.

Laura Gordon, with the Ontario Motor Vehicle Council, says that in Ontario "There is absolutely no cooling off period when leaving a deposit for a car purchase. There is an urban myth that there is, but there isn't." Gordon says consumers should never sign contracts unless they are sure they can fulfil them.

> Many people assume that if they leave a deposit for a car purchase and the deal falls through, they will get their money back. The dealer has no legal obligation to return your deposit if you have signed a contract.

She says one way to avoid confusion and prevent unwelcome surprises is by getting pre-approved financing. It's one of the first steps a consumer should take before going out and kicking tires on a car lot. "It's obviously a really good idea to know how much you can afford." By going to a lender first, you will know how much you can borrow, the interest rate, term and monthly payments. You can also use this data to compare other financing offers from dealers.

When signing a contract and leaving a deposit, be aware that you may be agreeing to other terms and conditions that may not have been fully explained to you. There may be freight charges, taxes, surcharges and other add-on costs that you have agreed to with your signature. While verbal promises may have been made, it's what is in the document you are signing that matters. Often people will sign contracts that includes the term "subject to financing." If you sign an agreement to purchase, you should spell out a specific interest rate in the contract. Gordon says, "if it isn't spelled out in the contract the dealer may be able to get you financing, but it may be in excess of what you want to pay."

By stating that the contract is "subject to financing at no more than 9%" you will be covering yourself.

Many dealers may choose to return deposits, especially in smaller communities, as a goodwill gesture to try and secure future business. However, it is legal for car dealers to keep a deposit or a portion of it to cover their costs. A car dealer who did not sell a car for two days while you tried to get financing, could have sold the car to someone else. A dealership also has overhead costs, loans and other expenses while waiting for cars to sell. However, the portion the dealer decides to keep must be a reasonable amount. For example, a person who leaves a $3,000 deposit only to change his mind within an hour should not lose the entire deposit. The dealership may decide to keep a portion of the deposit which it deems reasonable, but if the buyer disagrees he can seek action in small claims court or seek guidance from their provincial consumer affairs ministry.

The best advice is to *never* sign anything until you are absolutely positive you want the deal to happen. Don't be badgered into signing contracts or leaving deposits until you have done your financial homework. Even when a deal seems so good you worry that you just can't pass it up, taking a day to think about it without signing anything is a good move. Besides, if the vehicle is sold, chances are you will find a similar make and model with a comparable price just around the corner.

CAR RENTALS — Read the Fine Print

Francine planned to visit friends in another part of the country and arranged to rent a car upon her arrival at the airport. When she phoned ahead, she was pleased that the car rental company had a special rate of $19 per day. She rented the car and after three days, returned it to the airport. She was shocked when the bill came to $183. She complained saying there must be a mistake, but she was assured by the rental agency that the total was correct.

The daily rate is usually the first thing you are quoted when renting a car, but there are many extras that often double or triple the final rental cost. While the daily rate may be advertised in bold print, it's generally the fine print that will give you a more accurate indication as to what you will be charged when the car is returned. There may be additional insurance costs, airport taxes, surcharges that fund convention centres, excess mileage fees, refuelling charges, drop-off penalties and other hidden costs.

When renting a car, be aware that the advertised low rates almost always have add-on charges, so find out what they are upfront. The cheapest rates may also mean you get a car without air conditioning or an automatic transmission. Many car rental companies also entice consumers into paying for things they may not need. One of the most common extras that rental agencies add on is collision damage waiver insurance. Often staff at a rental agency will be very insistent that this insurance is necessary, because it's very profitable for rental companies. This insurance can add as much as $12 to $16 per day to a car rental and you may not even need it. Before renting a car, check with your own insurance company and credit card company to see if you are already covered for such damage. Chances are your insurance will provide coverage and this will save you a lot of money on a rental bill.

When you rent a car, the gas tank will usually be full and you'll be asked to bring it back with a topped-up tank. *Make sure you fill it up before you return it!* When you return a car with a half a tank of gas, most companies will charge as much as double the market price for a litre of gas. So, if your car is brought back needing $15 worth of fuel, you may be charged as much as $30 to top-up the tank. Other car rental companies may give you half a tank of gas to start off with and will charge you for it. However, you will not be credited for any gas left in the tank upon your return. Watch the clock when renting a car to avoid late charges. If it's supposed to be back at a certain time, don't be late! Even showing up an hour late could subject you to being charged for an extra day, possibly at a higher rate than the one you signed up for.

Before purchasing collision damage waiver insurance when renting a car, check with your own insurance company and credit card company to see if you are already covered.

When accepting the collision damage waiver insurance or when checking with your own insurance or credit card company, find out if you are covered for *anything* that could possibly go wrong. Does it cover chipped windshields, flat tires, roadside assistance and theft? Is there a deductible? Can you drop the car off at another branch of the same car rental company in another city? If so, will there be a charge for this? Is there a mileage restriction? How many kilometres do you get, and if you use up that amount, what is the fee for each additional kilometre?

Be careful when renting a car in foreign countries because it can be extremely expensive. When planning a trip, keep in mind that different countries have unique rules and regulations for car rentals. The quoted daily or weekly rate is likely to have additional charges that you should know about before making a reservation. Mandatory insurance coverage can more than double your rental bill. While your credit card or personal car insurance may cover collision damage waiver insurance in Canada or in the United States, it does not necessarily apply in other countries. Don't ever assume that you are protected. Read the rental agreement and if the contract is not in English, see if there is someone independent and trustworthy who can translate it for you before you sign it. Remember to factor in the price of gas when renting a car. In Europe gas is more than a $1.50 a litre, an added cost of renting a car.

Also, if you are travelling on business, ask for the corporate rate at a car rental agency. Corporate rates are usually a better deal, but a promotion could be cheaper, so compare the two rates. By checking ahead, reading the fine print and asking the right questions, you will save yourself time, stress and money.

CAR REPAIRS — Don't Get Taken for a Ride

Armand went to an auto repair shop when his car started performing poorly and black smoke was spewing out of its tailpipe. He was assured that he likely only needed a tune-up, but agreed that the mechanics could do whatever was necessary to get his car working properly. When he returned to the shop, he was told by the mechanic that the car also required a valve job which cost an extra $500. Armand was upset but he was reminded that he signed a repair order, that authorized the shop to do whatever was needed to get the car in working order.

One benefit to marrying a woman whose father is an auto mechanic is having someone you know and trust to do your car repairs. I must admit that I have shamefully used this to my advantage over the years to have brake jobs and tune-ups done on my vehicles. You may be fortunate enough to know a back-yard mechanic or a corner garage where repairs can be performed at reasonable prices by a person you have faith in. However, vehicles have become so complicated that they now require extensive diagnostic equipment found only at larger garages. Many garages offer free or low-cost 21 point inspections as a way to get cars into their garage so mechanics can look for and diagnose problems.

Complaints about auto shops consistently rank in the top five grievances logged by consumer protection groups almost every year. Most of us have only limited knowledge concerning the actual mechanical operation of a car, which means we have to rely on mechanics to do their jobs effectively and honestly. Many mechanics are trustworthy, diligent professionals, and cars by their very nature are expensive to own and operate. Still, there are mechanics who are ready and willing to take advantage of an ill-informed customer, so take safeguards to keep your repair bills from being higher than they ought to be.

If you can, choose a shop recommended by friends or family. It's also wise to have a shop in mind before your car actually needs repairs. If you find a reputable garage and are satisfied with the quality of their work and prices, stick with them. Don't have the brakes done at one garage and a tune-up at another. Staying with the same business will allow them to know the history of your vehicle and keep records regarding repairs done to your car. When you go to a mechanic, describe the symptoms but don't diagnose the problem. Ask what the labour rate is and if it will be calculated on a flat rate or hourly basis. To confirm that a new part has been used in your car, ask beforehand that the old one be returned to you for your inspection. If you have a newer car, always check to see if the repairs can be done under warranty.

> Always get a written estimate before agreeing to car repairs.

Many problems regarding car repairs revolve around car repair estimates. Never accept verbal promises. Always get a written estimate before agreeing to any repairs. Along with your name and vehicle information, the estimate should outline the parts that are to be installed and whether they are new, used or reconditioned. Reconditioned parts are those that have been refurbished, such as a used waterpump that has been rebuilt to new specifications. A garage may also use after-market parts instead of original equipment made by your car's manufacturer. After-market parts may be cheaper, but they also could be of inferior quality.

The price for parts and labour should be clearly stated separately on the bill. Make it known that you will only pay for work that is authorized. If you leave a car to be looked at, ensure that you will be contacted before any work goes ahead. If there is a fee for an estimate or a road test, you should be told about it beforehand. Also ask if the fee can be waived if you decide to go ahead with the repairs. Try to find out if the mechanics work on a commission basis, as this can mean an employee may earn more money if they can sell a customer additional parts or services.

Always keep copies of receipts and other paperwork relating to your vehicle by starting a separate file for each vehicle you have. This is a good way to keep track of repairs including oil changes, tunes-ups, tire purchases, fan belt replacement and other maintenance.

Different provinces have various rules and regulations governing car repairs and different mechanisms in place to deal with complaints. Find out more about the laws in your province by contacting your consumer relations ministry. Maintaining a car can be expensive, but by dealing with a reputable auto shop you can save money and be sure that your car will be in good running order.

THINK BEFORE YOU TINT

Jacques had the windows tinted on his car and was pleased with his vehicle's new look. However weeks after paying hundreds of dollars to have it done, he was stopped by a police officer who told him the tint job was illegal. He was fined, told to remove the film from his windows and report to police to show that he had complied. Jacques felt the tinting exercise was a waste of time and money.

Motorists tint their windows for a multitude of reasons. Tinting keeps a car cooler on a hot summer day, offers privacy and gives a car a cool look. But how dark is too dark? Each province has its own laws addressing after market tinting. Whether you are planning to do it yourself, or have it done at a tint shop, make yourself aware of the law in your region regarding window tinting by asking the tint shop or checking with the local police department.

For example, in Ontario any window behind the driver can be tinted as dark as you like. Allan Starkman of the tinting operation Tint King says "behind your head, you can have it as dark as you want. You can sit in there naked. You could paint the windows, as long as you have two exterior mirrors." It's a different matter when it comes to the driver and front seat passenger's windows and the windshield. These areas can't be obscured, but they can be tinted. How dark is too dark becomes the dilemma for consumers, tinting operations and police.

Some provinces leave it up to the police to decide "how dark is too dark," making tinting a subjective judgement. Other jurisdictions use what's known as a tint meter. This device will measure the percentage of light transmission that is blocked by the tint. Often there will be a standard which must be adhered to. The law may say, for example, that a person can use vision reducing material with a light transmission of 35% or less, plus or minus 3%.

Sergeant Frank Partridge of the Toronto Police Department says officers carrying out their duties want to be able to identify who is behind the wheel if they are trying to pull over a vehicle. Partridge says if an officer feels at risk — it's too dark. Police have safety concerns approaching cars with excessively tinted windows. "What are they trying to hide? Are they drinking, are they dealing drugs, do they have a firearm? Why do they not want the police or other motorists to see them on the roadway?"

Those in the tinting business insist tinting windows is not just about being cool. Starkman says, "we have people with skin cancer and glaucoma and they have prescriptions for tints. A tinted car can reduce glare and harmful ultraviolet rays." Tints can also make cars cooler on hot summer days and warmer in the winter. The tinting film can also help make glass shatter-proof. There are people who disregard the law and ask for tints that are illegal. It is the responsibility of the tint shop to make customers aware of the law in your province before applying tints. Some groups such as The Ontario Association of Police Chiefs would like to see tinting banned on all front windows and windshields of vehicles. Transport Canada also does not support the use of after market tints. If you are going to tint your car, just don't overdo it. Use common sense and for the side and passenger side windows use one of the lightest tints available.

ALERT

30

PAYING LESS AT THE PUMPS

With gas prices at an all-time high, Sasha noticed that it cost far more to fill up her car. The price at the pumps always seemed to be on the way up and she wondered if there was a way to cut down on her gas bill.

Almost every Canadian motorist has been affected by the rising price of fuel. While we have higher prices than our neighbours to the south, our gas prices are still substantially lower than what drivers in European countries must pay. Even if it's diesel you put in your tank, everyone can benefit from using common sense to save a few dollars at the fuel pumps.

Many motorists have been swayed to believe that higher octane fuel, which costs 10¢ or more per litre, will give your car increased mileage and power. The fact is, if your car is designed to run on regular 87 octane gasoline, that is all it needs! Currently about 94% of the cars, trucks and vans on the road require only regular gasoline; however about 23% of the gasoline sold in Canada is mid-grade or premium. David Leonhardt, spokesperson for the Canadian Automobile Association (CAA), says "if you put high octane gas in your car and you don't need it, all you are doing is wasting money." He contends that "there is actually a higher mark-up on high octane fuel than on regular gasoline."

To find out what kind of gas your vehicle needs, check the owner's manual in the fuel section. High performance and luxury cars such as BMWs, Corvettes and Jaguars do require 89 or 91 octane fuels. Someone buying a brand-new luxury car may not mind the added expense of premium fuel, but someone buying a used one may be surprised to find out a fill-up will cost them $5 or more per tank. The Canadian Petroleum Products Institute (CPPI), which represents Canada's major gas retailers, says consumers are getting an added benefit in high octane fuel. Bill Simpkins, spokesperson for CPPI, asserts that "petroleum fuels contain cleaners and lubricants which assist in cleaning the engine and removing carbon deposits." Both CPPI and the CAA are in agreement that higher octane fuels help correct rattling and pinging in older cars; however, if your car is making a lot of noise you may want to have it looked at by a mechanic.

The way you drive will greatly affect your car's fuel consumption. You should accelerate gently, brake gradually and avoid quick stops. A steady, even flow of acceleration and deceleration is not only good for your fuel consumption, it's also a safer way to drive and means less wear and tear on your vehicle. Driving your car 10 km/h slower can also reduce your gas consumption. If you speed, you will use a lot more gas driving your car at 120 km/h than you will at 100 km/h. Avoid heavy traffic, as the starts and stops of traffic jams will steadily deplete your fuel supply. Refrain from long periods of idling, even when warming up your car. Thirty seconds is long enough in warm weather and even on the coldest mornings a minute or two is enough idling time, unless you need to defrost your windshield and windows. You may want to drive your car slowly at first to let it warm up as you drive.

> Under-inflating your tires is one of the most common ways motorists waste gas. Driving on under-inflated tires is also dangerous.

Under-inflating your tires is one of the most common ways motorists waste gas. Under-inflated tires can cut fuel economy by as much as 2% for each missing pound of pressure. It's also dangerous to drive on tires that are under-inflated, as they are more prone to blowouts. Tires without enough or too much air pressure are also subject to uneven tire wear. It's a good idea to buy a tire pressure gauge to keep in the glove box, so that once a month you can check to make sure your tires are properly inflated. To find out what the tire pressure should be, check on the side of the tire itself or inside the driver's door for an information sticker. Keeping snow tires on when you don't need them can also decrease gas mileage as deep tread and heavy tires will cause you to use more fuel.

Keeping your car tuned-up is another way to ensure your car will save gasoline. A well-maintained vehicle that has regular oil and filter changes will increase your gas mileage and lower the emissions coming from your tailpipe. A tune-up may cost $150 to $250, but this may be saved in a few months on your fuel bills, if your car was not operating efficiently. A car that is streamlined will cut through the wind a lot easier than one that is not. Get in the habit of opening vents instead of rolling down windows. Open windows create wind resistance that will slow down your car. Running the air conditioner when driving at highway speeds is more efficient that driving with the windows rolled down. Remove ski racks when the ski season has ended and luggage racks after the holidays are over. If you have a truck, replacing the metal tailgate with a soft net tailgate will reduce drag. Any excess weight in your car will also cause you to burn gas. Always remove "junk from the trunk." In the winter a build-up of snow and ice in the wheel well area can add unnecessary weight to your car. Remove the ice with a shovel or a good swift kick, as the excess weight will drag down your gas mileage.

Consolidating errands and planning trips can be a time and gas saver, as a car works more efficiently when it's warmed up. Also, when you are buying a car, factor in long-term fuel savings. Do the calculations to see how much extra that mid-size car will cost you in gasoline over an economy model. You may still decide on the larger car, just realize there will be a price to pay at the pumps as well.

CHANGING YOUR OIL — How Often is Often Enough

Austin often had to drive his car as part of his job. He would occasionally put on more than 1,000 km a week. He was told he should change his oil every 5,000 km which brought him into an oil change shop almost once a month. He wanted to properly maintain his car but he wondered if the frequent oil changes were really necessary.

The engine is the heart of your car and the most expensive area to repair, so you should *never* put off an oil change too long. Having said that, a lot of good oil goes down the drain because people change their oil sooner than they need to. General Motors has devised an oil monitoring system, available on many of its 2001 vehicles including Cadillacs, Corvettes and Chevy pickup trucks. Faye Roberts, spokesperson for General Motors of Canada, says "the oil change monitoring system computes when it is time to change the vehicle's oil based on many factors, including the temperature of the engine and coolant, vehicle speed, number of starts and stops since the last oil change, as well as the driver's habits and routine." The oil monitoring system has an indicator to warn drivers when an oil change is due. The initial warning light will read "Change Oil Soon" and later, a second and final one will read "Change Oil Now." With the new system General Motors maintains that drivers will have a tool which enables them to change their oil only when necessary. Less used oil and filters is good for the environment and your wallet.

> Drivers who make many short trips, engage in extensive idling time, drive on dusty roads, tow a trailer or drive for long periods in hot weather should get their oil changed every 3,000 to 5,000 km.

Getting your oil changed every 5,000 km or every three months is usually recommended, but it's really your driving habits that should dictate how often you change your oil. The most wear and tear on an engine happens on start-up, so if you drive your car on long trips you may not need to change it as often. Some mechanics believe a car can travel much further than 5,000 km if the car is being used under normal operating conditions. Check your owner's manual, as 12,000 km is not unreasonable before needing an oil change, if the engine is running at normal operating temperatures.

You may wish to change your oil *more* frequently than every 5,000 km if you drive under what are called severe operating conditions. Drivers who make many short trips, engage in extensive idling time, drive on dusty roads, tow a trailer or drive for long periods in hot weather should get their oil changed every 3,000 to 5,000 km. Brian Holmes is a technical advisor with the Canadian Automobile Association. He says "short stop and start trips are harder on the oil than if you were to drive for an hour." Short trips cause car engines to repeatedly warm and cool off which is responsible for extra wear and tear. He recommends using 10W30 oil for most vehicles, but switching to 5W30 in the winter, as that oil has a viscosity which can lubricate engines faster in cold weather. "The more fluid the oil, the better it can help cars start in the winter."

If you have a new vehicle, you must get your oil changed as recommended and keep the paperwork. If you have a problem with a new vehicle, you may be asked to provide receipts to show you had your oil changed on time. If you cannot provide documents to prove this and you have engine trouble a dealer could choose to void your warranty. Be aware also that when you go to a lube, oil and filter centre, the shop makes very little on the actual oil change. Staff are encouraged to pitch customers extras products and services, such as engine shampoos, filters, wiper blades and lubricants which you may or may not need. Don't be persuaded to buy them, if you don't need them. Synthetic oils are more expensive but the companies that make them say if you use synthetic oils, you won't have to change your oil as often. There are also many oil additives on the market that claim to offer better gas mileage, increased performance and improved engine protection. It's difficult to know how beneficial the additives are, as the research behind the claim is usually done by the companies themselves.

This information is not to dissuade you from getting regular oil changes. The benefits of oil changes are well-known and documented. Frequent oil changes can help your engine have a long, trouble-free life. The benefits of frequent oil changes are most noticeable after 80,000 km. Just keep in mind the information behind the "rule of thumb" guideline by which consumers get their oil changed.

CAMVAP — an Impartial Arbitrator

Will owned a 2000 model pick-up truck. When the truck had 38,000 km on it, the engine seized. Will was surprised and disappointed but relieved the truck was still under a three-year/60,000 km warranty. When he had the truck towed to the dealer, he was asked to provide paperwork for all oil changes on the truck since he bought it. Will had several receipts for oil changes but not all of them. The dealership argued that Will was at fault for not changing the oil regularly and declared the warranty void. The engine would cost $4,000 to replace and Will was shocked that he would have to pay for it.

When faced with what Will felt was a grossly unfair situation, he went to The Canadian Motor Vehicle Arbitration Plan (CAMVAP) for help. The dealer refused to honour the warranty citing there was insufficient evidence that the oil had been changed regularly. Will argued he had changed his oil on schedule and since the seized engine was still under warranty, it should be replaced free of charge. An independent arbitrator listened to the case and decided in favour of the owner of the vehicle! Created in 1994, CAMVAP is Canada's largest consumer product arbitration plan which helps resolve disputes between automobile manufacturers and vehicle owners. Many Canadians are unaware of this free service which can resolve disputes regarding new car quality issues or how manufacturers implement their warranties.

CAMVAP requires that both parties must agree to accept the decision of an impartial arbitrator. CAMVAP will listen to both sides, weigh the evidence and make a decision that is binding and final. The arbitrators used by CAMVAP are not automobile experts, but rather good listeners who will compare facts and arguments. You can argue your case in court, or through CAM-VAP, but not both. A CAMVAP arbitrator can order repairs to a vehicle, a buyback of the vehicle, reimbursement of payments for repairs you have already made to your vehicle and out of pocket expenses up to $500. Of course, an arbitrator may also decide that there is no liability on the part of the manufacturer and award you nothing. The case could also be settled privately between the manufacturer and the consumer before the hearing takes place.

> CAMVAP will rule on disputes regarding manufacturing defects and the implementation of vehicle warranties.

According to CAMVAP's own statistics, about 68% of all cases brought before them have ruled in favour of the consumer. In most cases benefitting the consumer, there is usually not a buyback of the vehicle but the manufacturer is held responsible for the repairs. The entire process takes about 70 days, although some cases may take longer. CAMVAP will rule on disputes regarding manufacturing defects and the implementation of vehicle warranties. Your vehicle cannot be more than four model years old or have travelled more than 160,000 km at the time of the hearing. Your car must be used primarily for personal use and you must have first tried to resolve the dispute with the dealer and manufacturer before beginning the CAMVAP process.

This service cannot help you if your claim involves an accident, the vehicle was not built for the Canadian market, if the vehicle is a motor home or if the vehicle has been previously written off by an insurance company. CAMVAP will also not investigate if the dispute is about after-market accessories or if the vehicle has ever been used as a taxi, limousine, hearse, snowplow or for police, fire or municipal services.

The CAMVAP process is friendly and more informal then a courtroom. Proceedings may involve just you, the manufacturer's representative and the arbitrator. You will have to swear an oath or make a solemn affirmation to tell the truth. You should be well-prepared and have all pertinent documents to backup your case. Witnesses are allowed and you may have a lawyer, paralegal or any other person present to assist in presenting your case if you wish. CAMVAP's decision is final and both you and the manufacturer are bound by it. Best of all, the process is absolutely free and the only costs you incur are expenses related to calling witnesses or if you choose to have legal counsel. The plan is fully funded by automobile manufacturers, but the arbitrators are independent of the automobile industry.

Initially when you have a problem, you should try to settle it with your dealer first. If that fails, approach the manufacturer. You will have to follow the manufacturer's dispute resolution process which is outlined in the owner's handbook or warranty manual. Once you have tried these avenues and are still not satisfied, it's time to contact CAMVAP. There are different agencies across Canada that deliver the program to consumers. Call their toll-free hotline at 1-800-207-0685. Officials will tell you if your case is eligible and let you know what is required. Following the hearing, within 14 days both you and the manufacturer will be mailed a copy of the arbitrator's decision. If the arbitrator has awarded repairs, they must be done within 30 working days. If the award is for a buyback, the manufacturer has 21 days to comply with the ruling. If the award is for payment for repairs or out of pocket expenses, the funds must be sent to you within 21 days. However, if the arbitrator rules in favour of the manufacturer, the case is closed.

It is good to know that in the event you cannot settle a dispute with a car manufacturer that an independent free agency is there to help. For more information on The Canadian Motor Vehicle Arbitration Plan, check their Web site at www.camvap.ca.

BEST DEALS ON CAR INSURANCE

Dimitri and his neighbour Wei both own the same make and model of a 2001 minivan. One day when they were discussing insurance costs, Wei mentioned her yearly premium. Dimitri was shocked. He was paying hundreds of dollars more on the same vehicle. When Dimitri contacted his insurance company, he was told that his current rate was the lowest they could offer and that he would have to go elsewhere if he wanted cheaper insurance coverage.

If you drive a car in Canada, you must have insurance and depending on your circumstances, it can be expensive. I remember how shocked I was as a teenager when I went to insure my first $700 car and was told my yearly premiums would be twice what the car was worth! The Insurance Bureau of Canada says when you buy car insurance, you're buying financial protection and peace of mind. How much that peace of mind will cost depends on your age, marital status, gender, type of vehicle being insured and your driving record. Arguments that insurance companies are discriminating against certain drivers have been fought all the way to the Supreme Court of Canada — and lost. The insurance industry successfully argued that accident rates are higher for drivers who are male, single and under 25 and no amount of debate with an insurance agent will change this.

The Insurance Bureau of Canada guide *Automobile Insurance in Canada* states that few people really have a good understanding of their auto insurance policy until they are involved in an accident. Auto insurance is regulated by the province so how the system operates will depend on the rules and regulations where you live. In British Columbia, Saskatchewan and Manitoba, the government provides insurance coverage, while in other provinces auto coverage is provided by private insurers. In Quebec, auto insurance is a mixed-bag: physical damage and liability coverage is provided by private insurers, while bodily injury coverage is provided by the government. Some provinces have "no-fault" insurance, but this does not mean that drivers won't be penalized if they caused the accident. "No-fault" means that to avoid delays after a collision, claims are quickly paid out by your own insurance company. An investigation will follow to determine whose fault the accident was.

To keep your insurance costs as low as possible, the most important thing you can do is keep a clean driving record. At-fault accidents and driving convictions such as speeding tickets and other traffic violations will cause your rates to increase dramatically. Serious offences such as dangerous driving or impaired driving will cause long term harm to your driving record. Where you live will affect your rates also. A pleasure driver in Portage la Prairie, Manitoba, will pay a lot less than an employee commuting daily to downtown Vancouver, British Columbia. Many insurance companies provide low mileage credits if a vehicle is driven less than 16,000 km annually.

Retirees with no employment income are entitled to breaks. New drivers should take a driver trainer course from a recognized driving school as this could lead to savings of more than 30%. Companies offer multi-vehicle discounts and savings if you purchase your home and auto insurance from the same company. Your premiums can also be slightly reduced if you have your vehicle equipped with an anti-theft device such as a car alarm. Choosing a higher deductible will lower the premium; however make sure you can afford to pay the deductible in the event of an accident.

Never submit small claims, as an insurer keeps tabs on the number of claims you make, not just how much money is paid out. The dent in your car may be annoying, but you don't want to have your insurance company fix a $400 ding only to see your rates jump substantially for the next several years. The make and model of your vehicle has a big impact on premiums. Some cars cost more to repair, have fewer safety features, or may be targeted by thieves. The Canadian Loss Experience Automobile Rating (CLEAR) system rewards car owners with lower premiums for buying vehicles that experience fewer and smaller losses. For information on car ratings, contact the Vehicle Information Centre of Canada (VICC) at www.vicc.com.

Some insurers will allow one "at-fault" claim for clients, but others won't and even one at-fault accident can cause your insurance rates to jump. If you are switching insurance companies or renewing, ask if you will be forgiven a claim in the event of an accident. Also, be aware that when you lend your car, you also lend your insurance. If someone causes an accident in your vehicle, your premium could be affected.

Of all the factors taken into consideration, your driving record has the most impact on your insurance rates.

Some companies offer extremely low premiums but they may be difficult to deal with when you need to make a claim. When shopping for insurance talk to friends, family and colleagues who have had recent claims experiences to find out how they were treated and if their accident was settled promptly and without a hassle. While the law says you must carry at least $200,000 in third party liability ($50,000 in Quebec), it's advisable for all drivers to carry at least one million dollars liability insurance on any policy as the added coverage, which is usually just slightly more, offers protection against expensive lawsuits for collisions involving serious injuries to others.

Another area that is growing in popularity is group insurance through the workplace, auto clubs or alumni associations, as being part of a recognized group can also lead to lower rates. If you drive an older car, you may wish to drop collision and comprehensive coverage, but this should be done only after careful consideration because you may have to pay to repair the car whether the accident is your fault or not. Collision coverage pays to fix or replace your car if it's damaged in an accident; comprehensive pays to repair or replace your car if it's damaged by something other than a collision. In the event of a hit and run accident, you will also get stuck with the bill. Your insurance is valid as you drive coast-to-coast in Canada and the United States, but your insurance means nothing once you enter Mexico! You will need special insurance from a Mexican insurer to drive in that country. There are many variables that will affect your policy and due to the different insurance systems across Canada, you should direct any questions you have about your coverage to your insurer or for more information check the Insurance Bureau of Canada's Web site at www.ibc.ca.

ODOMETER FRAUD — Wipe Out the Miles

Richard was in the market for a used car and was searching used car lots for a suitable vehicle. He found one that he liked which seemed to be in good shape at a reasonable price. Its odometer read 98,000 which was higher than he wanted, but the salesperson told him the car was an excellent value which would sell fast. After about an hour of inspection, Richard signed a contract to purchase the car. When he drove the car off the lot, he noticed that the speedometer was in miles — <u>not</u> kilometres! He went back to the dealer and said he had presumed the odometer reading was in kilometres and demanded the deal be cancelled. The dealer told him that it was a done deal and basically to get lost.

The odometer reading plays an important role in helping a buyer decide a vehicle's true worth. What happened to Richard may seem far-fetched and unlikely, but it does happen! Our U.S. neighbours have a population ten times larger than ours, with about ten times more vehicles. Cars in southern climates last longer, as there is no salt used on the roads and some of them end up on Canadian car lots. Richard thought his car had 98,000 km when it fact it had more than 156,000! Often car dealers will spell out mileage on used cars in *miles,* not *kilometres.*

Of course the conversion is easily spotted on cars with a metric speedometer, but on an American car with an odometer in miles only, it could be missed by a consumer being given the hard sell by aggressive sales staff.

The majority of problems involving incorrect mileage on used cars are usually the result of odometer tampering or odometer fraud. As many as 5% to 15% of all used cars sold have had their odometers meddled with. Of course this is difficult to substantiate, yet you should be aware of it when shopping for a used automobile. If an odometer is turned back or unhooked for a while and then reattached, mechanical problems that affect safety could go undetected and unrepaired.

Cars from the southern United States last longer without the salt exposure and some end up on Canadian car lots.

Every province deems odometer tampering a crime and driving with a disconnected or inoperable odometer is against the law.

On average, most drivers accumulate about 20,000 km annually on their vehicles. If a used car's mileage is substantially lower than this figure, there should be a reasonable explanation why. When shopping for a used car, look for signs that validate the odometer reading and the car's condition. If buying a car from a dealer, try to contact the previous owner to verify the mileage and shape of the vehicle. If buying privately, ask to see the odometer reading on the contract the owner received when he or she bought the vehicle. Check for oil change stickers, request service records, inspect how well doors open and shut and make any other observations you can, if you have concerns about the odometer.

HOME
SWEET
HOME

BUYING YOUR OWN HOME

Bob and Carolyn were married and living in an apartment. They had been saving for the past three years to have enough money for a down payment to buy a house. They had many decisions to make! What kind of house should they buy? How much could they afford to spend? Where should they live? Should the home be in a new development or on a mature street? Would they be able to manage the added expenses of utilities, maintenance and taxes? How could they be sure that they were getting the best mortgage for their financial situation?

For most of us, buying a home is the single biggest investment we will make. That is why it should take months or even years of careful consideration and planning before actually jumping in and purchasing a house, townhouse or condominium. The most important part of buying a home is knowing exactly what you are looking for. Do you want an old home or a new one? Rural or city location? Does proximity to schools, shopping and entertainment matter? Is property size an issue? Square footage, privacy, type of neighbourhood and annual taxes are all considerations for the new home buyer. When buying a new home, you should get as much information as possible before diving into the real estate market. Don't count on a real estate agent or banker to take you by the hand.

I was extremely fortunate when buying my first home. A co-worker, who was also a friend, had to leave the country in a hurry and needed to sell his house. We had been contemplating buying a house and felt that this deal was too good to pass up. His house was relatively new, close to work and had all the features we were looking for. Better yet, by not using a real estate agent, we were both able to save thousands of dollars on real estate commissions. We even used the same lawyer to close the deal. To top it off the former owner had to leave behind the lawnmower, weed whacker, garden hose and other odds and ends I would have had to buy anyway. I know I will never have the same luck again when we buy our next home, but it was a case of being ready when opportunity knocked!

Many home buyers are not realistic about what they can afford or fail to think beyond the home purchase. There is a trend of city dwellers moving to idyllic small towns outside of larger urban centres. I knew one couple who thought they were fulfilling a dream by living in a small Ontario town and commuting to Toronto. Their dream quickly became a nightmare as they grew tired of spending more than two hours a day commuting to and from the city. They worked different hours, both had to drive their own vehicle to work. Before long they became fed up with traffic, snowstorms and time lost in commuting. The last straw came when their cars wore out from the travelling and had to be replaced. They soon decided to sell the house at a loss and move back to the city.

Complications can also arise when buying a new house from a developer. Just as there are advantages and disadvantages to moving into a mature established neighbourhood, the same is true for a new home built from scratch. One advantage is that as you can customize the house as you see fit and be the first one to live in it. But, after you move in, construction of other homes in the neighbourhood may continue for another year or more. There may be constant dust from the construction, no grass on your front lawn for a year and general mayhem in the area until the entire development is completed. You may have to wait to get your driveway paved, a fence put around your property and to have the asphalt poured on your street. For

someone determined to have a new home, these may be acceptable nuisances — just realize it beforehand so you will not have
any surprises.

Knowing how much you can afford is one of the key determinations you will have to make before you search for a home.
Wanting a palatial mansion with a winding staircase won't do you much good if
your income is $50,000 a year. Getting
pre-approved with a lender gives you the
ballpark figure of the home you will be
able to afford (see Alert 5 on mortgages).
Know your maximum purchase price and
how it will break down into monthly
payments. You should spend no more
than 32% of your gross monthly income
on housing, which includes your mortgage payment with interest, taxes and utility costs. If you have
a down payment of 25% or more, you can apply for a conventional mortgage but if you have less than 25%, you will require
default insurance from the Canada Mortgage and Housing
Corporation. The one time insurance fee will be added to your
mortgage and can cost you more than a couple of thousand dollars. It's a safeguard for the banks so that if you default on the
loan, the lender won't be out any money.

> Knowing how
> much you can
> afford is one of the
> key determinations
> you'll have to
> make before you
> start your search
> for a new home.

A realtor can help narrow your search through the home
buying process. Spell out your specific needs such as the maximum price you can afford, number of bedrooms and bathrooms,
general location, etc. Being upfront with the agent about the
homes you like and what you can afford will save you both time.
Be careful of the "love at first sight" phenomenon where you
feel you have found your dream home and then fail to think
clearly about asking price, repairs or location. Spend time in
the neighbourhood before locking into a deal. Park on the street
near the house at different times of the day. Are there sirens
down the street? Is the home close to a railroad track or airport
you weren't aware of? Do the residents appear friendly and affable? Also try to find out if the area is prone to flooding. Where
do you get your mail? Is there a police station, hospital or fire

department nearby? Put yourself in the neighbourhood to see if that is the place you are ready to spend the next five or ten years of your life.

Once you find a home that you like, find out how much other similar homes have sold for in the neighbourhood. This is referred to as a "Comparative Market Analysis" and will be done by your agent. With your agent you will make an offer, usually conditional on financing, sale of a previous home, whether you want a home inspection, the inclusion of goods or appliances and the date you wish to move in. Don't be pressured by the real estate agent or the seller and try to keep time on your side. If there are multiple offers on the home and you're sure it's no bluff, this may affect your timetable but don't rush into a home purchase you will regret later.

You will also have to choose a lawyer who will take care of the necessary paperwork for your agreement of purchase and sale. Once you have secured a lawyer, he or she will handle the paperwork and any legal problems that may arise as you complete the home ownership transaction. Whatever happens after you move into your new home, you will feel better if you are confident that you have made every effort to look after your best interests.

SELLING YOUR HOME — Reducing Fees

Eileen and Anthony met with a real estate agent to discuss putting their house on the market. The real estate agent required a 6% commission to list with his real estate company. An offer came almost immediately and the house sold within a week for $250,000, just slightly below their asking price. Eileen and Anthony had to pay the real estate agent $15,000 for less than a week's work.

The real estate market is a lot like farming. Good years bring bumper crops and hot real estate markets. Bad years bring poor yields and a sluggish economy. Back in the booming late eighties real estate agents made small fortunes as properties practically sold themselves. When a recession strikes, times get lean for the agent who has to hustle five times as hard to sell a property. There is no doubt a hardworking, attentive, professional real estate agent may be absolutely necessary when selling a unique, out-of-the-way property that needs special attention or fits a narrow clientele profile. In a large percentage of sales however, the real estate agent is simply the person who allows the seller to meet the buyer and make the deal. Of course this is a crucial step, but if buyers had access to the computerized multiple listing service on their own, they could independently access list prices and descriptions of properties and neighbourhoods; real estate agents wouldn't be necessary. Just as car manufacturers in Europe are allowing consumers to buy cars directly from the factory, Canadian consumers are looking for ways to lower real estate commissions.

In the past, a family may have purchased a home and kept it through marriage, child rearing years and later retirement. Today, some estimates suggest that the average homeowner will move every five years. Even if you move only five times, you could end up paying a real estate agent well in excess of $50,000! As I mentioned earlier, I was able to buy my first home without a real estate agent as I knew the seller. I realize that this was a fortunate scenario for me and one which saved me thousands of dollars. One of the most important things to realize when dealing with a real estate agent is that they are offering a service and their fee is negotiable. Some agents may ask for a commission fee as high as 7%. That doesn't mean you have to agree to it.

The Internet offers a cheaper alternative to the traditional method of buying and selling homes. Homes can now be easily showcased online and prospective buyers can take virtual tours and find out many of the details of the home themselves. Real estate commission rates are dropping and agents realize that more clients are seeking to negotiate a lower commission rate. It's becoming more common to see ads across the country advertising reduced commissions of 4%, 3% or even 2%. Real estate companies who refuse to drop their commission rates may argue that with the lower rate, you are getting cut-rate service and will not have an agent actively selling your property. By going with a lower rate, you may also have to agree to other services offered by the broker such as contracting to buy your next home through them as well.

Some people attempt to sell their homes on their own, but keep in mind that this can be a very difficult undertaking. There are several reasons why only about 1% of Canadian homes are successfully sold privately by an owner without a real estate agent. People selling their house on their own may have to rely on newspaper advertising, flyers or drive by clients. A person selling privately may try to get the same asking price as other similar homes in the area. But potential buyers realize that the seller is saving thousands of dollars by not using an agent and may want to knock down the price of the home by that amount. Also, while an experienced person may be inclined to wheel and deal with a private home seller, someone buying a home for the first time may wish to be under the wing of a real estate agent who fully understands the home buying process. Rightly or wrongly there is also a bit of mystery surrounding why a person is selling a home privately.

I don't mean to discourage someone from trying to sell a home without an agent. If you try it, good luck! Just keep in mind, it may be difficult. I watched a neighbour try for about four months to privately sell her house. She gave up, got an agent and it sold within two weeks. The real estate industry's communications network and multiple listing service may be the most effective way to get a sold sign on your lawn.

What's happening in your life will determine how you go about selling your home. If you have to transfer to another city, then you will likely have little choice but to sell your home quickly. If time is on your side, you may be inclined to try selling your home yourself or with a lower commission real estate agent. If these attempts fail, you can always move up to an agent who may charge a higher commission rate but who will sell your property. There are many good real estate agents who spend long hours working hard to sell homes. They also know the tricks of the trade and can steer the right clients in your direction. The point is you have a choice as to how much you will pay them. If you see homes in your neighbourhood selling quickly, negotiate a lower commission rate with your real estate agent. If the agent won't budge on their rate, try another one, maybe he or she will. Shaving just 1% off a commission rate could save you $2,000 immediately and much more when you consider the added interest charges to pay that $2,000 back.

GET THE MOST FOR YOUR HOME

Austin and Rebecca had lived in their home for eight years and with their growing family, they were ready to move up into a slightly larger house. They planned to put their home on the market in a few months and wondered what they could do to make it more appealing to a buyer.

Whether or not you have already had your home appraised or know its approximate value on the real estate market, there are ways to increase its worth and make it more appealing to a buyer. Just as you wash your car before selling it, there are many inexpensive things you can do to a home to boost its curb appeal. It's foolish to spend tens of thousands of dollars on a home prior to putting it up for sale, as you may find that you do not recoup your investment. Knowing what to spend where can help your profit margin. Spend money where it can be seen. Kitchens and bathrooms show improvements well and add value to your home. These may be good project areas while you are in a home, years prior to selling. Don't tackle large renovation projects just before you plan to move out.

The exterior of your home is most important because it is the first thing a buyer will see when they pull up in front of your house. Take a walk across the street and have a look at how it compares to other homes in the neighbourhood. Terry Light is an expert in the real estate industry and has some excellent advice on how to prepare your home to get the best possible price. Light says your home should have landscaping that is at least average for the neighbourhood. If your landscaping is lacking, Light says, "buy a few bushes and plant them. Do not put in trees. Mature trees are expensive, and you will not get back your investment. Immature trees do not really add much to the appearance value of the home." Mature abundant flowers create a favourable first impression and your lawn should be evenly cut, freshly edged and free of brown spots.

Depending on the exterior of your home, you will have to make a decision on whether or not to paint. A fresh coat can spruce up a home that looks old and tired. Choose a colour that fits with your neighbourhood. Light says, "it shouldn't be something too unusual. For some reason, different shades of yellow seem to elicit the best response in home buyers, whether it's the trim or the basic colour of the house." If your home has a leaky roof, you should fix it before you put it on the market. It is something that should be disclosed to a potential buyer and will likely be discovered by a home inspector. Not fixing it could result in a lower asking price for your home, which you may also find acceptable if you don't want the hassle of repairing the roof.

Light recommends that the backyard should be tidy and any pool or spa should be spotlessly clean. Children's toys should be put away and pets cleaned up after. The front door is the main entry way to your home and should be clean or freshly painted with a door fixture that gleams. Any screens with rips should be repaired. "If you have a cute little plaque or shingle with your family name on it, remove it. Get a new plush door mat, too. These are both things you can take with you when you move," suggests Light. Make sure the lock works easily and that the key fits properly. If your real estate agent has to struggle with the lock while everyone stands around, it gives a bad first impression. All sink fixtures in your home should look shiny and new. Taps shouldn't leak and should be easy to turn. Old faucets can be replaced inexpensively and washers can stop the drips.

Next, you have to decide if you should paint. Light is adamant that "painting can be your best investment when selling your home." He warns against choosing colours based on your own preferences, but instead suggests focusing on what might appeal to the widest number of buyers. "You should almost always choose an off-white colour because white helps your rooms appear bright and spacious."

Unless your carpet appears old and worn or is definitely outdated in style or colour, you should do no more than hire a carpet cleaner or do it yourself. If you do replace carpet go with a neutral colour. You may also want to repair or replace broken floor tiles but don't go to a lot of expense.

Doors and windows should open and close easily. A lubricant like WD40 can help get rid of squeaks. Any broken or cracked windows should be replaced before showing your home.

As much as possible, put away all family clutter, knick-knacks and personal momentos — you want the buyers to picture themselves in your home.

Smokers may want to smoke outside while trying to sell their home. Don't use scented sprays as it is too obvious and potential buyers may be allergic. Light says an ozone spray works better than fragrances as it can remove unpleasant smells without creating a masking odour. "Potpourri can be agreeable or a drop of vanilla on a stove burner will make it smell like you've been cooking." If you have a cat, keep the litter box clean and keep dogs outside as much as possible while preparing for a sale.

Your home should be available for viewing at all times even though this may be an inconvenience for you. You should always make sure you are *not* there when the home is being shown to a prospective buyer. Light claims "home buyers will feel like intruders if you are home when they visit, and they might not be as receptive toward viewing your home." If you can't leave, stay out of the way and don't shuffle from room to room.

Light suggests turning on all indoor and outdoor lights when you know someone is coming by to visit — even during the day. A well-lit house looks homey at night and during the day, lighting can prevent harsh shadows from sunlight and brighten dim areas. Keep tabs on your pets, especially any that may be unfriendly toward a visitor. You don't need a pet running out the front door and getting lost or running and jumping up on guests. Light advises that "if your kitchen trash can does not have a lid, make sure you empty it every time someone comes to look at your home. You want to send a positive image about every aspect of your home and kitchen trash does not send a positive image." Make sure beds are made, papers are picked up, dishes are put away and that the home is clean and dusted. "Try your best to have it look like a model home — a home with furniture but nobody lives there."

Your house should be free of clutter when you are expecting a potential buyer. Clutter collects on shelves, counter tops, drawers, closets, garages and basements. Light suggests creating the image of as much space as possible by clearing the toaster off the counter and getting rid of pots and pans you rarely use. Home buyers want to be sure there is enough room for their stuff and jammed packed drawers send a negative message. "Create open space and have as much empty space as possible."

As much as possible, depersonalize your home inside. Light says that when a potential home buyer sees family photos, sports trophies, or personal knick-knacks, it can shatter their illusions about owning the home. You want the buyers to picture themselves in your home. Using these tips to help your property look its best for potential buyers can increase its value, so you have more money for your next home. For more excellent advice from real estate expert Terry Light, check out the Web site www.realestateabc.com.

38

CONDOMINIUM CONUNDRUM

Roger and Diane had recently retired, their children were grown and they were considering downsizing to a smaller residence. They had always maintained their own home but since they didn't need the space of a large house anymore, they wanted to sell their property and invest some of the money. They didn't want to rent, so they were interested in finding out more about condominiums. They were unsure if purchasing a condo would be the best decision for their lifestyle.

Another blip on the baby boomer radar screen is the increased demand for condominium housing. Boomers looking to sell their homes and young urban professionals who are tired of renting are fuelling this latest mode of property ownership. A condominium, or condo, is a planned development where there is joint ownership of a building or complex. When you buy a condo, you actually own the interior space of your unit as well as a percentage of the development as a whole. While condos used to be viewed as retirement communities built on beaches or mountain resorts, they are now a staple of downtown city cores and suburban areas.

Condominiums appeal to residents who don't want to bother with cutting grass, shovelling snow and cleaning eavestroughs. They may also offer amenities such as tennis courts, fitness clubs and swimming pools. Some condos are designed for retirees or for those without children. As condos are run by a collective, there are rules or "condo bylaws" which serve the interests of everyone who owns a unit in the development. Find out if the condo is run by a property management group or if it's self-managed by a group of owners. What extras are available to you and when can you use them? Is there cable television or are you free to put up a satellite dish? Do you have to book common rooms in advance? Are there hobby groups or clubs within the development which may be of interest? Are pets allowed? Children? Can visitors bring either? Is there sufficient parking? Is there a storage area? In the case of a townhouse condo development, do you own the front lawn as well as the back?

> The last thing you want to do is to invest in a poorly maintained building. Check out all aspects of the development.

While there are benefits to condo ownership, there are drawbacks as well. In addition to mortgage payments you will also have to pay a monthly condominium or maintenance fee. The fee can be hefty too — ranging from $200 to $700 a month. Unit owners will also have to pay property taxes which could also add up to another $100 to $300 a month. Determine exactly what the maintenance fee includes. Does it cover snow removal, the fitness club and window cleaning? Some complexes are more efficiently run than others so you may wish to compare services and maintenance fees with similar buildings in the area to see exactly what you're getting for your money.

Some condos include utility costs in the condo fees. It may be beneficial if each user pays their own heating and cooling bills or you may end up subsidizing more wasteful users. Some condo developments lease common areas rather than own them. In this case, future increases could affect your fees. If you have a green thumb, you may have to check it at the door as many developments will not allow gardens, or other landscaping. You might not be able to put anything on the outside of your unit and you may have to use approved window coverings. Structural changes within your unit may also not be allowed.

The last thing you want to do is invest in a poorly maintained building. It will also make it more difficult to sell. Check out the lobby, sidewalks and parking lots. Try to visit the unit you are intending to buy and spend time in it. Who are the neighbours? Can you hear them? Does the balcony get sun? Speak to other residents. How do they like living there? Is it well run? Are they pleased with the responsiveness of their association? Do they feel like owners or merely tenants? If you can, visit inside other tenants' units to check out if they appear to be high end or low end spenders on their furnishings and surroundings.

Look into the finances of the condo development. Ask if you can attend the next meeting. Keep in mind that if the roof needs to be replaced or the landscaping upgraded, you will be paying for it along with the other owners of the complex. For example, if the parking lot was in a state of disrepair and this was not built into regular maintenance costs, there could be a special surcharge placed on all unit owners to cover the repairs. A well-run condominium organization will plan ahead for major repairs and emergencies and have a cash reserve. Find out if there have been major repairs in recent years and how much each owner had to cough up to pay for them. Do the condo fees go up each year? Are the increases the same as inflation or more? Make sure that the maintenance fees on your unit are paid up before you buy, otherwise you could find out that unpaid fees are your responsibility.

If you do decide to buy a unit, play hardball when negotiating a price and be aware of the following. When the real estate market fluctuates, condominiums are usually more vulnerable to downturns in the economy. They may be the first residential units to drop in price and the last to recover. This fact may not matter if you are staying long term, but it may affect your buying decision if you are planning a short term stay.

HIRING A HOME INSPECTOR

Ellen was buying her first home and wanted it checked out by a home inspector. She paid a home inspection company $300 to look over the house she was considering. The inspector toured the home from top to bottom. The house received a favourable review and Ellen bought it. After she moved in only two months later, she noticed a leak in the ceiling. She had a roofer survey the roof and was told it would require extensive repair work costing more than $5,000. When she complained to the home inspection company, they explained that their fee did not include a thorough inspection of the roof and that they would accept no liability for the repairs. Ellen wondered why she bothered with an inspection at all.

The home inspection field is growing rapidly and is virtually unregulated or self regulated by those within the industry. Home inspection services began in the 1970s when home buyers began to seek out professional advice. For most of us, purchasing a home is the biggest investment we will ever make. It's understandable that home buyers not familiar with plumbing, electrical and structural components, would want a professional opinion on a home's condition.

The Canadian Association of Home Inspectors (CAHI) was formed in 1982 to promote public awareness and confidence in home inspectors. There are various associations in most provinces across Canada that promote home inspection services, as well as offer accreditation services as evidence of an inspector's competence and professionalism. The CAHI's goal is "to advance the knowledge, skill and status" of home inspectors. While various self-regulating groups are working to raise the profile of the home inspection industry, in reality anyone can claim to be a home inspector. Charters Kenny of Baker Street Home Inspection Services, is a member of The Ontario Association of Home Inspectors. He admits, "to become a home inspector in Ontario, you don't require anything. You can have a business card printed up tomorrow and start inspecting homes." Consumers must be careful when they seek out the services of a home inspector. Most registered inspectors are required to be knowledgeable about all major components of a home including the exterior, roofing, plumbing, electrical, heating, central air conditioning, interior, insulation and ventilation.

A home inspection is no guarantee that your home is free of problems.

However, even when an inspector is well-qualified, there is no guarantee they will uncover all the problems in a home. There are limits to what an inspector can do while checking a building. Kenny says, "inspectors can't take things apart. The people looking to buy the home don't own it, so there are limitations." In fact, *The Standards of Practice of the Ontario Association of Home Inspectors* lists various limitations and exclusions. The guide says that inspections are visual and are not technically exhaustive. Inspectors are not required to offer warranties or guarantees of any kind. Inspectors are not to move personal items such as furniture or debris that may obstruct access or visibility. They will also not necessarily use their expertise to predict future conditions. Inspectors are not required to walk on roofs, observe the condition of household appliances or treatments on walls, ceilings or floors.

According to their *Standards of Practice*, the goal of the home inspection is to provide the client with a better understanding of property conditions as observed "at the time of the inspection."

Inspectors can only provide an opinion on conditions within the scope of their own "expertise, education, experience and profession."

So this begs the question — when you buy a home should you get a home inspector? It can be argued that if you're spending $200,000 on a home, it's definitely worth $300 or $500 to have a professional check it out first. Others may argue that if the advice given by an inspector is not guaranteed and not completely thorough because of limitations, that paying someone to examine your home could be a waste of money. Make up your own mind if you believe an inspection is necessary. If you are buying a new home, you would not require a home inspection because the home and its components will be covered by a new home warranty. If you are buying an older home that could need repairs and are unsure of your ability to judge major components yourself, you may wish to seek the advice of a home inspector.

If you do use a home inspector, grill a few first on their abilities and backgrounds. Are they registered with a home inspection association that can offer proof of some standards, conduct and ability? Do they have a background in construction or engineering? And always read the fine print in contracts and be sure they are checking every major aspect of the home. If there is one part of the home, such as the roof, that is not covered in the inspection, you may wish to have it checked by someone else before you sign on the dotted line.

SHARING A WALL

Audrey moved into a semi-detached home in a quiet neighbourhood. She thought the building was in great shape but before long she noticed water leaking down behind her cupboards and through her ceiling. When her home was inspected, she was told her roof was fine — it was her neighbour's half that had the leak. Audrey informed the people next door but they said they realized their roof was in need of repair but they didn't have the money to do it. Every time it rained Audrey had to put out pots to catch the water and she feared that her home would begin to mold and rot from the moisture.

With the high cost of housing, many people decide to purchase less expensive townhouses, duplexes or triplexes. Often the homes are still a fairly large size and savings can be realized through the sharing of the lot and in constructions costs, as it's cheaper to build one large unit with a shared wall than stand alone detached homes. Buying a home attached to another one can have cost saving advantages, but depending on your neighbours, it can also pose problems.

When buying any property having good neighbours is important, but when your home will actually be attached to theirs, this becomes especially critical. Who are the people next door? How long have they lived there? Is their property kept in good condition? Do they rent or own? How long do they intend to stay? Do they have children? Do they have pets? Even the best construction will not completely eliminate sounds coming from your neighbour's property. If you are in a townhouse between two other units, a barking dog, cranked stereo or loud children could make your dream purchase a nightmare.

Complications can arise when your neighbours fail to keep up their property to a reasonable standard. This is particularly true when their unit begins to affect your home's structure and property value. In the case of a shared roof, it's a good idea to approach a neighbour about having roofing work done at the same time. This will keep both sides looking similar and could also lead to cost savings as a roofer would be able to do both sides at the same time.

If a neighbour refuses to make repairs which are causing problems for you, municipal officials can request that the repairs be done.

If a homeowner doesn't fix up a property and it adversely affects another person's home, there is a remedy at hand. Most municipalities when advised of the situation will alert staff who deal with building codes and bylaw enforcement. If a neighbour refuses to make repairs which are clearly causing problems for another tax-paying homeowner, municipal officials can approach the offending neighbour and request they have the repairs done. Usually this is enough to have the problem looked after. If not, the municipality can then have an inspector order repairs and authorize contractors to do whatever is necessary to rectify the problem. The municipality will recoup its money by adding the cost of the renovations to the offending homeowner's tax bill.

Of course, it's a good idea to try to work out these issues before a problem arises. There would most certainly be increased and unwanted tension between neighbours if one were to call on a city inspector to force repairs. In the case of a shared driveway, staircase or walkway it would be prudent to talk to your neighbour well before any repairs are needed. Ask when it would be a good time for them to jointly finance a new fence for the entire property. What is their view on the crumbling patio stone or cracked shared driveway? If you are buying an adjoined home, try speaking with the neighbours before purchasing to get an idea of their views of splitting repair costs on items that affect both properties. Having a plan in place before improvements are needed will make it easier when it's necessary for them to be done. In the event your neighbour's decaying property has caused you to have to make repairs, check with your insurance company to see if the renovation costs are covered by your policy.

HOME HEATING HELP

Robert noticed a big increase in his home heating bill after natural gas prices more than doubled in 2000. He tried keeping the heat down and did his best to conserve energy, but it seemed his bills never got any lower. With energy prices continuing to rise, he wondered how to ensure that his home was as energy efficient as possible.

Many consumers are feeling the pinch as home heating costs continue to climb. An inefficient home not only wastes money in the winter, it also means wasted cooling dollars in the summer. Your heating and cooling bills could be up to 50% lower with even modest improvements.

Homeowners should check for drafts and air leaks around windows, doors, fireplaces and baseboards. Silicone caulking can be applied to fill cracks, while spray foams can be used in larger holes such as those around plumbing outlets. Weather stripping products don't last forever, so check annually around windows and doors to see if new draft proofing measures can help keep the wind from howling in. Check to ensure storm windows have been closed after the summer season. Window kits that use clear plastic film may help stop drafts but these should be used only as a short term fix. If your windows are letting in that much air, you will eventually need to repair or replace them. Many older homes lack sufficient insulation.

Check your attic to see how much insulation you have. If it's only a couple of inches, a few bags of insulation would easily pay for itself in saved heating dollars.

As homeowners struggle to make their homes more energy efficient, the federal government has devised a unique system to help rate houses on their energy efficiency. When you buy an appliance such as a washer or dryer, it will usually have an "EnerGuide" sticker which states its energy efficiency rating between one and 100 as it compares to similar products. "EnerGuide for Houses" is a new national home energy rating program created by the Ministry of Natural Resources Canada. The program is carried out by certified professional energy efficiency advisors across the country.

Homeowners pay a fee, usually around $150, to have energy advisors examine their home from basement to attic to conduct an energy efficiency test. This involves installing a blower fan system on your front door which essentially creates a huge vacuum inside your home. The fan blows up to 3,000 cubic feet of air out of the home which highlights any leaks or drafts you may have around doors, windows, baseboards or wherever they may be. An energy consultant may use a smoke pencil which is a device designed to detect air flow. They will make recommendations on insulation, ventilation and draft proofing and if necessary, a furnace upgrade. When the test is complete, your home will be graded on a scale between one and 100 on how efficient it is. Newer homes can score in the seventies and eighties, but many older homes average an efficiency rating of only 40 to 50, meaning valuable heating and cooling dollars are being wasted annually.

> Check your attic's insulation. If it's only a few inches thick, a few extra bags would easily pay for itself in saved heating dollars.

If a homeowner had the test done and corrected problem areas, they may be able to easily recoup the $150 fee paid to conduct the test. The company carrying out "EnerGuide for Houses" may offer to do the necessary repairs for a fee, or the homeowner may choose to make improvements on their own.

If the homeowner does decide to let the energy advisors carry out corrective measures, it should be negotiated beforehand. Houses with a high score on the "EnerGuide for Houses" test prove that they are less costly to operate, which can be a potential selling feature. If you are interested in finding out more about "EnerGuide for Houses," you can contact your local utilities for more information. You can also find out who may provide the test in your area from the federal Ministry of Natural Resources, listed in the blue pages of your phone book.

Many homeowners forget to change their home furnace filters which can cause problems at all times of the year. A clogged filter can be a strain on your air conditioning in the summer and cause your unit to malfunction. It can also cause poor air quality in your home. Check your filter frequently, but always when it's time to start your furnace in the fall or central air conditioner in late spring. Before winter settles in, you should put a cover on your exterior air-conditioning unit, not just to protect it, but to stop cold drafts from getting in and heat from getting out.

DEALING WITH ENERGY MARKETERS

Jamal heard a knock and met a natural gas broker at his door. The broker asked to see Jamal's gas bill and then told him that he could save hundreds of dollars a year if he switched from his current natural gas provider and signed a five-year contract. Jamal thought it over and declined. However, on his next gas bill he noticed his rate had increased and he had been switched to another natural gas supplier. It took him months to get the ensuing mess sorted out.

Deregulation is designed to benefit consumers, as in the past large utilities had virtual monopolies over electricity, natural gas and telephone services. It takes many years before deregulated industries run smoothly and consumers are usually caught in the middle, confused by what's happening and unsure if they are really getting the best deal possible. Deregulation has taken place in Ontario, Alberta and many other jurisdictions. As systems are already in place to transport energy through electricity transformers and natural gas pipelines, it wouldn't make sense to build parallel distribution systems. So your regular provider will still get the energy to your home, you may just decide to buy it from someone else. Deregulation will increase competition much the same way as long distance telephone charges decreased following the break up of telephone monopolies. The road to deregulation is filled with potholes and while there are potential savings to be had, consumers must be savvy when signing long term contracts to purchase energy.

Complaints about natural gas brokers have consistently made the top ten lists of consumer grievances over the past four years in Ontario. Thousands of people have had similar experiences to Jamal in the infancy of natural gas deregulation. Brokers were hired to sign up as many new customers as they could. Many worked on a commission basis and some unscrupulous operators would do whatever they could to get new customers. A broker asking to see your bill may have wanted it for the sole purpose of writing down your account number so he could switch you to the company he was working for. This widespread practice was condemned by Ontario's Energy Board which has tried to clean up the industry and make it more honest and fair for consumers.

The electricity sector is also undergoing deregulation meaning consumers will now have the option of purchasing their power from someone other than their regular supplier. This new era is a bit discomforting for some, as risk has now been introduced into the energy marketplace. No one truly knows what the future prices will be for natural gas, oil, electricity and other commodities. Brokers are market speculators who buy energy in bulk and then hope they will be able to sell it for a profit. Signing a contract to buy energy is similar to signing a mortgage at a bank. No one knows what the interest rate will be over the long term, so bank customers have a choice. They can take their chances on a short term six-month interest rate that could go up at any time, or they can pay a higher interest rate and lock in for five years or more. Signing a long term contract becomes a personal choice.

If you live in an area where natural gas or electricity has been deregulated, this means that it is being sold as a commodity and the market price will change according to supply and demand.

Natural gas is sold by the cubic metre and the gas supply charge is about 40% of your gas bill. The remaining portion of your gas bill, a delivery and customer charge, is the cost of transporting the natural gas to your door. Electricity is sold by the kilowatt but there will also be a charge to deliver the electricity to your home. When considering offers, make sure you are comparing "apples to apples" and that a lower price does not have hidden charges that could in fact make it less of a bargain.

Shop around and read contracts carefully. If you are approached by an energy marketer, don't get fast tracked into signing a contract. See what other companies are offering. You may also decide not to sign any long term contract and ride out the market. There is always the chance you could lock yourself into a three- or five-year agreement to buy energy at a set price and then the price could drop. You could end up paying more for your energy than if you had bought it on the open market.

In the late 1990s natural gas was selling at about eight cents per cubic metre, but in 2000 it shot up to 25¢ per cubic metre. I signed a five-year contract when the price was low with a broker who was offering a rate of 11 cents per cubic metre. When natural gas prices skyrocketed, I was in an enviable position. I wish I could say my decision to lock into a five-year deal was because I was a shrewd observer of the natural gas market situation; however I must confess it was more like dumb luck. Still, the locked in lower rate will save my family hundreds of dollars over the term of the contract.

Some companies may offer upfront rebate cheques as an incentive to get you to sign up with them. Read the fine print on these offers as cashing the cheque usually means that you have contractually agreed to whatever the offer says. Beware that a future cheque may not be a rebate for past business. It could be a new offer with a higher rate that will automatically take affect when you cash the cheque. Before you enter into an agreement with an energy broker, compare it with what other competing brokers are charging. An excellent Web site for this comparison is at energyshop.com. Be sure you understand what you are signing, read the fine print especially regarding exit clauses. Can you cancel the deal if you want to? Does the policy automatically renew and could the rate change at that time? If you wish to change to another broker in the future can you? Are there financial penalties for changing to another broker? If you have signed a deal with a broker and then want out of it, check with your province's consumer ministry to see what kind of cooling off period you have, and if you can cancel the deal.

Signing a contract to buy energy is similar to signing a mortgage. No one knows what the interest rate will be down the road, so you are always taking a chance.

In almost all cases, you will still get just one bill from your utility but the charges will be separated out and the broker named on your statement. Studies done in Australia and the United Kingdom show that electricity prices for residential users have dropped by about 15% under deregulation. A Harvard University study found that in the United States while natural gas prices decreased by 35% for large commercial and industrial customers, prices changed little for residential homeowners. There are other ways that consumers can benefit from deregulation. Utilities are now selling appliances, service contracts or the ability to choose where your power will come from. Someone who is an ardent environmentalist may not mind paying a premium price for electricity, a "green surcharge," if the electricity coming to their home is generated by wind machines or solar power.

PROTECTING YOUR POSSESSIONS

Chris returned home to find his house in flames. Luckily his wife and children escaped without injury but he was told by fire-fighters that almost all their possessions would be lost. What was not ruined in the blaze was destroyed by water and smoke damage. When it came time to add up all the losses and deal with the insurance company, Chris was in a quandary trying to remember everything his family owned. The following weeks would be stressful as he struggled to recall the countless belongings, products and heirlooms in their home.

Most homeowners have home insurance coverage which is extremely important in protecting your investment. Banks will not lend mortgage money to individuals unless they are sure that the property is protected. You should have "guaranteed replacement cost" insurance on your home to ensure there will be enough money to rebuild it in case of a catastrophic loss.

Often people who live in apartments, and have little property, are unsure why they should bother with tenant insurance. However, tenant insurance, like mortgage insurance, includes liability coverage which will protect you in the event of an unforeseen accident which damages another person or their property. It covers you for anything that you or your family becomes personally liable for that is not criminally related. It will protect you if someone slips and gets hurt while they are putting on their boots in your home or if you damage other units in a building by leaving the taps running in your bathtub. Home and tenant insurance will protect you if you accidentally knock over and injure a child with your grocery cart at a store, and cover you for a camera that is stolen from your car.

If you were to come home and find that you were the victim of a fire or break-in, would you remember the hundreds of items in your home? Would you be able to clearly convey to an insurance agent all of the things that you needed to replace — belongings that would be covered if you could just remember you had them? Most people in houses, condominiums and apartments have insurance to cover their contents, but few people have detailed lists of everything they own. If you have $150,000 content coverage and you have a major catastrophe you are not simply handed a cheque for $150,000 from an insurance company. You have to fill out a huge stack of paperwork that will be used to determine what was lost and what will be replaced. You will be closely scrutinized and while an insurance company will pay you what you deserve, they want as much proof as possible. When you think of the things in your home, you may easily recall your fridge, stove and television. But what about paintings, figurines, clock radios, toys, tennis rackets, pots and pans, curtains, tablecloths, etc?

It's important to understand your policy to know exactly what you will be covered for. Be clear on whether you have full replacement value on your goods or actual cash value. If you have only actual cash value, your eight-year old 25-inch television will not be replaced, but you will be given an amount of money for it based on its worth considering depreciation. Replacement value means a 25-inch TV will be replaced with a new 25-inch TV. Once you are clear on your policy, then you should make an inventory. It can be fairly time consuming to make a list but you should, and then from time to time update it. An easy way to make a quick inventory of your belongings is with a home video camera. Insurance officials say it's a good start, but they also want to see lists, receipts, serial and model numbers. The more information you have be it photos, receipts, or charge card statements, the better. All will help identify your goods if those items disappear.

Ideally you should make lists of individual items, such as compact discs or the computer software you own. The higher ticket the item, the more documentation you should have to support it. Special items such as jewellery or hobby collections should be appraised to give accurate assessments of their worth. If you have a prized baseball card collection worth thousands of dollars but don't have the proof to back it up, it will be hard to convince a claims adjuster that it's worth anything. You may wish to have additional insurance, known as a rider, on higher value items such as an expensive wedding ring, silverware, furs or mountain bikes (many policies will only pay a limited amount, about $250 per bike). Once lists are made, they should be kept in a safe place such as a safety deposit box. An inexpensive way to keep your lists safe is to swap them with a friend or family member. As well as keeping a copy for yourself, you keep their lists, they keep yours. Many insurance companies offer inventory lists to help you make an accurate record of your contents.

> If you raise your home insurance deductible from $250 to $500 or $1,000, you can reduce your annual premiums by as much as 30%.

There are certain things that home insurance will not cover. If your hot water heater breaks down and floods your home, in most cases your insurance company will pay for your damaged carpets and ruined items. However, if the flooding damage is caused by water from *outside* your home, you will not be covered. This includes a major rain storm that seeps through cracks in the foundation, or you accidentally leaving a basement window open. Damage caused by ice dams (water freezing and backing up on your roof) and sewer backups is not necessarily covered. Damage caused by a rotting roof, rodents or mud slides is also generally not covered. If you are away for more than four days and the water pipes freeze in your home and cause extensive damage, you will only be covered if you had asked someone to check on your home in your absence. You must check with your agent to know what kind of coverage you have.

Here is a money saving tip you may want to consider. If you raise your deductible from $250 to $500 or $1000, you can reduce your annual premiums by as much as 10 to 30%. Keep in mind that if you do have a claim, you will have to come up with the deductible which is an out of pocket expense. Don't claim for small losses. Take advantage of any potential savings offered by your company for having smoke detectors, fire extinguishers, a monitored burglar alarm system and deadbolt locks. It could add up to another 10 or 15% savings on your premiums. Shop around and see what other insurance companies are offering. If premiums are cheaper elsewhere, ask your insurance company why. Don't switch for the sake of a few dollars but make sure you are getting good value for your money. If you are not sure about something, ask your agent! Don't wait until you have a claim and then find out that you're not covered.

HOME RENOVATION RIP-OFFS

Raja wanted to renovate his basement and phoned a contractor whose number was posted at the grocery store. The man said he could do the job for $1,500 and no contract would be necessary if he was paid "under the table" to avoid taxes. Raja agreed and paid the renovator $3,000 upfront to start the job. A crew went to work on the basement the next day. A week later, the renovator said he needed another $7,000 to buy materials. After the cheques were cashed, the contractor never came back. Raja then realized he only had a phone number to a pager. His calls were never returned, the work was never done and he never got his money back.

Home renovation rip-offs can easily happen to the unsuspecting homeowner. A basement renovation project can cost as much as a new car. While many consumers will research a car purchase for months, some may entrust a complete stranger to complete a huge construction job in their home without knowing anything about them. While there are many hardworking contractors, the profession is unfortunately a haven for scam artists who start jobs without any intention of finishing them. Homeowners get caught with their guard down by not researching projects well enough, being too trustworthy and failing to get the work to be done in writing. Renovators can make it seem tempting to do a job "under the table" in order to avoid taxation, but this can lead to problems which could cost the homeowner significantly more in the long run. Dishonest or unprofessional home renovators also cut corners, use inferior materials and undertake shoddy workmanship.

When having major improvements done to your property, you should always get at least three estimates. Contracts are crucial and all aspects of the renovation project must be put in writing, as verbal promises mean little when a problem arises. Specify the work to be done in the contract and be extremely detailed so it cannot be open to interpretation. For example, if you want a shower, make clear the brand of shower stall you want and the specific type and model number of the plumbing fixtures. Simply stating that you want a new shower can allow a builder to use cheaper materials and products that you may not find desirable. If you can, buy the materials yourself so you will know how much building materials cost, as contractors often inflate prices when quoting a job. If you buy the materials and there is a problem, you will still have them in your possession if a renovator quits before the job is done. Also ask if you can write a cheque directly to the building supplies company and have the materials delivered to your home.

Never pay too much upfront! The bulk of home renovation problems happen when homeowners pay a contractor too much money in advance of a job. Usually dishonest operators will word contracts so that they are able to receive the bulk of funds before substantial work is done. They may say they need a 30% deposit and then another 30% when they begin the work. This means you could pay them more than half in advance before any work is actually done! Then, if the homeowner complains about their work, they will just leave with the money they have already been paid. They can also claim that they wanted to finish the job but the homeowner was being difficult and wouldn't let them. Most honest renovators do not require large, upfront deposits. They may need some money to purchase materials, but only pay what is reasonable. If a contractor is too eager to get money before starting a job, this could be a clear sign that they may not be legitimate. Insist on a contract and spend time going over it. How much is for labour? How much is for materials? Is the contractor responsible for the debris left behind from a major project. Will they transport it to the dump or will you? What is the warranty or guarantee? Is the contract enforceable? How can it be enforced? Is the quote a firm price? Is there any possible way it could change halfway through the job? How much experience does the renovator have? Can they prove it? These are all questions you should ask before sealing a deal.

Be aware that in the event of a problem with a home renovator, the police may be of little help to you as scam artists use the law to their advantage. If a renovator takes $20,000 from a homeowner and does absolutely nothing, this is considered fraud and the police will get involved. However, if a renovator begins a job and does some work and then leaves with your $20,000, in many jurisdictions this is not considered fraud. It becomes a dispute between the consumer and the contractor which could result in a long drawn-out and costly court fight. Even winning in court does not mean that the homeowner is assured of getting their money back. This is why it is so important to choose the right contractor. Before choosing a renovator, you must be absolutely sure you can get hold of them if you need to. It's fine for someone to give you a business card with a cell phone or pager number. When things are going well, your calls will be returned, but what if there is a problem? Do they have a home base, a physical address you can go to if there is a problem? Are they listed with the Better Business Bureau? Are there unresolved complaints against them? Make sure that you are not hiring someone who just has a pick-up truck and a pager, who can easily disappear with your money if things go wrong.

Word of mouth is often the best way to pick a renovator. If a friend or family member has had a good experience with a company, it increases the chances that you will too. If you're having a basement finished, ask the renovator if there is a job he has done recently that you can inspect. Be sure it is in fact an independent person's home you are seeing, and not the contractor's friend. If a contractor cannot or will not provide references, don't hire them. Often home supply stores can suggest reputable businesses. Avoid contractors who come to your door and offer a special price, who conduct "free home inspections" and then suggest repairs, or renovators who quote a price without seeing the job. A professional contractor will also have liability insurance coverage and be knowledgeable about building permits, so you won't have any unsuspected surprises.

> When having major renovation work done, always get at least two or three estimates. Then, make sure you have a contract and put all aspects of the project in writing.

A government inspector once told me about one of the worst cases of home renovation fraud he had seen, involving a senior citizen. A scam artist came to the senior's door and told him that it appeared his house was in a terrible state. He asked to see the senior's basement and then told him that without a new kind of sealant, the senior's home could fall into a state of serious decay. The senior agreed to have the work done. The scam artist went to a nearby hardware store and bought three cans of spray insulation for about $30. He sprayed the basement walls with the foam and then demanded $15,000, which the senior paid. While you may not fall for this obvious fraud, it did happen. Everyone should be aware of this type of criminal activity.

FURNACE AND A.C. START-UP

Hector tried to be frugal and every fall he waited until the last possible minute to turn on his furnace. As a cold front moved in one day and the temperature dropped Hector decided it was time for some warmth. He turned on the heat but it didn't come on! His furnace was broken. When he called to have it repaired, he was told that it would be at least three weeks as there was a long line-up of work orders ahead of him. It would be a cold fall.

In the winter of 1999, when cold weather swept into the greater Toronto area, home heating companies received more than 30,000 calls in *one day*! Hundreds of families were left in the cold for days and even weeks waiting for furnace repairs. Every year millions of Canadians turn on their heat at around the same time. The same is true in the summer when along with the first heat wave, a wave of Canadians want to cool off with their air conditioners.

Those in the home heating and cooling business say that a furnace or air conditioner is most likely to fail on start-up. In most regions of Canada, a furnace will sit idle for at least five or six months of the year. The same is true of a central air-conditioning unit. Equipment designed to heat up and cool down goes through various stages of expansion and contraction. Experts say after the machinery sits dormant for a period, it is at this time — at start-up — that they are prone to a breakdown.

Many people are creatures of habit, so it's wise to start a new habit of testing your furnace or air conditioner *before* you need it. If you usually turn on your furnace during the first week of October, why not test it during the first week of August? Just turn it on for a few minutes until you can feel the warm air flowing through the vents. By doing this you will be assured that your furnace will most likely work when you do need it. If your furnace doesn't work, you will be able to get it fixed in a timely fashion. The same can be said of your air conditioner. Why wait until June when the temperature is rising, when you can test your unit in May to see if it's blowing cool air?

> Start testing your furnace and air conditioner a month or so before you'll need it — that way, if it doesn't work, you'll have lots of time to get it fixed before you really do need it.

By finding out if you have a problem early, you will not only be more likely to get service, you may get better service. Often when companies are deluged with work orders, they may refer you to other companies that may be second-rate. You may also have to go with a contractor you know little about. You could be put in the position of having to accept an offer from a repair crew that you feel is unfair because you're caught over a barrel. There could also be additional charges during a busy period, such as overtime costs on a weekend or for a late night service call. By checking your unit early, if there is a problem you will have time to get estimates and shop around. Your furnace will likely work for you when you test it, but that one time it doesn't, you'll be glad that you checked and saved you and your family from cold nights waiting for a technician.

CAVEAT EMPTOR — LET THE BUYER BEWARE!

DONATING AT THE DOOR

Anita answered a knock at the door to find a young girl wearing an ID badge and holding a clipboard. The girl said she was canvassing in the area to raise money for the police department to help find missing children. Anita felt it was a reasonable cause and gave the teenager $5. She later decided to obtain more information about the campaign and called her local police department. She was told that there was no such program in place.

When I was young, against my mother's wishes, I sometimes visited the local pool hall. There I met a teenager who spent so much time at the tables, he practically lived there. One time he ran out of money and left, only to return a short time later with more cash, ready to play. "Where did you go?" someone asked. "I went collecting for the boy scouts" he said with a grin. This fellow had no shame and would go door-to-door, telling people he was involved in a campaign to help boy scouts finance a camping trip. When he had $20 or enough for a day's worth of pool, pop and chips, he would return. The next time he went "collecting," he would pick a different part of town.

The young woman collecting for "missing children" also came to my door. When she mentioned the program to help find missing children, I too thought it was a valid undertaking and gave a few dollars, not really thinking too much about it. The next day when I went to work, I was given a news release from the police department saying canvassers were going door-to-door claiming to collect money to help find missing children. The police said they had no affiliation with this group and asked me to warn the public that it was a scam. I realized then that I had been duped. It was the last time I gave a donation at the door.

It's unfortunate to have a "no donation at the door" policy for door-to-door charity solicitations, but it's one that many people are adopting. This is lamentable as there are many committed volunteers who spend countless hours going door-to-door in neighbourhoods across this country, raising money for worthwhile causes. However, for every person raising money legitimately, there is someone else trying to scam donations out of well-intentioned people.

Some fraud artists will hire young people to go door-to-door collecting money for various groups. The teenagers may not even realize they are taking part in a fraudulent activity. The perpetrator may take several teens in a van to various subdivisions where they will go door-to-door seeking donations. The teens may be given plastic badges to attach to their coats and clipboards to make their soliciting seem more believable. In fact, all the money being collected is going into the pocket of the fraud artist, who then pays the canvassers a minimal amount.

Many schools and athletic clubs sell chocolate bars to raise funds. Most people don't mind this kind of solicitation because you are at least getting *something* for your money. While this method of fundraising is used fraudulently, usually the scam artist wants to leave you *nothing* for your money. Often with deceitful door-to-door solicitations, the con artist may claim the fundraising effort is in association with the police, fire-fighters, a local hospital or some other worthwhile cause. They may use names that sound similar to reputable organizations to mislead potential donors. Often people feel put on the spot to give money, even though they have no idea where their gift will go.

If approached by someone soliciting door-to-door, ask for printed material explaining their organization and what the fundraising drive is about. Ask if there is a phone number where you can verify the information and if you will be given a proper receipt. If a door-to-door canvasser can't give you details as to precisely where your money is going, tell them you're not interested and close the door.

WORK AT HOME SCAMS

Sarah was a stay at home mother and was trying to find a way to generate some income. A newspaper ad that said she could earn a salary working at home stuffing envelopes caught her interest. The ad promised she could earn $1,000 a week and no experience was necessary. She responded to the ad and paid an $89 one-time fee to get started. In two weeks, she received a worthless plan that basically told her to repeat the scam on others. The package insert stated that there was no money to be made stuffing envelopes, and that she would not get a refund as there was no money-back guarantee.

Work at home scams are shameless and deplorable as they exploit money from people who usually are in dire straits. Ads claiming to need people to stuff envelopes, review manuscripts or assemble products have been in newspapers for decades. Newspapers may have a small disclaimer in the classified section advising readers to beware of companies that ask for money upfront; however, papers will print the ads to generate revenue. Often the ads are completely legal because of information hidden in the fine print and loopholes in contracts.

One of the most popular work at home scams is the one that Sarah fell for — envelope stuffing. A similar ad indicated that a person could earn as much as $5,000 a week stuffing envelopes. When the person answers the ad, he or she is sent some paperwork and an official looking document that says the envelopes and materials will arrive after a start-up fee is paid. Once the fee is paid, the person is sent a package that amounts to a slap in the face. One that I witnessed said, "envelopes are being stuffed by machines at a rate of $1 per hundred. Why then would any company send you envelopes to be addressed?" It usually states as well that you were never offered a money-back guarantee, so don't ask for a refund.

Most of the scams are run out of a post office box. The perpetrators may try to make the operation appear legitimate by including in its address a suite number. When a person is sending something to Suite 238, it sounds more official than P.O. Box 238. Canada's postal system will not allow someone to use a post office box and call it a suite, but private companies specializing in renting post office boxes will. Some scams advise the person who is duped to simply take out their own ads and con others the same way. Other work at home scams may promise money can be made assembling products. Respondents may have to invest in a kit to learn how to do the assembly, but the work never materializes. They may be promised money-back guarantees *if* they are accepted for the job. Of course, they never are.

One ad, a staple of Canadian newspapers, offers people the chance to earn money in their spare time reviewing manuscripts for book publishers. The person receives, for $45, a list of publishers and is invited to canvass them for work. Large publishers would never consider using novice reviewers to critique book proposals. Other ads in newspapers may ask you to "test your voice" for work in broadcasting. There is usually an upfront fee and a career in broadcasting never materializes. The adage "if it's too good to be true, it probably isn't" can be applied to all these various schemes. Be leery of any job proposal that seeks money upfront for application or set-up fees. In her mind's eye, Sarah imagined a large truck coming to her home and dropping off thousands of envelopes for her to stuff. In the end, she felt foolish to have believed a work at home job could have provided such easy wealth. She and many other people deceived in these scams don't bother telling others for fear they will be thought of as stupid. The perpetrators of the scams may be morally bankrupt but unfortunately, they continue to make money collecting "application" fees from thousands of wishful people.

THE DEEPEST CUT — Identity Theft

Surjit was surprised to receive a call from a collection agency demanding that he repay a $10,000 line of credit. Surjit asked which bank was claiming he owed them money and found out it was one he had never dealt with. He explained that he was never a customer of the bank but the agency insisted they had the right person. They had his name, address, date of birth and social insurance number. Surjit then learned of other purchases and credit cards taken in his name that he had no knowledge of. Surjit was the victim of identity theft.

Identity theft is one of the fastest growing crimes of the new millennium. It's a criminal activity that began in the 1990s and already it's estimated that hundreds of thousands of people in North America have become victims. It's a racket responsible for hundreds of millions of dollars in fraud each year and major credit card companies claim that identity theft is now responsible for the vast majority of its fraud losses.

Criminals will use various tactics to get credit card numbers, social insurance numbers, drivers license information and other highly personal data. They may break into mail boxes and steal mail. Others go "dumpster diving," a practice where a thief will go through the trash hoping to find discarded credit or bank statements. They may steal purses or wallets. Some thieves have obtained low level jobs in financial institutions to gain access to records. They may also fraudulently obtain credit card information from inside sources such as waiters or gas station clerks. Thieves also fill out change of address forms through the post office (see Alert 63, Mail Redirection) to divert your mail to another location.

What identify thieves can do with your information is endless. They can take out loans, credit cards, cell phone service, or open bank accounts and then write counterfeit cheques. They could buy or lease a car in your name or file for bankruptcy under your name to avoid paying debts.

Usually an identity thief will impersonate a consumer and run up as many bills as quickly as possible. When they find credit cards are no longer accepted or cheques are refused, they simply move on and do the same thing to someone else. Thieves can also use the personal information to create driver's licences, social insurance cards, or passports to sell on the black market.

Destroy pre-approved credit card offers or loans. Never give out credit card information over the phone unless you know exactly who you're dealing with.

Don't carry your social insurance number, birth certificate or too many credit cards in your wallet or purse, unless you will be needing them that day. Always keep a close eye on your credit card when it is being used and take your credit card receipts with you. Don't simply leave them behind with the clerk or throw them in a nearby trash can. Be creative when deciding on a pin number for your bank card. Don't write down your passwords in your wallet. If it's lost or stolen, it will be easy for the thief to figure it out. Also be careful whom you give your social insurance number to. Why is it necessary they have this important number?

Personal shredders, once thought to be a tool for government or big business, have now become a new appliance for the home. Shredders have dropped in price and now sell for as little as $20 or $30. They can be used to destroy your paper trail, so there are no concerns after personal statements and bills go out in the trash. Once documents are shredded, it's extremely difficult to piece them together. If you buy a shredder, keep in mind that the cheaper shredders do a straight cut, shredding the paper in vertical strips. Higher-priced models do a cross cut, making it harder to piece shredded paper back together.

Shred or at least carefully tear pre-approved credit card offers or loans. Never give your credit card information over the phone unless you know exactly who you're dealing with. Identity theft victims are not held liable for the fraudulent charges, but the crime can create an ongoing financial nightmare for them. It can take consumers years to get back their good name and credit rating. They can have difficulty obtaining new loans, writing cheques or even getting a cell phone. If you become the victim of identity theft, call the police immediately as well as your bank and other creditors. You will most likely need to cancel your bank accounts and credit cards and acquire new numbers.

Proving your innocence can be a frustrating part of being an identity theft victim. Often consumers feel re-victimized when they are grilled by bank and credit officials. You may be required to fill out affidavits declaring you are not responsible for the charges that have been made in your name. This investigative period can be very frustrating but the interrogation process is usually a necessary part of the investigation. The consumer's main concern is to maintain a good credit rating.

MODELLING SCAMS — Not a Pretty Picture

Jennifer had always dreamed of becoming a fashion model. She answered a modelling agency's ad and was amazed when they told her that she had the potential to make thousands of dollars a month. She was told she would only have to pay $1,200 for a photo shoot to build her portfolio and then the offers would come rolling in. After she paid, she had a session with a photographer and waited for her career to begin. She never heard from the agency again.

Many of us would like to think that we or our children have the right qualities to become a high-priced model, actor or broadcaster. Whether it's for the glamour or the money, every year thousands of men and women try out for careers in modelling. Many more sign up their children hoping they will have success modelling in catalogues and magazines. Unfortunately our vanity can be used against us and as Jennifer found out, there is no guarantee in the modelling world. Modelling can be a ruthless business in which it is very difficult to succeed.

Dozens of modelling agencies may operate in urban centres. Larger, well-established ones offer legitimate services. Some even have "call days" where young women and men can drop in to be briefly checked out by talent scouts free of charge. The majority of modelling agencies are small businesses that may boast of being well-connected to the fashion industry. However, too often they are more interested in lining their pockets than helping aspiring models. They operate by placing ads in newspapers, the Yellow Pages and by approaching possible clients in shopping malls and on the street. Agencies are also popping up on the Internet. Some companies will offer to post your photos on the World Wide Web, so that potentially millions of people can see them. While it may sound like an interesting sales pitch, it does not necessarily lead to lucrative contracts.

> If it's happening too fast, be careful. If you have to sign a contract or pay money in advance, that is a sign that you should be very leery.

Like thousands of other aspiring models, Jennifer was told by the modelling agency that she was exactly the kind of woman the fashion industry was looking for. Agency employees told her she had potential to become the next Cindy Crawford or Claudia Schiffer and that they had clients lined up for her kind of "look." By making an investment in herself she was told she could earn a living as a sought after model. Even men and women who may not have classic features are often told that they are needed to fill roles representing normal or average looking people. Not all clients are charged the same price to sign up. The agency may try to get a feel for how much money a client is willing to spend by assessing clothing, jewellery and their desire to "capture a dream." Agencies can set their fee as high as $2,000 for someone who looks like they can afford it, to as low as $300 in an effort to get people to sign up.

After an aspiring model pays an agency, it's common for a photographer to take some pictures. However, by fashion standards the photos usually aren't very good, as the photo shoot is just carried out as part of the ruse. Models who pay to sign up with an unethical agency are in reality buying an expensive quick session with a photographer. They are left with a few pictures and no work. When a person realizes the true nature of the deal and confronts the agency, they are told to read the fine print on the contract. The agency may have suggested a person had potential to become a famous model, but the contract will state that they only agreed to take some pictures. That's it. If an aspiring model has still not caught on that they have been duped following the photo shoot, an unscrupulous modelling firm may also try to extract additional funds by saying they require more money to help promote them within the industry. They will attempt to swindle as much money as possible from the unsuspecting person.

Elite Models in Toronto is one of Canada's top modelling firms. Scouting Director, Elmer Olson, says people get caught all the time paying money to agencies hoping that they will become rich and famous. Olsen says aspiring models should be extremely careful when dealing with any agency. "If it's happening too fast, be very careful. We never have our models sign anything upfront. If you have to sign a contract or pay money in advance, that is a sign that you should be very leery." Olson says women can be beautiful and men handsome and still not have what it takes to make it in the modelling world. The man who looks for the perfect face says, "you're born with it. It's in your genes. You have to be tall and willowy. You can be beautiful and just not right for modelling." Olsen adds that there is not a demand for plus-size models or for people to represent the average consumer. In Toronto, there are as many as 20 modelling agencies and Olson maintains he would recommend only three or four to the serious, aspiring model.

Fraud divisions in police departments across Canada have been dealing with modelling scams for years. Often the same agencies will close up shop, move to a new location and open under another name. They may even attempt to bilk the same client again! Anyone interested in modelling or acting should be extremely careful before signing contracts. Agencies may be misleading, but because of the way contracts are worded, often these unscrupulous activities are completely legal.

DON'T GET FLEECED AS YOU GET FIT

Patrick had wanted to get into shape for years and finally decided to join a fitness club. He signed a one-year contract with a gym, but after working out for only several months, he was unable to keep to his workout schedule and had to quit. Patrick paid for his membership authorizing monthly payments on his credit card and since he signed up for a year, he would have to pay even if he was not using the gym. However, after a year had passed, he noticed monthly payments were still being deducted from his credit card. When he contacted the gym, he was told that the monthly fees would continue until he cancelled his membership in writing.

Whether it is as a result of a New Year's resolution or a sudden burst of new-found vigour, many of us have good intentions to get into shape. Unfortunately, not all of us stay with a fitness program once we start it. Grievances with health and fitness clubs usually rank in the top ten categories of consumer complaints across the country. In the past, many gyms would offer lifetime memberships, only to close down and declare bankruptcy not long after opening. Some clubs would reopen under a different name and repeat the practice. Some provinces, including Ontario, have banned lifetime memberships, but do allow what are known as automatic renewal contracts. It's this clause that caused a problem for Patrick and many other club users. Some consumers have had monthly payments deducted for years from their bank accounts before they noticed them coming out.

When joining a health and fitness club, extreme care must be taken when signing contracts and making arrangements to pay for memberships. Clubs often advertise special offers to entice new members to sign up. When customers tour facilities, some clubs may use high pressure sales tactics to encourage people to sign long-term contracts or to pay extra for a "personal trainer." A personal trainer is a gym employee who will work with you one-on-one to help you get in shape. The trainers can cost an additional $200 a month and are used to help a gym generate extra revenue. While the trainers may offer good advice, just be sure you really want one. If you agree to a year-long contract, you will have to pay for the trainer's services even if you quit the club, or decide later you don't want their help.

> When joining a health club, be sure to ask if the contract includes an automatic renewal clause. This feature is a legal method of turning one-year contracts into long-term ones.

While there are good health clubs in operation, one must be extremely cautious during the most important part of joining a gym — signing the contract. Be vigilant in watching out for hidden costs in the form of initiation fees, health check-up charges or other extras you may not want or need. Find out if there is an escape clause in the contract, in case you have a change of heart about working out, or become ill, or dissatisfied with the club. Ask how long the business has been at its current location and what would happen to your membership if the club closes down or moves to another location. When joining a fitness club, try to sign up on a limited or trial basis, so you can see if you're pleased with it. Visit at the same time you plan to use the gym, so you can see how busy it is and ask other members if they have experienced any problems.

A very important part of the contract is the "automatic renewal" feature. When signing up, be sure to ask if there is an automatic renewal clause built into the contract. This is a legal method of making one-year contracts into long-term ones. The clause says in effect that one party — the club or the member — can automatically renew the contract after one year is up. The club almost always renews and then if a member wants out, he or she must cancel their membership, in writing, usually within 30 days. This can be a good feature for someone who wants to stay with a club and keep the original monthly rate without an increase, but it's an underhanded way to continue taking monthly fees from someone who has quit working out and is unaware that he or she is still being charged. One person I spoke with did not notice that monthly membership fees were coming out of his account for more than four years. Also, you must fill out the proper paperwork to end your contractual obligation. Simply refusing to pay is not an option, as some fitness clubs are not afraid to play "hardball" and will use collection agencies to get payments or monies owed. If you are having trouble getting out of a fitness club contract, you should contact your provincial consumer ministry to seek advice.

In my community, our municipal centre offers an excellent work-out option that could possibly be implemented in your community. Rather than signing long-term memberships, individuals can buy five visits to the gym for $20. This way you can use the gym when you have the time and not feel pressured or guilty if you miss your weekly workout. Another thing to consider is working out at home. Quality exercise tapes can offer excellent fitness programs if you stick to them. A workout bench or treadmill in the basement is also a lot cheaper to use over time than going to the gym. Working out at home could save you membership fees, babysitting costs, travel expenses and keep you out of the grasp of fraudulent fitness clubs.

DON'T LOSE MORE MONEY THAN POUNDS

Deirdre was slightly overweight and was looking for a diet plan to help her slim down. She saw pills advertised that promised to help her drop pounds without dieting or exercise. The ad featured testimonials from satisfied customers who said the plan worked for them. She ordered the diet aid and paid for the pills on her credit card. When she got them, she thought the weight would melt away within a few weeks, but as time passed she noticed no difference.

Many of us would love to find an easy way to lose weight and get in shape. The problem? There is no way to do it easily. In our weight-conscious society, there is tremendous pressure to look slim and many people are looking for an effort-less way to achieve weight loss without practising a sensible diet and daily exercise. Despite the advertising, there is no magic remedy that will help "the pounds melt away" and many advertised products are not only ineffective, they may be harmful as well. With the Internet, consumers have access to products that have not been cleared by Health Canada for use in this country. Some products on the market are unsafe and constitute really nothing more than strong laxatives or diuretics.

One of the main factors that determines our weight is our genetic make-up, which is something we can't control. Of course our habits, caloric intake and exercise regimen will have an effect on our weight, but no one should believe that there is a miracle product that will help us slim down. While some products may offer the slightest of benefits, the vast majority are just complete rip-offs. Companies are making tens of millions of dollars selling weight loss powders, pills, wraps, teas, sauna belts, electronic stimulators, appetite patches, sprays, subliminal tapes and even earrings that claim to help you lose weight. The gadgets and products usually declare they can flush, melt, block or burn the fat away and guarantee that you will effortlessly, easily and permanently lose weight — all without exercise.

> Companies are making tens of millions of dollars selling weight loss powders, pills, wraps, teas, sauna belts, electronic stimulators, appetite patches, sprays, subliminal tapes and even earrings.

Beware of any product using terms like miraculous, medical breakthrough, ancient secret, herbal remedy, or doctor developed. To add credibility, some products are sold by "health advisors" or doctors, but keep in mind they may be guns for hire who will say anything because they are being paid to or because they have vested interests. Ads that rely heavily on undocumented case histories with before and after photos are difficult to authenticate. With computers, photos can easily be manipulated by putting an overweight person's head on a supermodel's body.

Many people who buy fraudulent weight loss products don't complain about being ripped off as they may be embarrassed or worry that it could just draw more attention to their weight. Also the consumer may feel that he or she is to blame and that the product probably could have helped others. Weight loss fraud is harmful in many ways, as it takes people's hard-earned money, exposes consumers to increased health risks and interferes with responsible programs that could really help people. Talk to your doctor about your weight if you are concerned, and speak to friends about weight loss strategies that have worked for them before looking for a miracle cure.

TIME-SHARES — A Vacation Nightmare?

Graham entered his name in a draw and was excited when he got a call saying that he had won a free vacation. He and his wife Irene agreed to go to a presentation to collect their prize. When they got there, they were given a high pressure sales pitch to buy a time-share vacation plan. It sounded like a reasonable investment and before they knew it, they signed a contract agreeing to pay the company $12,000. The next day after further review, they decided they really couldn't afford it. They went back and asked to cancel the contract but the time-share company refused. They never did receive a free vacation.

Many people don't realize that when they fill out ballots to win a free prize at a car show, home exhibition or mall, their names are often used to create what some in the high pressure sales industry refer to as a "sucker list." Instead of winning a dream vacation or a new car, the person's name, address and phone number are really being collected so that they can be sold to companies looking for victims to exploit. Often these lists go to time-share or vacation points plan companies, which are essentially the same thing.

People who fill out a ballot will usually get called by a smooth talking operator. They are told they have won prizes which can be picked up at a pre-determined time. When the "prize winners" arrive, they are greeted warmly and are asked to sit through a presentation. It's a high pressure sales pitch usually accompanied by loud music, aggressive sales staff and promises of a deal that's too good to pass up. Participants are urged to make a quick decision and are usually discouraged from reading the fine print, by saying the details can be worked out later. In some cases, companies use two way glass so that senior sales staff in the organization can pick the easiest marks in attendance — the most likely candidates to whom they can sell a time-share package. Often the "prize" — a free vacation offer has so many strings attached such as extras for airfare, taxes, set-up fees, higher rates for popular destinations and additional charges during peak travel times and other charges, that it's not worth taking.

> Before signing any contract, find out about all additional charges including airfare, taxes, set-up fees, higher rates for popular destinations, additional charges during peak travel times, and maintenance fees.

When a contract is signed, it usually must be accompanied by a down payment and an agreement to finance the rest later. When the consumer has time to reflect the next day on what has been purchased, many want to cancel the deal. Of course, marketers who operate in this fashion are not willing to allow consumers out of the contract. While the tactics of aggressive time-share companies may be questionable, they are technically not doing anything illegal. Some companies will even close down their business completely and then open it up under another name, at another location.

Many consumers incorrectly believe that they have a cooling off period to change their minds and cancel the contract. This is true in British Columbia and Alberta where the government has legislated a seven-day cooling off period for time-share purchases. In other province such as Ontario, sales are final. In these jurisdictions, there is a 48-hour cooling off period for door-to-door sales, but when a consumer leaves her home to sign a contract somewhere else, the cooling off period does not apply. Provinces that don't have a cooling off period for these kind of high pressure sales realize that consumers are being defrauded by unscrupulous companies. In Ontario, as I write this book, the Ministry of Consumer and Commercial Relations has proposed instituting a ten-day cooling off period and disclosure rights which would ensure that consumers get an adequate description of exactly what they are purchasing. Legislation such as this would give consumers time to reconsider contracts signed in the heat of the moment.

Some vacation resort plans may be beneficial to consumers. Speak with individuals who have already purchased the plan to see if they have found it to be advantageous. All verbal promises should be written into the contract. Make sure you know about all additional charges such as financing costs, membership and maintenance fees. Compare what you would normally spend annually on vacations and consider if you want to be locked into a structured vacation regimen.

Check with your consumers' ministry if you want to know the law regarding cooling off periods in your province. When entering contests, be extremely careful giving out personal information like your address and telephone number. Who is putting on the contest? Is it a reputable group or agency? Can you be assured that your name will not be given to telemarketers or time-share companies? As always, if any deal seems too good to be true, walk out before signing on the dotted line.

USING THE PHONE TO DEFRAUD

Bonnie was pleasantly surprised when she received a phone call saying that she had won a big screen television set. She would just have to pay a $200 shipping and handling charge and the TV would be shipped to her within the week. After she sent a cheque, she received another call saying there had been a mistake and that she had actually won a new car. Bonnie was thrilled. She was told to send another cheque, this one for $2,000 to cover taxes and to have the car delivered to her door. After she paid the money, she didn't hear from the company again. She never received a TV or car.

Many of us may find it hard to believe that people can be conned out of their money on the telephone but it happens all the time! According to the RCMP's Commercial Crime Branch, Canadians are defrauded out of $60 million on the phone every year, with an average loss to victims of $2,000 each. It's well known that Montreal is a hub for telemarketing fraud in North America and investigators with Quebec's RCMP fraud unit say there are 40 to 50 fraudulent telemarketing operations active in that city. These rackets, also known as "boiler rooms," operate in one city but their victims can be anywhere. Telemarketing fraud has been labelled one of the most widespread white collar crimes in North America.

Telemarketing fraud generally refers to any scheme used to dishonestly get money from victims over the telephone. According to the RCMP, criminals that run telemarketing boiler rooms are well organized and highly structured businesses, usually with links to organized crime. There are staff known as "openers," who make the initial call to people. Their job may be to open with a sales pitch, offer prizes or try to solicit a small amount of money. The "closers" are the professional scammers who have their techniques finely honed to extract as much money from the victims as possible. The closers are often allowed to keep a large percentage of the money obtained through the con.

Often when a con artist finds an easy mark, he will return again and again, known as "reloading," until the victim finally realizes that she is being duped.

When victims are asked to send money to collect their prizes, the cheques or money orders usually end up at rented mailboxes, apartments or even vacant buildings. According to Quebec's RCMP there are more than 300 addresses in Greater Montreal used by fraud operations.

Many in law enforcement feel the laws are too lenient for fraudulent telemarketers as convicted criminals often get off with only a fine or short prison term. It's also difficult to get convictions and even when officials do, the fraud artists often just start up a similar operation at a different location. The RCMP says punishment for this kind of crime is much more severe in the United States, where an offender found guilty of using telemarketing to defraud people over the age of 55 could be sentenced to five years in prison for each victim. The U.S. is now working with Canada to try and stop telemarketing fraud, in part because U.S. citizens are being defrauded by illegal operations in Canada.

Victims of telemarketing fraud are often trusting seniors who live alone, but anyone caught with their guard down can be a potential fraud victim. There are countless cases of victims being taken for their savings, life insurance benefits and even home equity. Often when a con artist finds an easy mark, she will return again and again known as "reloading," until the victim finally realizes he is being duped. Some telemarketers may contact victims as often as 30 times to talk about their lives, age, religion, even where they get their hair cut! Shockingly, there are also organizations that sell lists of likely target groups to telemarketers. The RCMP has seized lists of names of people with Alzheimer's disease, amputees, widows and widowers. There are also lists compiled of people who have given money in the past to telemarketers. These lists are known as "leads" and are sometimes sold at $10 or even $100 for each name!

Be extremely cautious on the phone with any call that comes out of the blue. Free gifts, prizes or unbelievable offers are often used as hooks to reel victims in. There is almost always the pressure of a deadline and telemarketers will usually insist on advance payment before the consumer can receive the gift or service. Telemarketing firms may also give the caller names of "touts" or "singers" who will praise the telemarketers' services, but they are actually part of the scheme.

Ask the caller questions such as how did you get my name? Can you send me written information? Can you explain your offering to my lawyer? Never let yourself be hurried and never provide your credit card number to someone you don't know. If you get a call saying you've won a prize, just hang up or proceed very cautiously when listening to the pitch. If it sounds too good to be true — it is.

1-900 NUMBERS ARE NOT TOLL-FREE!

Gabrielle received a flyer in the mail telling her that she had won a free vacation and that all she had to do was call a 1-900 number to claim her prize. When she phoned the number, she heard a recording that did not sound promising, so she hung up. She forgot about the call and thought no more about the prize. Later that month when she got her phone bill, she received a $50 charge for phoning the 1-900 number. The charge surprised and angered her.

"1-900" numbers are sometimes referred to as "pay per call" services, because you end up being charged for the call as well as the information or service provided. Charges for 900 number calls are set by the 900 number companies themselves and are often much higher than regular long distance rates. In provinces across Canada, many people have been victims of scams involving 900 numbers used in lotteries, vacation proposals or other prize offers.

Sometimes consumers will have messages left on their answering machines or pagers telling them they've won free vacations and that they should call a 1-900 number to claim their prize. When they call back, they may get a machine or a person, but in each case they could be charged $20, $30 or $50 for the call. If a free trip was offered, usually it never materializes.

Misleading scratch and win cards are also used in a similar fashion. A person may get a scratch and win card in the mail, believe he has won a prize, and call a 1-900 number to collect his winnings. He may then find he has been charged for the call and realize after reading the fine print, he has in fact not won anything. Consumers must be alert as even though these contests are morally questionable, companies are able to skirt the law because of legalese in the fine print.

Concerned about others at your household making use of 1-900 numbers? Your phone company can block these outgoing calls, usually for a monthly charge.

It should be pointed out that 900 numbers are also used by legitimate businesses to charge their customers for information services. Usually, fair companies will make the charges clear for consumers, so there will not be any surprises on their phone bill. 900 numbers are also used by phone sex services. Anyone concerned about access to 1-900 numbers from their home, such as their use by children or a babysitter, can order a call blocking service. This is available from the phone company and will effectively restrict outgoing 900 calls, although there may be a charge for this feature.

1-900 numbers should not be confused with toll-free numbers such as 1-800, 1-888 and 1-877 numbers. These toll-free numbers allow you to make calls to government offices or business services without paying long distance charges.

YELLOW PAGES SCAM

Margaret was in charge of accounting for a small business. She was puzzled when she received a Yellow Pages invoice that she thought she had already paid that month. Believing she may have forgot, she sent off a cheque for the amount. She realized later after checking the books, that she had paid the yellow pages bill and had mistakenly sent money to a copycat directory that her company didn't advertise with.

Small businesses across Canada must spend a lot of money to advertise in the Yellow Pages. To complicate matters, they routinely get solicitations that appear to be invoices from their local Yellow Pages Directory, when in fact they are look-alike bills sent by rival companies. The bills are copycat invoices of the genuine Yellow Pages bill and often have a similar layout as a *bona fide* statement. They may include such symbols as the walking fingers logo and the words "Yellow Pages" somehow worked into the billing material. The look-alike bills may come from a Yellow Pages directory soliciting new business, a company planning to print only a few thousand copies or a fraudulent party that has no intention of publishing a directory at all.

Some companies phrase the wording of the bill in a manner which is deceiving, although technically legal. The invoice may look as though the company is requesting a payment, but only the fine print will clarify that it's not a bill and that no money is due. Therefore, the business should only pay if it wants to. A bookkeeper shuffling through piles of paperwork could easily pay a look-alike bill in error, which is what the sender hopes! Paying the bill could also lead to future billings or an unwanted commitment.

Look-alike Yellow Page schemers may send out bills hoping that an unsuspecting bookkeeper will pay a look-alike bill in error.

Advertising in the competing Yellow Pages directories may seem cheaper than an advertisement in the directories offered by the mainstream phone company. Before joining up with any Yellow Pages directory, ask to see a copy of their current directory. Who will be getting copies of it? How many will be distributed? Are they free? How long has the company been in business? If a directory isn't going to help your bottom line, then why bother signing up? Clearly, anyone paying company bills should be aware that copycat Yellow Page schemers may be hoping to make a quick buck off an unsuspecting bookkeeper.

TELEPHONE "TESTING" SCAM

Jasmine worked for a large firm. One day she answered the telephone and a representative of the phone company said they were testing lines in the area and asked if Jasmine could help them with a simple test. Jasmine said sure. The representative asked her to dial one, plus zero, plus another number. She did, the person on the line thanked her and asked Jasmine to hang up. On the company's next phone bill, there was a long distance charge of $68. While Jasmine thought she was talking to a representative of the phone company, she was really being tricked by a prison inmate who used the scheme to make a free long distance phone call.

With the high cost of long distance charges, some unscrupulous people want to make long distance calls and charge them to an unsuspecting business. It's a scam that can be pulled on any company large enough to have a switchboard. A person claiming to be a representative of the phone company will telephone a business and ask an employee to help them test the phone line to make sure it's working properly and free of static. They will ask you to push three numbers. The employee presses these three numbers and hangs up, but because of the current technology, the phoney phone representative remains connected to your business's phone system. The scam artist is then able to make a long distance call anywhere in the world and charge it to the unknowing company's phone number.

By pushing the three numbers, an employee is in effect giving the swindler full access to their company's phone line. This scam cannot be pulled on residential phones as there must be a switchboard for it to work. Phone companies say their technical staff would never perform any kind of legitimate test on phone lines this way. Phone companies do monitor for this illegal activity and the problem is not considered to be widespread. Some of the illegal calls have been traced to prisons where inmates have been using this scam to get free long distance phone calls! Be leery of anyone who phones and asks you to "test your phone line" by pushing certain numbers. Hang up or call back to see if the company is legitimate.

> Phone companies say that their technical staff would never perform any legitimate test by asking you to dial three numbers.

MATCHMAKING — Magic or Misery?

Alicia moved to a new city and with her busy schedule, she found it difficult to meet men socially. She had a few dates with co-workers but nothing really worked out long-term. She was thinking about trying a dating service but was unsure if it was the right thing to do. She was concerned about her safety, she didn't want anyone to find out and she didn't want to waste money on a fly-by-night matchmaking operation.

What may surprise people most about dating services is the number of people who actually use them. Most don't broadcast the fact that they have used a matchmaker to try and find true love, but in our busy world thousands of people are turning to dating agencies. Matchmaking has become big business. While there has been a stigma in the past to using dating services, this way of thinking is changing. In fact, the vast majority of people who use dating services are often caring, intelligent and articulate people, who truly wish to find a mate for long-term companionship.

Like every other business, a dating service operates to make money. Often they will use a high pressure sales pitch to get you to sign up. They may also use statistics to try and impress you with their success rate with cupid. Many companies will use misleading advertising, stating that they have a "90% success rate." Just because a company is able to set up a date between one non-smoker and another non-smoker, this hardly constitutes a success. There have been cases of dating services closing their doors, only to open another service under another name. They will then solicit former members of the failed service to try and collect more money from the same people!

Peter Crocker operates the dating service Partners Personal Introductions and has written *A Consumers Guide to Dating and Introduction Services in Ontario.* Crocker says that in post-war Germany there was such a man shortage that single women anxious to find a husband would use vending machines at railroad stations to dispense their photos and addresses. Now there are dating services that use telephone mailboxes, videotape introductions and the Internet. Crocker estimates that as many as 40,000 to 50,000 people inquire about dating services each year in Ontario alone. Many dating services lack the experience and knowledge to provide reliable service, he says. "If a dating service says to you, come in and meet with one of our counsellors — think commission salesperson." Crocker admits that finding a mate using a matchmaker is hit and miss, but he says it can lead some people to Mr. or Ms Right. "A dating agency, if it is well-run, can be a good way to meet others and weed out the socially challenged and weird and wacky people. But, like anything, you've got to do your homework," he claims.

Crocker says singles dances, bars, personal ads and telephone dating services can improve your odds, but they require a lot of time and effort to screen out the insincere and the secretly married. Many services won't even tell you their price over the phone, and only get down to the fees after a high pressure sales pitch. Rates can vary from several hundred dollars for an annual membership to tens of thousands dollars, just to sign up.

Crocker says the dating service industry is becoming more specialized with some agencies specializing in "queen-sized" people, older women and the younger men who love them, people with HIV, people who wish to remain celibate and even services for people who are already married. Matchmaking is more than a numbers game and large companies that use only criteria such as age range, height, weight, drinker, smoker, musical tastes, education, income, marital status and personality traits are doing their clients a disservice. Odds are slim that two clients will possess all of the characteristics that the other is looking for. He says if a company is too large, it will not have the time to know "what makes a person tick." A client's information is often tucked away in a file with their photo paper-clipped to their folder. Crocker is not in favour of a company that decides who you will date based entirely on your answers to a questionnaire. This method frequently results in mismatched blind dates and wasted time.

A dating agency, if it is well-run, can be a good way to meet people and can weed out the socially challenged, weird and wacky people. But, like anything, you've got to do your homework.

Crocker says that consumers looking for a dating agency should look for one that can offer personalized service. A smaller company may have more affordable fees and only take on members whom they feel confident they can match. Rather than matchmaking based solely on the information on file, it's also important to match a couple based on intuition and life experiences. Because no one can predict chemistry, the clients should have the final say over whom they will be meeting. After a matchmaker describes the potential date, the member should be able to see a photo or video before they decide if they want to accept or reject the match. Only if both members approve, will the matchmaker then exchange first names and phone numbers.

If you plan to sign up with an agency, ask how long they have been in business. Do they belong to the Better Business Bureau and, if they do, are there unresolved complaints against them? How much are the fees and exactly what will you be getting for your money? Is there any way to get your money back if you are not satisfied with the service? Dating services are not regulated. One of the biggest problems facing the industry is the high number of agencies that go bankrupt. Can you put your membership on hold if for any reason you can't use it? Do they check to see if a person has a criminal record? Will the service be hands-on and personalized, or after paying the fees will your information be tucked in a filing cabinet? Ask to see proof of the agency's successes. They should have clients who have found true love, that are willing to tell their stories to show that the service can work.

Not everyone who uses a dating service will find happiness. One should be aware of that fact before joining one. Having said that, some dating services do match people who eventually marry. Some of these married couples may never reveal how they truly met. Crocker is a believer that dating services do play a positive role in helping people meet. They attract sincere people looking for long-term relationships or marriage, who tend to be well-educated and have good jobs. "A good service will weed out the undesirables for you and introduce you only to people you really do want to meet — saving you time and aggravation," he maintains. For more information, you can check Crocker's Web site at www.partnerspi.com.

BANK CARD FRAUD

Sanchez received a call from his bank asking why he had overdrawn his account by $4,000. He was also accused of putting a blank piece of paper in a deposit envelope and claiming that it was a cheque for $2,600. Sanchez was shocked and told his bank that he had no idea what was going on. He was later cleared of any wrongdoing, but it took weeks of stress and hordes of paperwork before he got his money back. Sanchez was the victim of bank card fraud.

Credit card fraud is a huge problem for consumers and businesses in Canada with more than $200 million being defrauded from credit card accounts every year. However, bank card fraud is also a growing concern and is causing major inconveniences for an increasing number of bank customers. In most cases, financial institutions will cover the losses caused by fraudulent bank and charge card activity. Still, consumers are put on trial for weeks until it can be proven they were not involved in the fraudulent use of their bank card. Then there is paperwork, new cards and the possibility that the consumer will be the target of more fraudulent activity in the future. What happened to Sanchez is becoming increasingly common and customers who use their bank cards at debit keypads in stores and restaurants must be aware of the potential for fraud.

Unlike a credit card, a bank card's four digit personal identification number or "PIN" offers extra protection when accessing your bank account. But there are still ways criminals can get it. Be extremely cautious if you ever use a swipe keypad for a debit card that is bolted down to a desk or counter top. Criminal investigations have found some cases where the keypad has been secured under a pinhole camera in the ceiling! The hidden camera records your PIN as you punch it in. The criminal element then swipes your card to get the information contained in its magnetic strip. Often the deceitful waiter, gas station attendant or clerk will ask for your debit card and swipe it under the counter or in a place you won't be able to see it. After swiping it once through the bank machine, they will swipe it again on an illegal magnetic reader known as a skimmer or scanner. By having both the information from the magnetic strip and your PIN, criminals can now create a fake bank card and access your account. Reproducing bank cards is a highly technical operation and could not be done by a couple of juvenile delinquents in a basement. This type of activity is often associated with organized crime.

Never lose sight of your bank card and make sure it isn't swiped through more than one reader.

In most cases of bank debit fraud, the bank will cancel the customer's card immediately, issue another card and a new PIN. Customers will usually be reimbursed the money they have lost personally through bank debit card fraud, but they will be asked to sign a declaration that they have had nothing to do with the missing funds, have never given out their PIN and in no way have benefited from the fraud.

To prevent being a victim of bank card fraud, never divulge your PIN to anyone. One man complained to his bank that someone had taken almost $1,000 from his account. He further explained that he had spent the night with a woman he had met in a bar and given her his bank card and PIN to go to get $20 from a bank machine. When she didn't come back, he realized later that she had withdrawn almost $1,000 from his bank account! Since he was the one who gave the woman his PIN, the bank refused to cover the loss.

When entering your PIN at a banking machine or store counter, take a moment to ensure no one can see it. Use your hand as a screen to protect the confidentiality of your transaction. Most importantly — never lose sight of your bank card when it is being handled by someone else. Your card should be slid through a reader only once, possibly twice if it was not read correctly the first time. However, your card should not be swiped through a second reader, as this could be a scanner making a copy of your bank card information.

Question why any merchant would have a card reader that is not visible to you. It is proper procedure to always have the readers in a conspicuous place. You may wish to pay cash when you are in unfamiliar, questionable or undesirable surroundings. Don't write down your PIN in a wallet or purse; avoid obvious PINs like your date of birth or telephone number; and always take the debit transaction record when provided. Also, while robbery is rare at bank machines, it does happen. Check out your surroundings before using a bank machine and don't bother if you are concerned about your safety.

VACUUM CLEANER SALES — a Dirty Business

When Loretta answered the door one day, she was met by a salesperson selling vacuum cleaners. The salesperson told her that the company was overstocked and for a limited time they were selling their product at $500 off. She was told that the vacuum was the finest machine on the market with amazing cleaning abilities. The salesperson stayed at her home for hours describing the benefits and in the end she signed a contract to buy the vacuum for $1,400. After the salesperson left with her money, she reconsidered her purchase and tried to call the salesperson to return the vacuum. She never heard from him again.

Everyone has to make a living, but the tactics used by some door-to-door vacuum cleaner sales staff are appalling. Salespeople have been known to target lonely seniors and shockingly, even those suffering from Alzheimer's. In one case, a salesperson sold seven vacuum cleaners to an elderly victim. He would sell the senior a vacuum one day, and return the next day to sell him another one, taking the vacuum he left previously as a trade-in! In another case, a salesperson sold a vacuum to a senior who was unable to use the vacuum because he had no legs! One aggressive salesperson was known to even sell vacuums to seniors without carpet. In his pitch, he would tell seniors the vacuum also worked as an air purifier! The senior was told to run the vacuum for ten minutes before she went to bed to help her sleep better.

The aggressive marketing of vacuums is a problem across the country. In 1997, there were 1,500 complaints regarding door-to-door vacuum sales just in Ontario and 95% of them involved senior citizens. Investigators with the Ministry of Consumer and Commercial Relations say seniors are often targeted because they are vulnerable, trusting and lonely. There are salespeople who will spend an entire day on a sales pitch with a senior, because one sale can earn the seller as much as $1,000 commission. Many seniors who end up buying expensive vacuum cleaners suffer from senility or poor health. Others may sign a contract under pressure, just to get the salesperson out of their home.

An aggressive salesperson may "size up" the potential buyer to see what that person can afford.

To understand the business of selling vacuum cleaners, one must understand the perspective of the seller. A salesperson may get vacuums for only $300. Whatever they can charge a buyer over this amount is their profit. An aggressive salesperson may "size up" the potential buyer, to see what that person can afford. They may sell the same make and model of vacuum cleaner to one person for $1,200 and another customer for $2,500. The salesperson tries to get a sense of how much money the person has, and if that money is readily available in a chequing account.

Be cautious of sales staff who say the offer is good that day only, or that your neighbours just bought one, or that there is a free gift with purchase. Often door-to-door sellers will get names and addresses off of ballots used in prize draws. In one case, a ballot box for a free trip was set up outside a drugstore that had a special seniors day. The names were then taken from the ballots and used to track down potential customers. Products sold door-to-door are generally overpriced. Do you really need to spend $1,500 on a vacuum cleaner? Many vacuums sold through department stores at one-fifth the price and may do a far better job.

Every province in Canada has a cooling off period for door-to-door sales that allows the consumer to back out of a deal. In Ontario, consumers have two days to cancel a deal if they bought an item worth more than $50 from a door-to-door salesperson. This is only if the item has not been received, or paid in full at the time of purchase. Door-to-door sellers know this, so they get all the money and deliver the goods on the spot to skirt the cooling off period. Sales staff may also make themselves unavailable for the 48-hour period after a sale. They may not provide the proper name or address of the company they work for. To find out the length of the cooling off period for door-to-door sales in your province, contact your consumers' protection office through your province's consumer ministry. Ask them about your rights, if you're having difficulty locating the seller during the cooling off period.

If an aggressive salesperson refuses to leave your home, call the police. Calling the police or the threat to do so will usually be enough to get a salesperson to pack their bags and get out. This is good advice to pass onto ageing parents or loved ones. To get into your home, vacuum cleaner sales staff may offer "free gifts" on the phone or ask you to take part in a carpet cleaning demonstration. This is almost always a pitch to get you to buy something. It's better just to say "no thanks" and hang up.

AVOIDING CYBERFRAUD

Marlon enjoyed his Internet e-mail and used it to stay in touch with friends and family. However, he was annoyed by the constant flow of e-mail from questionable sources that he had to sift through. He was continually being pitched business opportunities, chain letters and work at home schemes. He did find one investment opportunity in his e-mail that interested him and he was curious if it was legitimate.

The Internet has given marketers a whole new way to pitch their wares, services and *scams* to the public. At one time, the snake oil salesperson had to drive from town to town but no more! Now they can simply use bulk junk e-mail to communicate with millions of consumers directly in their homes and businesses. Junk e-mail is more than just a nuisance. Every year, thousands of unsuspecting consumers fall victim to questionable rackets and schemes on the Internet and lose millions of dollars to fraudulent companies.

Bulk e-mail operates similarly to junk mail in your post office box. The companies don't really know exactly who is going to get their offers, but they do if you answer them. The same is true of e-mail. Often an e-mail may say that if you don't want to receive more e-mail from the company, advise them to stop by answering them back with an e-mail. This is often a trick to find

out more information about you! By sending them an e-mail
back, you have shown them that you have read their e-mail and
acknowledged their existence. Don't expect this tactic to get
you removed from a junk e-mail list. You also run the risk that
you may have your e-mail address sold
to other companies operating on the Internet. Legitimate companies do not operate
using bulk e-mail. In some jurisdictions,
it has become such an annoyance that
lawmakers are moving to ban or regulate
unsolicited e-mail.

> Legitimate companies do not operate using bulk e-mail.

Any business opportunities on the Internet should be viewed
with suspicion. How is one to know if the business exists outside
of cyberspace? There are many e-mail opportunities that claim
you can make $500 a day with limited investment and without
selling, attending meetings or personal contact with others.
Usually the offers claim you can profit in Internet related businesses and advises you to e-mail or phone them. Often what
appears on the surface to be a legitimate business opportunity
is a pyramid scheme, designed to separate you from your money.
The envelope stuffing work at home offers you see on the
Internet are no different from the scams operating in the classified ads in newspapers. Similar scams claim you can get rich
quick by trading money on world currency markets, buying real
estate or investing in offshore banks. Others claim to offer easy
credit repair, free vacations or guaranteed loans. Don't bet on it.

Chain letters have found new life on the Internet and many
people get sucked into this scam because the amount of money
involved is relatively small. You may be asked to send $5 or $10
to five names on a list, which in turn will be paid to you if you
don't break the chain. This is just an old scam operating with a
new technology. Some e-mails may claim that the letter is completely legal and has been approved by authorities, but this does
not make it so. Almost all chain letters are considered illegal and
most people that participate lose their money. If you ever get
one, don't be fooled — break the chain!

Junk bulk e-mail also takes aim at areas where consumers feel vulnerable — diets, smoking cures, hair loss and other health related issues. Can a pill over the Internet really melt fat away without exercise? Can a new cream really stop hair loss? Is there a miracle procedure to reverse the ageing process? You can bet the answer is always no. If someone had invented a way to grow hair on a golf ball, they wouldn't be hawking it on the Internet through junk e-mails. Companies that offer free phone cards or music CDs usually have hidden fees that make the offers no bargain. The bottom line — the Internet may be the new communications nucleus for business, but companies that are legitimate and trustworthy are not dropping unsolicited e-mail in your mailbox.

If you use the Internet often, one way to try and reduce junk e-mail is to have two e-mail addresses. One can be for private use with co-workers, friends and family. The other can be used for purchases online or going into chat rooms. You can also purchase or download software to block unwanted e-mail. While it's always nice to get e-mail, be sure you view any bulk junk e-mail with cynicism. You may want to delete it without even reading it.

61

LOST PHOTOS

After saving for years, Miriam finally realized her dream vacation of a safari in Kenya. It was everything she had hoped for and she took incredible pictures of elephants and lions that she was sure would be suitable for framing. Upon returning home, she dropped her film off for developing. When she went to pick up her photos, she was told there had been a problem and that the film was lost. Miriam was heartbroken. Worse than that, the film developer was only offering to provide her with replacement rolls of film, for pictures she felt were priceless.

Losing precious photos can be upsetting and the realization that others may believe them to be of little value can also add to one's distress. With the high volume of films going through film developing centres, some films are lost or damaged. A picture may be worth a thousand words but how much is it worth financially? This becomes a sticky issue as a photo of my little girl taking her first steps may be a precious memory for my family, but it may be of little value to anyone else. Photo developers try to cover themselves to avoid disagreements or lawsuits over missing or mutilated photographs.

There is a lost or damaged film policy warning printed on most envelopes that developers use for their film processing. Warnings may also be posted in the store. The warning is usually along the lines of the following: "If any such film or print is damaged or lost by us, it will be replaced with an equivalent amount of unexposed film and processing." This policy can seem very cold and uncaring to someone who has just been told that their photos of a memorable trip or relative's wedding are lost forever. Most developers are reputable and work diligently to trace lost pictures, but every developer also depends on a similar policy as it's almost impossible to assess a photo's worth. Developers also want to limit their liability.

If you have important photos to be developed, you could take your film to a one hour, developing on-site facility. This may increase the odds in your favour that your pictures would not be misplaced. If they are misplaced, it would be easier to track them down than if they were sent out for developing the week before. You could also take your film to an independent film developer who may specialize in photography and darkroom work, although this could be expensive. If your photos are ever lost, don't expect too much from the developer because of their disclaimer. Still, it never hurts to be an effective complainer. You could demand more than the store's policy calls for, such as free photo finishing in the future for your trouble. Most stores will want to keep customers happy. If they don't offer some sort of appropriate compensation, let them know that you will take your business elsewhere and tell everyone how they lost your precious photographs.

If your photos are ever lost, don't expect too much from the developer because of the company's disclaimer. But it never hurts to be an effective complainer.

ALERT

62

BULK FOOD BUYING — Is It a Deal?

Martha saw an ad to buy beef in bulk and thought that bulk purchases might be a good way to save money on her grocery bill. She was told that if she signed an agreement with a freezer food company, she would save hundreds of dollars a year. After she joined the plan, she was surprised when the first order of meat she received was in smaller portions than she had expected. It was also of poorer quality than what she could buy at the grocery store. She tried to cancel the deal, but was told she couldn't as she was locked into the contract.

Bulk food buying from a reputable service can be a good way to save money, but shoppers can also become victims of "bait and switch" tactics used by unsavoury operators. Consumers could end up spending more on a single purchase of bulk beef than if they bought the same meat products individually at their local grocery store. Buyers must make careful decisions and read the fine print to ensure that they don't sign a food deal they will later regret.

Some consumers such as seniors or the disabled may prefer the convenience of home shopping as often food is pre-packaged in serving sized portions. Some bulk food plans may pitch special offers such as a free freezer, but the price is usually worked into the food deal. Find out the make and model of the freezer being offered so you can determine its true list price and comparison-shop with other similar sized freezers on the market. The ads for bulk food buying can be persuasive, but as always, it's the fine print that will determine if the purchase is a good arrangement. There may be additional charges for cutting and wrapping meat. The prices could also be based on gross weights, meaning the true weight after trimming the meat could be a lot less than you bargained for. There may be special discounts on bulk food purchases, but a 10% discount on food that is 30% overpriced is no deal at all.

It's important to know exactly how much fat will be in the ground beef. Will it be lean or medium grades? What cuts will the steaks be? Get this information in writing and ask for a complete price list of the exact quantity of food you will be getting. Before committing to a large order or signing a long-term contract, make sure that you try out the products you'll be getting to ensure the taste and quality is satisfactory. Don't be pressured into signing any contracts. If the company is above-board, it will allow you to shop around and compare what other similar services are offering. Make sure you understand any deal before signing and don't pay a lot of money upfront. If the contract is to provide groceries over a set period of time see if you can pay for the food as you receive it and check the contract to make sure you can exit from the deal, if you are not completely satisfied.

Situations can arise where it may not be prudent to have a freezer full of meat or other foods. Over time, meats can suffer from "freezer burn," a gradual dehydration which makes meats dry and tough. You could also lose a large quantity of food if there was ever a power failure. Be aware of the door-to-door selling of meat. A distributor may say that she has meat left over from a local restaurant that is of excellent quality and that it is being offered at a bargain, but for all you know it could be old, poor quality cow meat. It just makes no sense to buy meat from someone selling door-to-door when you can't get in touch with them later. Consider checking out a bulk food company with the Better Business Bureau or the consumer ministry in your province to see if there have been complaints.

ILLEGAL MAIL REDIRECTION

Jonathan noticed his regular mail flow had slowed almost to a stop. He didn't think much of it until he realized even utility bills and charge card statements weren't being sent to him. He contacted Canada Post and asked why he wasn't getting his mail. The post office told him that his mail was being sent to his new address as he had requested. That's when Jonathan realized that someone had illegally redirected his mail. He lost important documents, bank statements and products that he had ordered off the Internet. Worse than that, someone now had his personal information at their disposal.

Mail redirection is one of the latest scams being used by criminals to get private and confidential information about consumers. Mail fraud is happening with increasing frequency across the country and Canada Post says hundreds of Canadians have had their mail illegally redirected in recent years. It's more likely to happen in large urban centres where post offices are not familiar with their customers on a first name basis. Once a consumer's mail has been redirected, criminals then have access to their credit card numbers, bank statements and any other information that happens to come through the mail before the consumer realizes what's happening.

The thief will simply go to Canada Post and pay a fee, currently $32, to have the unsuspecting consumer's address changed. Usually the mail is redirected to a post office box. The criminal can get a person's address from various sources such as off a piece of mail or through the phone book or Internet. In a perfect world this scam wouldn't work. When changing your address, you must provide two pieces of identification along with photo credentials. In a busy city like Toronto, as many as 15,000 people will change their address every month. Chris Bartsch with Canada Post says that some thieves use false identification to dupe postal employees into making the switch. Bartsch says, "unfortunately in this day and age computer graphics can be used to falsify information."

An unsuspecting postal employee may allow a person to make a change without the proper identification, although this should never happen. Canada Post is now aware of this new type of fraud and postal employees are being told to follow proper procedure. Bartsch maintains "our corporate security has put out bulletins to remind workers to be extra vigilant when it comes to redirection of mail." Police say that mail redirection is a criminal activity that in many cases is linked to organized crime. It's a way that the criminal element can have access to private information that allows them to forge credit cards, make passports and sell identities.

Even after Jonathan had his mail flowing regularly again, the incident still caused major chaos in his life. He had to cancel all credit cards, change bank accounts and make frequent checks on his credit rating to make sure someone was not using his name to take out loans. He would also have to go through additional checks and balances in the future, when applying for any kind of credit so that financial institutions would know that he was the true Jonathan and not an impostor using his personal information.

If your mail ever comes to a stop, contact your local post office immediately. Never leave letters in a mailbox outside your home for an extended period. If you are taking a vacation or plan to be away for any length of time, see if a neighbour or friend can collect your mail so it's kept in a safe place.

PREVENTING PAVING PROBLEMS

Susan put off having her driveway paved and was surprised when a paver came to her door offering to do the job. His rate was only $600, a fraction of the price she had been quoted by other companies. She was leery but the paver explained that the low price was as a result of the fact he was doing a number of driveways in the neighbourhood. Susan agreed and the paver did the job. Within only a few months, she started to notice her driveway crumbling, cracking and grass growing through the asphalt. When it was hot, her car would actually start to sink into the driveway. Susan tried to contact the paver who did the job, but he was nowhere to be found.

If you get what you pay for, this is especially true when having your driveway paved. If Susan had done more research, she would have been suspicious when the paver started pouring hot asphalt right onto the ground. Be extremely leery of any paving company going door-to-door soliciting business. Companies that offer a much lower price than the competition may use inferior materials or skimp on proper paving techniques. Warranties may be offered, but they are useless if the paving company goes out of business or is nowhere to be found.

There are various ways that homeowners get caught in driveway paving scams. Companies may offer an extremely low price and then come back and ask for more money to complete the job. Salespeople often go door-to-door taking deposits promising to come back, but then disappear. Some firms do the work, but they do a terrible job. In one case, an unprofessional paver actually used wooden paddles tied to an employee's feet to flatten the asphalt! In extreme cases, driveways have actually washed away with the first rainfall.

Even reputable firms will get complaints, but usually these companies will honour warranties to protect their good name. Many consumers are satisfied with work done by paving firms they've found on their own, or through references from friends and neighbours. Always get at least two or three estimates and never accept an estimate over the phone. If you deal with a company some distance from your home, and there's a problem you may have trouble enforcing the warranty.

If a paving job is inferior, most problems will surface within a year. When you check a company's work, try to find a driveway that was paved a year ago, not last week. A good paving company will ask you questions. They may want to know if heavy vehicles will be parked on the driveway and the age of your house. Owners of new homes are advised not to have driveways paved until two years after construction to give the ground time to settle. Make sure the estimate includes all the work to be done. The contract should fully describe the size of the area to be paved, the materials to be used and whether it includes digging out existing materials.

Be leery of any company going door-to-door, claiming to be working in the neighbourhood.

Never sign a blank contract. Many people are fooled by a shrewd salesperson who has business cards and a prepared contract. Keep in mind that a quick sales pitch may be designed to deceive you. Before signing a contract, make sure all the prices are broken down, and that the materials and work specifications are spelled out. Always make sure the contract includes the name and address of the contractor. Ask about the warranty and make sure it is spelled out in writing. Most reputable companies offer one- to three-year warranties.

Most veteran driveway pavers who do quality work say if you get a cheap price, expect a cheap job. If you want a driveway done right, you need to excavate about eight inches in depth. You should have six inches of gravel and then two inches of compacted asphalt. This formula may differ slightly depending on certain variables. A professional job doesn't come cheap. Susan's driveway should have cost about $1,500 instead of $600. However, now that her driveway is falling apart, she says she would have paid more to have the job done right. Instead, she is out the money and has a cracking, crumbling, sinking mess that will eventually have to be replaced.

MAKING YOUR CASH COUNT

SAVING MONEY ON GROCERIES

Alexa had a growing family to feed and often had to spend hundreds of dollars a week to keep food on the table. She tried to look for sales, cut coupons and stick to a budget. Still, she wondered if there was more she could do to try to save money.

Many people will spend weeks comparison shopping for an item like a camera yet they will spend hundreds of dollars a week on groceries without a second thought. It's true that groceries are a necessity, but it's an area where consumers could save considerable money with even moderate efforts. Even trimming your food bill by $20 a week can save you more than $1,000 a year. The typical family spends about 15% of their income on food. Consumers with higher incomes may spend more dining out in restaurants and eating higher priced foods at home.

One of the best ways to save money grocery shopping is by planning ahead. Using a shopping list, meal plans and generally being organized *before* you step into a grocery store can save you time and money. Being organized can prevent repeat trips to the grocery store and prevent impulse buying which quickly can add to your food bill. Go grocery shopping only when you need at least five or ten items. Studies have shown that a shopper entering a store to pick up one item will buy at least three things, and that 20, 30 or even 50% of food purchases are unplanned. Keep in mind that coupons are marketing tools designed by companies to draw attention to their products. Only use coupons for items that you had planned to buy anyway. If you saved 50¢ on an item that you weren't planning to buy, have you really saved any money?

Buy non-perishable items in larger quantities if possible. A one litre bottle will almost always be cheaper than buying the 300-ml version of the same product. Consider store brands or generic brands which are often just as good and much cheaper. It's a fact that manufacturers that make batteries for large brand name companies often make no name batteries for other stores as well. The same corn that is packaged for the more expensive national brands often goes into the cans marketed by store brands. I once toured a water bottling factory and saw this practice first-hand. There were several different brands of water being bottled for sale at a wide range of prices; however the water going into each bottle was from the exact same source!

When items that you use regularly are on sale, try to stock up. It may be convenient to shop at the grocery store closest to your home but if you can drive five minutes further to a store with lower prices it will be well worth the drive. It's an old saying but it's true — never shop while you are hungry! Stopping in a store after work when you are tired and famished could see you buying junk food, snacks and other products that you wouldn't normally buy. Shop after the dinner hour when the stores are less crowded. Also, only buy items that you know you will eat. Many of us buy foods we think we should eat, but when we don't, it's just wasted money.

Don't forget about checking out the top and bottom shelves when you are shopping. One common grocery store marketing tactic is to put the most expensive items at eye level. Don't be distracted by attractive displays and fancy packaging as these extra purchases lead to a more expensive food bill. Deli counters and fresh flowers are other big profit generators to be aware of. When you use a flyer for grocery shopping, keep in mind that not everything in the flyer is necessarily on sale. Watch for multiple item discounts; you may only get the deal when you buy three of them! However, you also may be able to buy one item and get the lower price. Check!

If you really want to save money, you should consider cooking from scratch, stretching meat by cooking casseroles and including at least one vegetarian meal per week in your schedule.

Remember that coupons are marketing tools designed by companies to draw attention to their products.

Also eat less! Many of us take part in "recreational eating." Cutting out high-priced snacks is not only good for you, it can lead to substantial savings on your food bill. Many people don't like budgeting but if you can stick to a food budget, the savings will add up. Some stores now allow food to be purchased on credit cards. Always try to pay cash for food as it's easy to fall into a credit trap if you are constantly buying food on credit. You may also be less inclined to shop wisely with a credit card. If you are constantly amazed by the high total price when you get to the cash register, bring a calculator to ring up your purchases as you shop, so you won't have any unexpected surprises.

USED GOODS —
Good for You
and the
Environment

Gerry decided to take up golf and wanted the latest
equipment for the game. The most current clubs,
complete with an expensive driver, shoes, a pull cart
and other accessories cost him nearly $1,000. He saw
used golf balls for sale but decided to buy new ones at a
cost of about $6 each. He golfed several times, wasn't
very good at it and now the expensive golfing gear sits
in his garage gathering dust.

There is no doubt that most of us would like to buy
new whenever we make a purchase. Most of the time we have
to. However, just as a new car drops dramatically in price as it
rolls off the lot, the same is true for many other items. Manufacturers can be commended for making many articles more
durable than ever. Many businesses are also looking to profit
from this recent recognition that second-hand is acceptable.

While this type of consumerism has been around for decades
in pawn shops and yard sales, modern franchise stores are now
selling used items and trying to market them as "experienced
goods." Of course pre-owned merchandise is not appealing to

all consumers and the choice is also limited. Still, for those on a tight budget, it is an option. For new parents with limited means, stores specializing in used baby goods can be a great place to look for bargains. A new crib, stroller and rocker for instance can cost more than $800. A store dealing in pre-owned baby goods may have these same items for less than half that amount. Stores that sell used baby products must by law guarantee that they are safe for children and are without defects. Of course used goods may not always make appealing gifts, but depending on the receiver, they just might.

Consignment stores are also growing in popularity. They can be a place to find pre-owned video games, compact discs, weights and stereo equipment. Items such as tables, instruments and speakers are usually a more reliable purchase than goods with moving parts, such as appliances and video cameras. Still, many goods will come with at least a limited warranty.

Used sporting goods stores are enjoying tremendous growth. A parent having to outfit a child for hockey can save hundreds of dollars by buying used. Used skates, skis and golf clubs can be purchased usually at a fraction of their original price. Buying second-hand is a good idea for people trying a sport for the first time. If you lose interest, the investment was not as great. If you end up loving the sport, you will know the kind of equipment you should get in the future when you are more knowledgeable about the activity. An astute shopper can find gear that will pass for nearly new and be safe to use.

Gerry was right to wonder about used golf balls. Picture this. A golfer pays $35 for five golf balls. He tees up a shot and drives it into the woods. Later that week, the ball is picked up and sold on the side of the road for only 50¢. Does the lower price make it a bad ball? According to golf pros, manufacturers are now making golf balls that can last for years and be every bit as sound as new balls straight out of the package. Balls really only lose their compression after being underwater for long periods of time. Kevin Thistle, a golf pro at the prestigious Angus Glen golf course in Gormley, Ontario, says, "if a ball is in a pond for a couple of weeks, there is usually not a problem. However, if balls are underwater for years, they will usually have a yellowish colour." When consumers are looking for used golf balls, they should look for balls that are bright white with a brand name. For a fraction of the price, used balls will usually perform as well as new ones. In addition, knock-off of expensive clubs can often be substituted for the real thing. A representative of a large golf equipment supplies company once told me that 90% of good golfing is the golfer's ability. Only 10% is due to the equipment. Many professionals also say a couple of golf lessons can be a better investment than expensive accoutrements.

Buying used sporting equipment is a great idea for people trying the sport for the first time.

The want ads are also a great place to find deals if you shop carefully. With the high divorce rate and people moving long distances because of employment transfers or other life changes, often newer household goods end up for sale in the paper. When my wife insisted that it was time that we purchase an expensive dining set and china cabinet for our home, I admit I was apprehensive about spending $4,000 or $5,000. I was able to convince her to check the classifieds in the paper before we would buy new. She found a beautiful oak collection to her liking that was only three months old. A young executive paid $3,500 for the set, only to find that she was being transferred to a high-tech job in British Columbia. She was getting a pay raise and decided that instead of shipping her furniture, she would sell it. We bought the set for $1,900 — with no tax! Sure we got lucky, but we wouldn't have if we didn't look.

Buying used goods also forces you to pay cash for items instead of putting them on credit at stores where you may be charged a high interest rate for borrowing. Buying used goods is obviously not for everyone, but depending on your stage in life or financial situation, it may be something to consider.

RENTING TO OWN

Gordon needed a washer and dryer but couldn't afford to get a set right away. He decided to rent until he could afford to buy. Time passed and Gordon actually rented the set for years. By the time he had fulfilled his rental contract and owned the washer and dryer, he had almost paid four times what the set was worth.

There are few financial arrangements more expensive than renting to own. While it's obvious that it's less expensive to buy a piece of furniture or stereo outright, consumers are lured into rental agreements because of low weekly or monthly payments. A person who decides to rent to own may have no savings, a poor credit history or just an insatiable itch to get a big screen television the fastest way possible. In many, but not all, instances renting to own should be used only as a last resort.

Rental centres may offer free delivery, instant approvals and free repairs on items to make the deal seem worthwhile. However, basic math shows that the total cost of renting-to-own the item is at least two and possibly three to four times what a consumer would pay if they had simply purchased it. Before renting to own, shop around to get an idea of the true cost of the item that you wish to acquire. Compare the cash value of the product you are about to rent to the actual price you will pay over the life of the rental contract.

If you do decide to rent to own, find out exactly at what point you will own the product. Will you be penalized if you return the item, or want to cancel the deal partway through your obligation? Often with rent to own agreements, there will be additional surcharges. Ask the sales representative to highlight all charges. Is there an insurance fee? If delivery is free, is it also free when it's time to pick it up? Find out if you are liable for loss or damage to the product while it's in your possession. Can you purchase the product before the end of the rental agreement? If so, how will the price be determined? Will you get credit for payments already made? If the rented item breaks down, will you be given a replacement item until it is repaired? If you are late with a payment, will the item be repossessed or will there be a penalty?

Most importantly when you plan to rent to own, find out whether the product is new or used. Often the appliances have been rented before to other customers so you could end up paying three times the price for an appliance and still get one with sufficient wear and tear so that it breaks down shortly after you own it.

It can be difficult to get a straight answer on what the interest rate is when you rent to own and exactly how much the rent to own arrangement will cost you, so it's important to do the calculations yourself. For example, if you rent to own a 32-inch television set for $26 a week for 96 weeks, the total rental price is $2,496. If the set could be purchased outright for a price of $1,199, you have then paid $1,297 more for the TV along with the other fees set out in the contract.

Some rent to own operations have been criticized for making money off the backs of the poor. However the rent to own industry insists that it provides a valuable service. Is there ever a time when renting to own makes sense? The answer is yes. If you are starting a small business from scratch, renting office equipment and furniture may be necessary to get your business up and running. The expenses are tax-deductible and a business may trade up to newer and more modern equipment until it is self-sufficient enough to buy the items unconditionally.

Many people have to relocate for work and renting to own could be a viable alternative for someone who has to move to another city for a short period of time. This could save a person having to move all their appliances from one end of the country to the other, only to have to ship them all back again. It would also save a person from having to buy the items and then sell them at a loss when their stay is over. If you are going through a marriage break-up, you may want to rent appliances until you receive your share of household articles under the divorce settlement. Also, if your refrigerator broke down and you couldn't afford one right away, a short term rental might make sense to keep you from eating out until you can buy one.

> If you decide to rent to own, find out exactly at what point you own the product. Will you be penalized if you want to cancel partway through your obligation? And what are the additional charges?

Except for the above circumstances, you may be better off buying used goods from the classifieds or from a used appliance store than renting-to-own. If you can't wait until you can save up to pay cash for the item, you may be able to buy it on a layaway or an instalment plan. Even if you agree to a high interest loan, it still may be a cheaper alternative than renting-to-own.

THE HIGH COST OF DYING

Even though Sandra struggled with her illness for quite some time, her family believed she would make a full recovery. They were shocked when she died and were not prepared for her funeral. Overcome with grief, Sandra's family placed the arrangements in the hands of a funeral home and left many of the details to their discretion. The service and burial went well and the family approved the best casket, lavish flower bouquets and a beautiful service. When they received the bill for Sandra's funeral, it approached almost $15,000. It would affect their finances for years to come.

Losing a loved one is a difficult, emotional and stressful time. Often those close to the situation are unable to think clearly about finances. Many families also want their spouse, child or parent to have the best service available and do not want to be perceived as being cheap. Even the most basic funeral service can cost $5,000, $10,000 with a cemetery plot and monument. Additional products and services can cause funerals to become extremely costly. While it is best to make arrangements ahead of time, the majority of Canadians don't. At the time of a death, a relative or friend should be put in charge of the funeral arrangements. Decisions will have to be made regarding the casket; if the body will be embalmed; if it will be buried or cremated; and what type of funeral would be appropriate.

Many funeral homes are family-owned businesses that have operated for years in cities and towns across Canada. At such places, the price of a casket can account for half the cost of a funeral. Now there are funeral supply stores operating in some larger centres that sell caskets directly to the public. Don Flynn is the author of *The Truth about Funeral's — How to Beat the High Cost of Dying*. It's a self-published insider's perspective on the funeral business which Flynn says takes in billions of dollars every year in North America. "We all have consumer skills, but we tend to forget them when we shop for funerals," says Flynn. The former funeral director claims that many funeral homes operate as profit factories and that some funeral directors use high pressure sales tactics to cash in on people's grief. "Some funeral homes use a professional sales team to sell products and some caskets can be marked up by as much as 800%," he claims. "When you see a $4,000 casket sitting there, remember it may have only cost $1,000," says Flynn. The average price for a casket is in the low thousands, but most funeral homes have more expensive models for sale. A funeral home in Chicago was actually selling a solid copper casket for $42,000!

Many in the funeral business disagree with Flynn and contend that the vast majority of funeral homes are run by trained professionals who are there to help people in their time of need. While this may be true, all funeral homes should provide a price list so that consumers can shop around. Flynn says there can be thousands of dollars in difference between funeral homes in the same community, and that many funeral homes have a vested interest in elaborate traditional services as they are more profitable. According to Industry Canada, casket prices can range from $100 for a plywood casket, to several thousand dollars for metal, cloth-covered or hardwood caskets. Ask to see less expensive caskets, not usually on display. You may be able to save money by using a decorative shell during the funeral and graveside service, which is then removed before burial. Some funeral homes will also allow you to use a lavish casket for viewing and then a more modest one for burial. Depending on where you live, you may be able to purchase a casket through a casket retailer for thousands of dollars less than you would through a funeral home. Just be aware that some funeral homes don't like it when you supply your own, and may pressure you to buy one through them.

Embalming uses chemicals to temporarily preserve the body for cosmetic and sanitation reasons. In most cases, embalming is not legally required, but funeral homes will move ahead with this procedure unless you inform them otherwise. Flynn points out that even the inventor of modern-day embalming left instructions that he did not want to be embalmed. While burial has been the traditional way to deal with remains, cremation is gradually becoming more accepted. A casket is not needed if the body is to be cremated, meaning the funeral usually costs less and a cemetery plot is not required. If a casket is required for the service, it can usually be rented. Urns for cremated burial services cost an average of $300, but Flynn says there is nothing wrong with bringing your own urn which you can buy elsewhere at a fraction of the price.

When pre-arranging funerals, ensure the funeral home has a good reputation and it's likely to remain in business. Compare plans offered at different funeral homes and make sure all goods and services for the funeral are spelled out in the contract. Check if you will have to pay interest on payments and if your plan covers the increased costs of a funeral in the future due to inflation. Cemetery plots can vary widely in price. When buying one, find out what will happen if you move or change your mind. Will you be able to sell the plot? Also, make sure a guarantee is in place to ensure the plot will be there when you need it. Prepaying for your service with a funeral home can be a good idea, but Flynn suggests investing an equivalent sum of money separately. You may get a higher return and the money will remain under your control.

While most of us don't like to talk about death, planning ahead makes it easier for everyone. Consider what you have liked or disliked about funeral services you have attended. Do you want to be buried or cremated? If you wish to be buried, where would you like it to be? Do you want a religious service? Do you want organ music at your funeral? Do you want flowers or a donation to a charity dear to you? Do you wish your organs to be used for transplants or medical research? Are you partial to a lavish ceremony or will a simple one do? By giving this information to your executor, a friend, or family member will ensure that your wishes are carried out and that it will be less likely that your loved ones will be talked into expensive extras.

MAKING REBATE OFFERS WORK

Samantha was planning to buy a computer and while shopping she noticed that some brands were promising mail-in rebates on the purchase of their products. She wondered why the companies didn't just have a sale and take the money off at the cash register, rather than make her go through the hassle of sending away for her cash. Still, the rebate offers were tempting as they did substantially lower the price when factored in.

Rebate offers are widespread in the marketplace as manufacturers try to sell us appliances, tires and computer equipment. For the most part, manufacturers honour their rebate offers; however the biggest complaint is that it can take many months before you receive your cheque in the mail.

Randy Scotland with the Retail Council of Canada, says that companies use rebates as a marketing tool. "One thing that rebates do is draw attention to your product on the store shelf," he says. Scotland says unlike a sale, a rebate allows manufacturers to give customers a break without dropping their price point. "By offering a rebate, the manufacturers can reward a customer for choosing one model over the competition." Rebates also allow companies to find out demographic information about their customers when they fill out and return the rebate cards. Rebates also end up being very advantageous for companies when customers either forget or don't bother to send in for their money.

If you have to mail your rebate card to the United States, or another country, it may take longer to get your refund. When applying for your rebate cheque, make sure you fill out the information correctly and attach the proper documentation. This can affect how quickly you will get your refund. If all goes well, most rebates should be processed in eight to 12 weeks. Read any rebate offer carefully, as some have fine print that stipulates the product must be purchased within a certain time period. Some offers may also require that the rebate be mailed by a specified postmark date.

> When applying for a rebate, make sure you fill out the form correctly and attach the proper documentation. Watch for time limitations and postmark requirements and keep copies of everything.

Make photocopies of important documents so that you will have copies for your own reference if there is a problem and the rebate doesn't arrive. If the allotted time passes and you still have not received your rebate, refer to the original copy which may have a phone number or a Web site where you can inquire about your refund. Also, keep in mind that the rebate offer is between the customer and the manufacturer, not the store where you bought the product. So if you do have a problem with a rebate, don't expect much help from the retailer.

There are cases of people not receiving their rebates due to bankruptcies or companies just failing to honour them. When buying any product with a rebate offer, be sure to view the product on its merits and not just because of the money back offer. Beware of conditional rebates such as those that include cash back on a computer *only* if you commit to a long term contract for Internet service. Technology is changing fast and you may find yourself tied to an agreement with a service provider that is slower or more expensive than what the competition is offering.

SAVE MONEY ON PRINTER REFILLS

Helen had purchased a computer and wanted to buy a printer as well. When she went shopping, she noticed that prices varied widely, but there were printers that did a good job for less than $100. She bought one for only $89 that came with a $40 rebate. A printer for only $49! Helen thought it was a great deal — until she had to buy an ink cartridge that cost $55 — more than the printer was worth.

There is an open secret in the bargain printer business. Some companies make more money selling ink than they do selling printers! Inexpensive printers may seem like a great deal on the store shelf, but when you get them home they can have hidden costs. Bargain printers are also more expensive to operate because they are not as efficient. For example, when printing in colour some $80 printers may cost as much as 50¢ per page to print. A $250 dual cartridge printer may be able to print the same page for 10¢ and produce sharper and higher quality images. Another drawback is that while the fastest ink jet printers can print more than six pages of text a minute, inexpensive printers take a lot longer.

Consumers often don't think about the price of ink until their printer runs dry and they have to replace the cartridge. That's when they find out that their $80 printer requires a $50 cartridge. Due to the high price of replacement cartridges offered by printer manufacturers, other companies have entered the market to provide a cheaper alternative that not all consumers know about. Kor-Rec-Type, one of the companies that manufactures "ink refill kits," claims that they can save consumers a bundle. Ko-Rec-Type's Howard Gutterman says, "for the most part, the kits are simple to use. Obviously there is a little patience required, but refilling old cartridges will save consumers hundreds of dollars over time." When a printer cartridge runs out of ink, there is basically nothing wrong with it. The kits come with syringes that allow you to squirt new ink into the empty cartridge. With colour cartridges, there are three inks and three compartments to fill. Just follow the instructions. "Basically you inject ink into the cartridge, it migrates into the sponge and within minutes you can put the cartridge back in your printer and print away," explains Gutterman. Most cartridges can be refilled five times or more before a new one is required.

The kits sell for between $25 and $50 and will refill a printer cartridge three to five times. You may get your fingers dirty while filling them up, but do the math. Buying five cartridges at $50 each is $250. Buying one kit with five refills is $50. Refill kits are available at most computer stores in almost every format. Depending on your printer, some kits work better than others. Printer manufacturers also claim that the kits can be messy, leak inside your printer and contain poorer quality ink. Some companies may even void your warranty if you use the refills! I personally have used the refills for years and found them to be of good value. If you don't want to mess with ink, you can also buy "compatible cartridges" which will fit your printer but cost a lot less. Be aware that most printers have settings that will allow you to use less ink depending on the job at hand. While you may want the darkest quality print job for a special report, you may wish to use less ink for other documents.

When buying a printer, find out how much the replacement printer cartridges will be so when the ink runs dry you won't have any expensive surprises. Also, check if refill kits and compatibles are available for the printer you're considering. Check if the printer comes with one or two cartridges. Inexpensive printers only come with a colour ink cartridge, so if you want a black cartridge for printing letters, you will have to pay extra for it. Colour cartridges used to print in black may give you a more purplish black, than a true black.

You may get your fingers dirty while refilling a printer cartridge, but do the math. Five cartridges at $50 each is $250. One kit with five refills is only $500.

It may be worthwhile paying a little more for a higher quality printer. If it comes with both a colour and a black ink cartridge, you will save money on ink and it will be cheaper to operate in the long run. Of course, if you use your printer only occasionally, an inexpensive printer may be feasible. However, if you own a small business or think you will be using a printer often, it may make sense to pay more upfront to save money on printer ink in the future.

PILL SPLITTING

Irene was on a fixed income and required medications for various ailments. While a drug plan used to cover some of the drugs she needed, now she paid for most of them out of her own pocket. Some of the pills were extremely expensive but there was no way she could do without them. Still, she wished there was some way to cut down on her monthly medicine bill.

There is no doubt that medications can be expensive. This may be less of a concern if you have an insurance plan through your employer that can help cover the costs of your drugs. If you don't have a plan, you may be looking for ways to reduce your medication costs. Pill splitting is a way to cut your pills and some of your medication bills. Before continuing to tell you about this technique I must strongly advise that this should never be done without *first discussing it with your doctor and pharmacist*. Pill splitting is not something that will work with every medication. However, if you are on a fixed income and it could work with even one of your medications, it could save you a substantial amount of money.

When you buy a drug it is often priced the same, or close to the same price, regardless of the dosage. For example, a single pill of the male sex enhancement drug Viagra is priced at around $13 whether it is 25, 50 or 100 milligrams. If a doctor felt that a patient could benefit from taking 50 milligrams of the drug Viagra, a money saving option would be to ask the doctor to prescribe 100 milligram tablets of the drug, which you could then split in half for the optimum dosage. Janet Cooper is a pharmacist and director of practice development with the Canadian Pharmacists Association. "The practice of pill splitting can be a practical way for consumers to cut down their medication costs," she says. "There are many drugs that can be split in half to save patients money and still have the desired positive health effects."

Antidepressants, heart medications and other popular drugs can be candidates for pill splitting. Another example is the high blood pressure medication Prinivil. One 20-milligram tablet of Prinivil costs about $1.07. It's about 89¢ for the 10 milligram dose, 74¢ for 5 milligrams, and 62¢ for the 2 milligram pill. Depending on your prescription you could ask your doctor to double the dosage, split the pills and save substantially. Some drug makers accommodate pill splitting by scoring tablets in the middle, so that they are easier to break in half. Cooper says "Some pills actually have to be split because the drug manufacturer may not make the dose that the doctor is prescribing."

It is extremely important to note that *not all drugs can be split*. Some pills are formulated to release medication over a period of time, so splitting the pill could cause a patient to accidentally get the whole dose at once, or not at all. Drugs with a protective coating are also not candidates as such coatings are meant to prevent the pill from dissolving in your stomach. "You can't split a pill that is enteric coated which means it is designed to be released in the intestines. Long acting or slow release medications should also never be split," Cooper says. If you split pills, you should use a pill splitter which can be purchased at most pharmacies for less than $10 or so. Pill splitters are not 100% accurate, so if your medication requires an extremely precise dose, pill splitting is not recommended either. "It really depends on the medication. Some tablets are very brittle and may shatter when you try to split them. If you cannot accurately split pills, then it's not recommended," explains Cooper.

Another way to try and save money on drugs, especially if you take the same medication over a long period of time, is to buy more at one time to reduce dispensing fees. When you go to a pharmacy, in most cases you will be charged a dispensing fee which is a commission the pharmacist gets for selling you the medicine. If you can, have your doctor prescribe your medication for a longer period to avoid constantly paying dispensing fees to get your pills. Some drug stores also give senior citizens a break by not imposing dispensing fees. Finding such a drug store can mean significant long term savings for seniors.

Different dosages of the same pill are often similarly priced. With many drugs, you can ask your doctor to prescribe double dosage tablets, of which you could just take half.

Some doctors are against pill splitting because some patients may forget to split the pill or split it incorrectly. Pill splitting could lead to mistakes if a patient is elderly, has poor eyesight or impaired dexterity. If you are having difficulty paying for your drugs, don't be shy telling your doctor or pharmacist about it. They may have other suggestions that could help save you money such as switching from name brand drugs to less expensive generic drugs. While pill splitting can save money, your health must come first. If you consider pill splitting, keep in mind you should never attempt to split pills unless you consult your doctor and pharmacist.

WATER IS LIFE

Despite assurances from city officials that his water was completely safe, Jacob was interested in getting a water filtration system for his home. He considered buying bottled water but found it expensive and cumbersome to constantly be transporting. One water treatment specialist told him for peace of mind he should install a system worth thousands of dollars. One day while shopping, he noticed water pitchers with charcoal filters that promised to remove contaminants and improve taste, selling for about $20. The different claims and wide price range left him perplexed.

Currently in Canada, almost half of all homes have some kind of water filtration system even if it's as basic as a water pitcher with a filter in it. With recent concerns about water quality, many people are interested in upgrading to systems that claim to remove even more potentially harmful contaminants. In June 2000, in Walkerton, Ontario, seven people died and another 2,000 people became seriously ill after drinking water contaminated with *e-coli* bacteria. It was one of the worst tragedies in North America in recent memory that was caused by unsafe drinking water.

Bottled water is safe in Canada, according to the Canadian Bottled Water Association, a group that oversees water bottling companies. The Association says there has never been a case of anyone becoming ill from drinking bottled water. Water from groundwater springs is tested and disinfected before bottling to ensure that it is safe for consumption. Bottlers in the United States have been caught selling bottled tap water labelled "spring water." In fact, there are now brands of water on the market that are labelled purified drinking water. You should know that this is just tap water that has been treated again by the bottling company. The vast majority of water sold in Canada is spring water.

Bottled water falls under the *Food and Drug Act* and every bottle must have the water source printed on the label. The bottled water industry is enjoying tremendous growth in Canada, as well as profits, so there is no need for bottlers here to cut corners on safety. Still, buying bottled water can be costly over time which is why consumers are looking for alternatives.

When buying a water filtration system for your home, take several things into consideration, the first being where you live. Health officials across this country assure us that whether we are on a municipal water system in Halifax, Toronto or Vancouver, safe water is flowing from our taps. Safeguards are in place to ensure that water is treated and monitored daily. People who live in rural areas and rely on private water sources such as wells or water from lakes have different parameters to consider. Water filters can improve taste and remove contaminants but they *cannot* treat microbiologically unsafe water — such as water with *e-coli* bacteria.

On safe, municipal water systems, people use water filters to make their "safe water, safer." The most common in refrigerators across this country is the water filter pitcher. A water filter pitcher with a charcoal filter does a good basic job of filtering tap water at a cost of around $20. Independent studies have shown that these pitchers can make water clearer, taste better and remove any foul odours. They can eradicate the chlorine taste and contaminants such as lead and copper.

The pitcher's filter needs to be replaced every two months or so. The pitchers can be cumbersome, take up room in the fridge and be a hassle to constantly fill-up. Some consumers like to use filtered water for juices and cooking. That's when you may want to upgrade to a filter that goes right on your faucet or under the sink; there are different brands starting at around

$50. These filters will usually do everything the pitcher filters will do. Some filters also claim they will remove additional contaminants and parasites such as *cryptosporidium* and *giardia*. Faucet systems also have a filter that needs to be replaced.

If you want the benefits of a faucet filter but do not want to have a filter attached to your tap, you can have an under the counter faucet filter installed. They start at around $100 and offer the same type of filter protection, but they come with their own faucet and can be hidden under the counter.

More expensive filter systems promise better protection against a wider range of contaminants. They claim to offer bottled water quality at a fraction of the price. One system, considered by many in the industry to offer superior protection, is called the Reverse Osmosis water filtration system. It promises to remove 99% of the contaminants, as well as 25 harmful elements including things like cadmium, magnesium and barium. They sell for $400 and up. These systems are larger and take up more space. You may also require professional help to install them. While all of the above filter systems do a favourable job of filtering and improving the taste of your water, *they will not* protect you from microbiologically unsafe water, such as water contaminated with *e-coli* bacteria.

Across Canada, millions of people rely on groundwater as their main source of domestic water. This includes people living in the country on private wells, because they are out of reach of municipal water systems and cottagers who rely on lake water or groundwater sources. Following the Walkerton *e-coli* scare, where chlorine pumps failed on the town's water system, there have also been other cases of *e-coli* contamination. *E-coli* is found in animal manure, an agribusiness by-product of meat production, which is used as fertilizer on crop farms. There is growing concern as some farmers move to super farms or factory farms. Some of these farms include barns that are a kilometre long, housing 5,000 cattle. One barn can produce the same amount of waste as several small towns. If the waste is not spread over a wide enough area, health officials say that groundwater can end up contaminated with *e-coli* bacteria.

Water treatment facilities use chlorine or ozone to disinfect water to make it safe. These are not practical methods for the residential home owner. One product that has tripled in sales since the Walkerton tragedy is a water system that *can* kill *e-coli* bacteria and can be installed in your home. It uses ultraviolet light to kill the deadly bacteria. One business that makes this product is Trojan Technologies of London, Ontario. Diana Cunningham with Trojan says, "ultraviolet light alters the DNA make-up of *e-coli* bacteria. It can no longer reproduce and then dies." While UV light is a proven way to treat microbiologically unsafe water, Cunningham cautions that you will still need to buy a water filter system to pre-filter water before it is treated with the ultraviolet light. This is so the bacterium does not hide behind other particles in the water. This UV system will cost $300 to $1,000 depending on size. You will also need to pay a professional to install a filtration system.

Often you can have your water tested for free by contacting your municipality or health department. If you are on a municipal water source, you may want to consider the filtration systems that are designed to make "safe water, safer." If you have a private well or a cottage, then you may want to consider the added UV protection to safeguard your water supply against problems that cannot be filtered out. You can get more information from water treatment specialists who can be found in the yellow pages.

At the time of the printing of this book, thousands of residents of North Battleford, Saskatchewan, have become ill due to the town's water supply. The municipal water system has been infected with cryptosporidium, a parasite that causes diarrhea, cramps and fever. It is potentially deadly for anyone with a weakened immune system. Many home water filtration systems are able to filter out cryptosporidium to make drinking water safe.

WHAT'S AN APPROPRIATE TIP?

Alex always felt awkward when it came time to tip the server when dining out. He wanted to leave an amount that showed he was appreciative, but at the same time he didn't want to pay too much. After all, he was already paying for the meal and he knew that the waiter was being paid by the restaurant. He didn't want to appear cheap, yet he was trying to keep an eye on his budget.

Tip — To Insure Promptness. Many waiters, door staff and valet parking staff earn only minimum wage and depend on tips to increase their salary to a liveable level. Different cultures have varying opinions on tipping and many consumers are confused about leaving the appropriate amount. Some argue that tipping is just a way for employers to pay their staff poorly so the paying public will have to subsidize their salaries. Others suggest that it is a way for hardworking staff in the service industry to be appreciated and rewarded by customers. Tipping is meant as a thank you, but if it's done before any service, it can also be used as a subtle bribe for special treatment. I have a friend who always tips the room service staff at the beginning of his vacation, in an effort to make his stay more comfortable.

In the early 1900s in the United States, there was actually an Anti-Tipping Society of America established by travelling salespeople who managed to have tipping abolished in seven states. However, tipping is a part of today's culture and an expected cost of dining out. Shannon Smith is the President of Premiere Image and an expert in manners and dining etiquette. She says, "tipping is a big dilemma for people. They don't know how to tip or how to pay a bill graciously in a restaurant." Smith says that in a casual restaurant, before taxes, you should tip 15% of the bill. For upscale dining, the appropriate tip moves up a notch to 20%. These amounts are for excellent service, and Smith says as service declines, so should your tip. If you get bad service in a restaurant, Smith believes "it should be brought to the attention of the manager or supervisor and you should leave no tip."

Servers don't keep all the money they collect. Policies differ, but in a casual restaurant they often apportion 1% of their final sales to the kitchen, 1% to the bartender and 1% to the serving assistants. In upscale restaurants 75% of the tip goes to the waiter and 25% to the maitre d' and bus persons.

Smith says that it is rude not to tip, but it may be appropriate if you get bad service. "There is nothing that aggravates me more when I'm trying to order and the waiter is walking away with the order book in his hand," she says. Only give a tip if you feel the person deserves as bad service shouldn't be rewarded. Many waiters are insulted if you don't tip. While a thank you may be appreciated, it is the tips that make up the bulk of their salary.

If you are on a trip and have to tip various service staff, it's a good idea to have change or small bills at the ready. Keep in mind that tipping practices vary in different countries. While 15 to 20% is an expected tip in Canada and the United States, in countries including Italy, Mexico and Malaysia, a tip of 10% is considered generous. In some countries, the tips are included in the service charges or menu prices so there is no need to go beyond this. Check with your travel agent beforehand, or simply ask the server or check the menu to see if tipping is included. Even if tipping is included in the prices, sometimes a small tip could be left to show your appreciation when service is superior. Tipping should also make the giver feel good because while tipping is expected, it's also considered a gift that should be appreciated.

74

EFFECTIVE COMPLAINING

Larry bought a barbecue at a major department store. It worked well for a while but then it started heating unevenly and failing to light. Since it wasn't working properly, he took the barbecue back to the store. He was told that 30 days had passed and that he was out of luck. They refused to take the barbecue back and had no parts to repair it. Larry got extremely upset, blew up at the clerk and stormed off with his defective barbecue.

To get what you want in life, it's extremely important to be an effective complainer. Most people will take the time to listen to a reasonable, level-headed person explain his or her side of an issue or argument. No one likes a whiner or a bully! Who wants to listen to someone shouting in their face? The answer is no one! You will almost always be treated better when you address others in a respectful, even tone with a well thought-out argument.

A good habit to get into whenever you buy something, is to ask what the store's return policy is. The Retail Council of Canada says there is no return policy legislation in Canada and that businesses set their own criteria for what they take back and why. The Council says when consumers buy products in good faith, they own them, and that stores are really doing consumers a favour when they allow returns.

It is the consumer's responsibility to understand a store's return policy and to keep receipts and warranties in case they are ever needed. The return policy is usually posted in the store or on the receipt. Is there a time limit on returns? Does the package have to be sealed? Are there restocking charges? Is it money back or store credit? Does the product have to be in its original packaging? Be aware that some products such as cosmetics, medicines and personal care items such as undergarments cannot be returned for health and safety reasons. Some stores may take back goods without receipts to try to secure long term business, but others stand firm. One woman complained that after she bought a $3,000 computer, she took a two-week holiday and then decided she didn't want it. Even though she had the receipt and the computer was still in the box, the store stood by its one-week return policy and refused to take it back. Also, be aware that demonstration models or used items may be sold as is, and may not come with the same warranties that a new product would.

You should not be afraid to complain if you are unsatisfied with a product or a service, as a good business will want to correct any problems to keep customers coming back. If you do have a problem seek a remedy immediately; hesitating will only create problems. Give the returns department the first chance to solve your problem and if that doesn't work, ask to see the manager. In a polite but firm tone, tell him or her your complaint and ask what will be done to correct it. Write down the details of your conversation, including dates.

If speaking with someone at the business does not garner results, ask for addresses and phone numbers so you can write or phone the general manager, owner or public relations division of the company. Detail your problem in reasonable length using even-tempered language. Depending on your complaint, you may wish to include that you will also inform the media of your situation. This should be used only as a last resort, as it can inflame the matter.

If you have contacted company brass about your complaint and you still receive no satisfaction, you may wish to contact your provincial consumer ministry, Better Business Bureau and other consumer groups. Going to court should be used only as a last resort as it can be time consuming and expensive. Use the following sample complaint letter from Industry Canada's *Canadian Consumer Handbook* as a guide for your complaint.

(Your Address)
(Your City, Province, Postal Code)

(Date)

(Name of Contact Person, if available)
(Title, if available)
(Company Name)
(Consumer Complaint Division, if you have no contact person)
(Street Address)
(City, Province)
(Postal Code)

Dear *(Contact Person)*

Re: *(account number, if applicable)*

On *(date)*, I *(bought, leased, rented or had repaired)* a *(name of the product with serial or model number or service repaired)* at *(location)*.

Unfortunately, your product *(or service)* has not performed well *(or the service was inadequate)*. I am disappointed because *(explain the problem: for example the product does not work properly, the service was not performed correctly, I was billed the wrong amount, something was not disclosed clearly or was misrepresented at the time of the sale, etc.)*.

To resolve the problem, I would appreciate your *(state the specific action you want — money back, charge card credit, repair, exchange, etc.)*. Enclosed are copies *(do not send originals)* of my records *(include receipts, guarantees, warranties, cancelled cheques, contracts, model and serial numbers, and any other documents)*.

I look forward to your reply and resolution of my problem, and will wait until *(set a time limit — usually 10 working days are sufficient)* before seeking help from a consumer protection agency or Better Business Bureau. Please contact me at the above address or by telephone at *(home and/or office number with area codes)*.

Sincerely,

(your name)

Enclosure(s) *(copies of your records)*

cc: *(indicate to whom you are sending a copy of this letter, e.g. product manufacturer)*

TRAVEL TIPS

Bernice was travelling in a foreign country and was having a great trip until her hotel room was broken into. Thieves stole everything she had, including her cash, credit cards, identification and passport. Bernice was overwhelmed by her situation and didn't know what to do. She could barely speak the language in the country she was visiting and was now broke, afraid and unsure of where to go for help.

Canadians are now exploring the world in greater numbers than ever before, whether it's to suntan on a sandy beach, trek up a mountain trail or trace their family tree. Each year, Canadians make more then 100,000 trips abroad and while most vacations are trouble-free, some end in illnesses, accidents or legal problems. You can solve most minor problems yourself, but if you run into serious trouble or need assistance, Canadian help is available in most regions of the world. Canada's Consular Service of the Department of Foreign Affairs and International Trade has put together an information guide, *Bon Voyage,* for the Canadian traveller. This brochure contains excellent information to help you before or during a trip.

Preparation is important when planning a successful trip. Learn as much as you can about your destination, its weather, currency, crime rate, health care system and any possible problem areas. Know generally the political, cultural and economic situation of your destination and make an effort to learn at least a few key phrases in the country's main language. Even know-ing a few phrases such as "hello" and "thank-you" will go a long way and show respect to the people you are visiting. Be aware that when you are travelling, the laws of the country you are visiting apply to you too.

Your passport should be a treasured document and is proof of your Canadian citizenship. If your passport is due to expire within six months of your arrival in another country, check to make sure it will be accepted. Some countries will not let you enter if a passport is about to expire. Also, be sure to complete the "in case of accident or death" portion of the passport, so your relatives or friends can be contacted quickly if an emergency arises. Before going on a trip, make two copies of your passport's identification page. Leave one at home in case you lose your passport, as this may help speed up the replacement process.

You need a visa to travel to certain countries and your travel agent should be able to advise you if one is necessary. You may also have to prove that you have enough money to support your-self during your stay and that you have a return ticket. If you are considered a national, you may be required to pay taxes or do military service. That would be quite a shock on a vacation! If you have special needs such as a wheelchair, be aware that not all countries have services for the disabled, hearing- or sight-impaired. There are excellent travel guidebooks for people who may require special considerations.

Travelling can be strenuous and you will want to ensure that you are in good physical condition before taking a trip. A check-up with your doctor may be in order. You also may require vaccinations depending on your destination. Check well in advance of your trip if vaccinations are required, as some must be taken six to eight weeks before you leave. Some countries also require proof of a negative AIDS test. If this is the case, have the tests done and obtain the results before you travel. When travelling, take the same precautions as you would at home, and don't assume that condoms will be readily available. Even if they are, they may not meet Canadian standards.

If you take medication, pack extra in case you are away longer than planned. Carry a duplicate of your original prescription when travelling to a country that is especially sensitive about drugs. An extra prescription that lists the generic and trade names of your medication may come in handy if your medication is lost or stolen. This is also a good idea if you wear glasses or contact lenses, as having the prescription will make it easier to replace them if they are lost or stolen.

Make sure that you have extra photocopies of your passport's identification page, any prescriptions, and proof of any necessary vaccinations or test.

You may also want to find out if your medication is sold in the country that you are visiting. If you require syringes for a condition such as diabetes, have an adequate supply and carry a health certificate that indicates they are for medical use. If you have a pre-existing condition, you may wish to wear a MedicAlert bracelet. Through the MedicAlert Foundation, your medical information becomes part of a database that can be accessed 24 hours a day, from anywhere in the world. For more information on MedicAlert visit their Web site at www.medicalert.ca.

If you are pregnant, check with your doctor before travelling and realize that some vaccinations may not be recommended. Carry an antidiarrheal agent because such pills may not be available in the country you are visiting and they could come in handy. Canadian currency and traveller's cheques in Canadian dollars are not widely accepted, so before taking a trip find out the most appropriate currency to carry and if your bank and credit cards will be accepted.

Women travelling alone should take extra safety precautions. If you are travelling with a child, it may be necessary in some families to review custody arrangements. If the child is travelling alone, the child should have documentation stating that the trip is permitted by both parents. Pets are not allowed in all countries and may require shots, or to remain quarantined for a period of time. There are also certain restrictions on plants and foods that may be brought in or out. Never take any parcel that is not yours across a border, or cross a border with a traveller you don't know well, such as a hitchhiker. Drug trafficking crimes are taken very seriously and ignorance of the law is no excuse. There are currently more than 2,300 Canadians imprisoned outside Canada for various offences (68% of them are in the United States). If you do find yourself in trouble, contact the nearest Canadian consulate immediately or have someone else do it for you.

Many people are now using the Internet to book holidays but if you book trips on-line, and find the hotel in a state of disrepair or even closed, you may not be able to have your money refunded. You might get your money back if you booked through a registered travel agent. Also, check many different web sites and speak to a travel agent before booking online as some studies have shown that there can be huge differences in pricing, even on the same flight! Ensure you have proper health insurance coverage while on your trip (see Alert 78 on travel insurance).

The Canadian government provides "Consular Services" abroad to help Canadians deal with travel problems. The service operates 24 hours a day, seven days a week. There is a network of 271 service points around the world for Canada's consular services including embassies, high commissions and consulates. In some jurisdictions, Canada may share services with other countries.

For general information on consular services before a trip, contact the Department of Foreign Affairs and International Trade Canada at 1-800-267-6788. If you have trouble during a trip, contact a foreign affairs office. Canadian officials abroad can contact relatives or friends on your behalf, help during emergencies such as natural disasters or civil uprisings, assist in medical emergencies, replace passports or take citizenship applications and direct you to information about the country you are in. If you are arrested, Canadian officials can ensure unbiased treatment under local laws and inform relatives of your situation but they cannot apply pressure to drop charges. They are also able to notify next of kin regarding accidents or deaths and help locate missing persons.

Travel reports providing details on safety and security conditions, health issues and entry and visa requirements for more than 215 travel destinations can also be accessed by calling the

Department of Foreign Affairs at 1-800-267-6788 or by fax at 1-800-575-2500. When travelling abroad, you can use Canada Direct, an automated long-distance access service that allows you to call home to Canada or to other countries using the Canadian telecommunications network. Simply dial the access number for the country you are in and follow the voice prompts. For a list of Canada Direct access numbers, call 1-800-561-8868.

If you have any questions about passports, you can call 1-800-567-6868 or check the Passport Office Web site at www.ppt.gc.ca.

You can obtain free copies of *Bon Voyage* by calling 1-800-267-8376 or by writing to Enquiries Service, Department of Foreign Affairs and International Trade, 125 Sussex Drive, Ottawa, Ontario, K1A 0G2, or by checking their Web site at www.dfait-maeci.gc.ca.

QUIT SMOKING — Your Doctor Can Help

John had smoked cigarettes for 20 years and had made up his mind to quit once and for all. He had tried quitting in the past without much success. After a short time away from cigarettes, he usually found himself craving a smoke. One cigarette led to another and before long, he was back in his regular smoking routine. He wondered if there was a way to quit for good.

There is no doubt that quitting smoking is extremely difficult. I know. I had to do it myself. Decades ago, smoking was considered glamorous and society was unaware of the terrible toll smoking can take on our health. Now, everyone is aware of the dangers of tobacco. The federal government has increased the warnings on cigarette packaging to include more graphic warnings and photos. Even though smoking is harmful to our health, smells terrible and is a daily expense, millions of Canadians can't or don't want to kick the habit. Some people are aware of the problems associated with smoking and don't care — they love to smoke. However, if you are looking to get off the smoking treadmill, there are some drugs and techniques that could help.

Of course if you never start smoking, you will never have to quit. I smoked for about 10 years and I know the craving for nicotine and the sweet smell of smoke wafting across a room can be intoxicating for the ex-smoker. I admit I still occasionally dream about having one. It's been said that quitting smoking is equivalent to heroin withdrawal. While most of us would not be able to make that comparison, it is widely recognized in the health community that even smokers who genuinely and desperately want to quit may find it almost impossible to do so.

Most health officials agree that someone can only quit smoking if that person truly wishes to do so, a process that may take years. If a smoker believes that she can quit just by using a nicotine patch or gum, without a determination to stop smoking, she is wasting her time. Questionable businesses are also eager to take money from smokers desperate to quit. Some claim they can use hypnotism, acupuncture or lasers to help smokers quit. In one case, a huckster was selling what he claimed were nicotine patches, when it fact they were really just stickers!

When a smoker has finally decided that he is serious about quitting smoking, he may try to tackle the addiction himself, by weaning off cigarettes or by quitting cold turkey. This method is effective for some, but many people quit several times before becoming a smoke-free citizen. Many smokers need help and rather than seek it through the want ads, they should get it first and foremost in their doctors' offices. There are many different medications that can aid a smoker kicking the habit. A smoker does not want to replace one habit with another, but gum, patches and prescription medication may be just enough to help a smoker triumph over tobacco.

One drug now being used to help smokers quit is the prescription medication "Zyban." You must discuss this drug with your doctor but I personally know of three long-time smokers who have used it with success. Zyban, which is also known by the generic name "Bupropion," is an antidepressant. The drug is intended for the heavy smoker who has tried and failed other means to quit smoking. There is medical evidence that Zyban alleviates some of the withdrawal symptoms and that quitting rates doubled as compared to placebo pills. It is available by prescription through your doctor.

There are side effects to Zyban and not everyone is a candidate for this drug. The most common side effects are insomnia and dry mouth, but there have been cases of seizures and eating disorders. Treatment with Zyban begins one week prior to quitting smoking and lasts for seven to 12 weeks. By taking it before actually quitting, the smoker has primed his body for nicotine withdrawal. The smoker may or may not notice that her will to quit has increased as a result of being on the medication. This drug may be a good alternative for people who have tried nicotine patches or gums without success.

Many smokers need help and rather than seek it through the want ads, they should seek it in their doctors' offices.

While smokers must change their routines while quitting smoking, one of the most difficult challenges is nicotine withdrawal. That is why there is a wide range of products on the market designed to replace the nicotine from cigarettes in a precise way. The idea is to slowly taper the smoker off cigarettes while at the same time allowing some nicotine into the body through a carefully controlled source. One of the most popular is the nicotine patch. It is a self-adhesive that looks like a bandage, however, it contains nicotine that is slowly released into the body. Unlike cigarette smoke which immediately goes into the bloodstream for a nicotine "hit," the patch allows the user to have a constant level of nicotine in their system.

You should never smoke while on the patch, as this could double your nicotine intake and be dangerous. You may also notice a skin rash under the patch and have trouble sleeping. Twenty-four hour patches allow nicotine to enter the body when the smoker is asleep (you usually don't smoke when you're asleep!), causing bizarre, colourful dreams. Sixteen-hour patches solve this problem but can leave users waking up with a craving for a smoke.

Nicotine chewing gum is also widely used to help with cravings. The gum slowly releases nicotine as it is chewed or kept in the mouth pressed between the teeth and cheek. Many people who use the gum fail to follow directions and may chew the gum too little or stop using it too early. Some health insurance plans may cover the cost of all these products — but often only once! So don't try them until you've worked up the gumption to quit.

There are other nicotine replacement products such as the nicotine inhaler, nicknamed the puffer. Similar to units that are used in the treatment of asthma, the puffer contains nicotine that can be inhaled into the mouth. There is also a nicotine nasal spray whereby the user gets nicotine by inhaling spray through the nostrils. The downside is that the spray can cause nose and throat irritation. When quitting smoking, your body will go through changes as it heals itself and gets used to being nicotine-free. Using a nicotine replacement will also help ex-smokers through "trigger times" such as talking on the phone, having a drink or driving.

Someone once told me that the most difficult periods when quitting smoking are the third day, third week and third month. Although is seems improbable, I noticed too that this is when cravings for a cigarette seemed strongest and getting over the third month is a successful milestone. If you can get this far, don't smoke again! Not even one! Quitting will be one of the best things you have ever done. You will save money, live longer, food will taste better, you'll be more productive (you won't need those eight-minute smoke breaks) and you will set a good example for your children and loved ones. Good luck!

BEYOND THE BARE NECESSITIES

PLASTIC SURGERY

Eva was never quite happy with the shape of her nose and how it made her look. She decided she would consult a doctor about having cosmetic surgery. The procedure, known as rhinoplasty, is commonly referred to as a nose job. The surgeon she consulted said her nose would look excellent after the procedure and Eva was pleased that for about $2,000 she would have the face of her dreams. But following the surgery, she was not happy with the outcome. In fact, she was convinced her nose looked worse then before. When she consulted the doctor, he told her it was fine. She felt cheated and ashamed. She later had to have surgery done to correct the doctor's work and it cost her more than $8,000.

Cosmetic surgery can conceal the signs of ageing or change facial features to give someone a more attractive appearance. It is not limited to women as more men are now having cosmetic surgeries performed. While many people who have had plastic surgery are delighted with the way it has changed their looks and in some cases their lives, not everyone is pleased with the outcome. Rhinoplasty is one of the most difficult of plastic surgeries to perform and there are many surgeons who lack the experience to get it right. There are many cases of patients having two, three or even seven nose jobs before they are satisfied with their appearance. Cosmetic surgery is not a perfect science and it takes years of practice to master it.

In fact, there are now surgeons who specialize in fixing other doctors' mistakes. Dr. Krzysztof Conrad, one of Canada's leading plastic surgeons, teaches facial surgery at the University of Toronto. He admits, "there are a number of patients who are dissatisfied with the appearance of their nose after surgery." Conrad says that as much as 40% of his practice is fixing nose jobs performed by other doctors. He says some surgeons are performing rhinoplasty without having the experience to produce a predictable outcome. As well as knowledge of the body, a skilled surgeon must also have artistic ability. "Nasal surgery being so complex, you must have knowledge of the inner structure of the nose and be able to sculpt the nose to have a natural unoperated look. It is a difficult operation," explains Conrad.

While a nose job is a common cosmetic surgery, plastic surgery can be performed on all parts of the body, including the buttocks, thighs, breasts, face, neck, ears and hands. If you are considering plastic surgery of any kind, consult at least two or more doctors. Find out their qualifications, see photos of their work and ask to speak with their past patients. If doctors do not want you to meet patients they have operated on, this may be a warning sign. Conrad says different surgeons will also end up with different results. As beauty is in the eye of the beholder, what one doctor may consider appealing another one won't. Prices can fluctuate between $2,000 and $10,000 for rhinoplasty. Be leery if the price is too low. "Generally speaking if the surgeon is charging very little that means the surgeon is in the stage of learning and needs experience," advises Conrad.

If Eva could turn back time, she may not have had plastic surgery in the first place. She had to pay $2,000 for the original surgery, then another $8,000 for the corrective surgery. There were also pain and stress she had not anticipated. Plastic surgeons do have malpractice insurance, but a patient may only have a case in a situation where a doctor has made a glaring error in the procedure, that would be obvious to a judge and jury.

There is also growing concern that some people are having plastic surgery done for the wrong reasons. In some cases, patients have become obsessed with their body image. There have been incidents of people getting countless plastic surgeries. For example, one patient, who got a nose job, several eyelid surgeries, a tummy tuck, liposuction and a breast lift, had an obsession with body image that was due to underlying psychological problems. A doctor should only ever perform surgeries that are necessary and that will benefit the patient's health and well being. Be sure you want cosmetic surgery for the right reasons. There is evidence that a well-done nose job or other plastic surgery can dramatically improve a person's self-esteem. Some patients elect to have plastic surgery after being disfigured in a car accident or by disease. Plastic surgery can be very beneficial and life-changing. If removing an unsightly birthmark or straightening a crooked nose can improve someone's confidence, it can be argued that plastic surgery can have an extremely positive affect on a patient's life. Still, in all cases you must carefully select a surgeon who can get the operation done correctly the first time.

There is no easy way to find the perfect doctor for you. The Canadian Academy of Facial Plastic and Reconstructive Surgery, an organization of specialist plastic surgeons, can provide you with some information on plastic surgeons in your area. You can check out their Web site at www.facialcosmeticsurgery.org. Remember also that different doctors have different specialities. As in other areas of medicine where doctors concentrate on feet or eyes, the same is true of cosmetic surgery. Some doctors may be good at breast implant surgery but are not experts at doing facelifts. Make sure that the doctor can prove to you that he or she is a specialist who can be trusted. Don't try to find a surgeon who is a bargain! A surgeon charging a lot of money is no guarantee of a satisfactory result, but it may mean that the doctor has the experience to perform the surgery to your expectations.

TRAVEL INSURANCE

Edgar and his wife, Melissa, planned a three-week vacation to Florida. When they arrived, all was going well until Edgar became ill. He needed an emergency operation and required a one-week hospital stay. The couple didn't have out of country health insurance and the medical bills quickly added up to $90,000. The hospital demanded the money and the couple had to sell their home to settle the account. The costly error would affect their finances for the rest of their lives.

More and more Canadians are taking extended stays in warmer climates during winter months or are setting out to exotic places around the globe. Young or old, it is an absolute *necessity* to have proper medical insurance coverage when travelling outside Canada. Whether it's a trip to deepest, darkest Africa or a weekend car trip to the United States one *must* have adequate health coverage. While we live in a country with excellent government-funded health care facilities, this is not the case in many parts of the world. Being properly insured is especially crucial for snowbirds who make annual treks south. Currently the top snowbird destinations, in order are Florida, Arizona, Texas, Southern California and Mexico.

Douglas Gray is the author of the best-selling book *The Canadian Snowbird Guide*. He says many snowbirds fail to purchase proper insurance while travelling, a costly mistake. Gray advises, "you need to have out of country medical insurance whether you are across the border for a day, a week or a month." Private health care facilities in the United States can be extremely expensive and hospitalization costs astronomical. For example, it can be as much as $15,000 a day for intensive care in a hospital. The cost of a triple bypass operation can easily top a quarter of a million dollars. Even treatment for a broken arm can be $25,000.

Provincial plans in Canada may pay a very small portion of a U.S. medical bill, but the vast majority of the debt must be paid by the individual. When you have adequate health insurance coverage and you get sick or in an accident, your bills will be looked after by your insurance carrier. Too many people travel without proper health coverage and end up in severe financial difficulty. If you use the services of a private hospital and end up with expensive medical bills, you will be expected to pay in full. Gray says, "if you have a house with a clear title in Canada, they will commence action. They are very proactive to seize and sell your home. They want to be paid and will go after your assets."

Make sure you fully understand what your policy covers and take details of the policy with you. You may also want to tell a friend or family member how to contact your insurer.

Another costly mistake some travellers make when taking out medical insurance is keeping current health problems a secret. You should never try to get a lower rate by concealing a health matter. Be totally upfront or it could cost you later. "Don't leave anything to the imagination and go to excess to make sure you've disclosed everything. Not revealing that you take an aspirin once a day could be enough for an insurer to void your policy when you need it most," says Gray.

Health insurance coverage can be purchased through the workplace or from an independent provider. Premiums will range from a few dollars for a day trip, to hundreds or even thousands of dollars for a six-month stay. The amount you pay for coverage will depend on your age and medical condition. Make sure you fully understand what your policy covers and take details of the policy with you. You may also want to tell a friend or family member how to contact your insurer. Also, will your insurance provider pay foreign hospital and related medical costs upfront, or do you have to pay and get reimbursed later? If you do have to pay, get the proper documentation so you will be reimbursed promptly on your return. If you require medical evacuation back to Canada, will you be covered? What if a nurse must accompany you — is that included? If you die, will your insurer cover the cost of shipping your remains home? Is there a 24 hours, seven days a week telephone operator standing by who will be able to assist you in your language if you need help?

"Snowbirds who want to enjoy the warm weather, sandy beaches and southern climates must ensure they have adequate insurance coverage to protect themselves or a single medical emergency could cause them serious financial hardship," warns Gray. Whatever the insurance will cost you, it's far better to pay out a little money before a trip, than have to pay tens of thousands of dollars in medical bills during one.

INTERNET SHOPPING

Mohammed used the Internet to buy products that he couldn't find locally. He used his credit card on-line to buy a blow-up raft from a specialty store in the United States. A few months later, his credit card bill contained more than $700 in charges he hadn't made. When he contacted his credit card company, he was informed that the charges were for downloading pornographic material. Mohammed denied using the pornographic service and following an investigation, it was determined that Mohammed's credit card number had somehow been stolen in cyber-space.

There is no doubt that the Internet has changed our lives and this is especially true when it comes to retailing in the new millennium. There is no need to get dressed up to shop now when you can enter thousands of cyberstores from home with the click of a button. The Internet is especially helpful when trying to order items not available locally. Some argue that shopping on-line with a credit card is as safe as swiping it at a gas station. However, the Internet is an evolving marketplace that is only as safe as the businesses you deal with and there are precautions you need to take. Also, purchases that initially seem like a great deal on-line can quickly become less of a bargain once buyers consider currency exchange rates, shipping and handling costs and duty fees at border crossings.

Corporations want consumers to be comfortable shopping on the Internet because it's good for business and e-commerce. Using your credit card on-line is usually safe, as in most cases the number is scrambled as you send it. A credit card number sent as 123-4567890-12 would be encrypted into gibberish that wouldn't make sense to anyone who purposely or accidentally intercepted it. Having said this, be sure that you are in a secure environment before using your credit card. The site should assure you that it is a safe place to do business by displaying a closed golden padlock icon or unbroken key at the bottom of your browser window. An Internet address starting with "http" is also an indication it is a secure Web site. As more consumers move toward buying on-line, credit card companies are working with retailers to make the Internet a more secure place to do business.

When ordering goods from outside Canada, consider also the cost of converting your money, duties, taxes, custom brokerage fees, shipping and handling.

Before spending a lot of time e-shopping at a particular site, make sure that they actually deliver to Canada and find out how much it's going to cost you. You don't want to buy a $40 item that will add up to $90 by the time you have it shipped to your door. Shipping costs will be determined by size and weight, the number of things you buy, where you live and how quickly you want your purchase. If the package is coming from the United States, you may have to pay duties, taxes and custom brokerage fees. Goods less than $20 are duty free. Custom brokerage fees often surprise consumers when they are added to the cost of shipping and they must be paid before you will receive your goods. The post office and courier companies use brokerage services to get parcels through customs at the border and the charges are passed on to the owner of the parcel. You will also have to pay the federal Goods and Services Tax and provincial taxes (Harmonized Sales Tax in New Brunswick, Nova Scotia and Newfoundland) on your purchase.

More important is the reputation of the company you are dealing with when shopping on-line. You should use the same precautions on the Net as you would at a store. Who is the retailer you are dealing with? What is their reputation? Do they have a "bricks and mortar" location or do they exist only in cyberspace? How did you find out about them? Do they have a phone number, address and company sales staff you can talk to? It's usually a good idea to call ahead and talk to the retailer, before making a purchase to make sure you can get through if there is a problem. It will also give you a chance to get a sense of the professionalism of the operation.

Canadians are becoming more comfortable in cyberspace and if you plan on shopping frequently on the Internet, it's a good idea to get a separate credit card just for on-line purchases. That way you could have a card with a $500 limit to use specifically on the Internet. A separate card will allow you to easily keep track of your on-line shopping, keep an eye on possible misuse of your credit card number and if there were ever a problem, the most you could be held liable for is $500.

DON'T GET TAKEN TO THE CLEANERS!

Amanda had taken her clothes to the dry cleaners for years without incident. She was very upset when a dry cleaner lost her expensive gown that she had planned to wear to an upcoming wedding. She was more shocked when the dry cleaner offered her only a small amount of money to replace it. She explained that the dress was worth hundreds of dollars and demanded more financial compensation. Even though she persisted, the dry cleaner told her to check the disclaimer on her dry cleaning stub and take it or leave it.

The dry cleaning industry cleans millions of garments each year and has a good record of keeping track of the countless suits, blouses and dresses that pass through its steamers and presses. When you drop off your clothing at a dry cleaning store, it usually ends up at a laundry plant with potentially thousands of other articles of clothing. Clothing does get lost from time to time and some say you can judge your dry cleaner by how well they deal with you if your goods are lost or damaged.

Groups including Ontario's Fabricare Association say there is no hard and fast rule on what happens when clothing is lost or ruined by a dry cleaner. When there is a problem, it is up to the individual dry cleaner to resolve the issue with the customer.

Dry cleaners who have been in the business for decades say there are many different approaches taken by businesses to try and satisfy the customer. Large reputable dry cleaners will do whatever is necessary to please the customer. This may involve trying to find the true price of the garment when new and then subtracting for wear and tear.

What more often happens when clothing is lost is that the dry cleaner will try to get the customer to accept free dry cleaning for the amount of the value of the lost article. So if an $80 shirt is misplaced, the dry cleaner may offer $80 worth of dry cleaning or even more, to try to satisfy the customer. Veteran cleaners say this is also a way for the dry cleaner to try and win back the trust of the customer. They fear just paying off a customer could mean they won't come back.

What happened to Amanda is common. Many dry cleaners will often print on the receipt their policy that they are only responsible for a limited amount of the garment's value, regardless of its true cost, even if they lose or ruin it. It may say something like: "The limit of any claim will not exceed eight times the price of washing or cleaning any single garment." Some dry cleaners may pay ten times the value of the bill. This could prove acceptable for an inexpensive or worn shirt, but if it was an expensive suit, this may be a paltry amount compared to its true value. If a dry cleaner did lose an $800 suit and was offering to pay only $40, it could be a case for small claims court. However, that approach could be time consuming and expensive.

Check with your dry cleaner beforehand to find out their policy on lost or ruined goods. While most dry cleaners have it on their receipt, not all do. Some have it posted in their stores. Others don't. Also, sometimes a small independent dry cleaner will be able to clean your clothes for far less money than the competition, but this may be because they won't reimburse customers fairly when they lose or ruin items. This could affect where you would want to leave certain items for cleaning. You may decide to take regular clothing to the local cleaner with cheaper rates, whereas you may pay a little more for the dry cleaning of an expensive dress or suit — just in case something happens to it.

MICROCHIPPING — Safeguarding Your Pet

Sade loved her Labrador retriever "Molson" and decided to get him microchipped in case he ever went missing. One day during a run in the park when Molson was off his leash, he ran off and never came back. After a frantic search, Sade gave up. She was relieved that she had him chipped and waited for a call from animal control officials or whoever found her pet. A call never came and Sade never saw Molson again.

Microchipping pets has been around for more than a decade and is now one of the most popular ways for people to identify their dogs, cats, birds and other pets. It costs around $60 to get your pet microchipped. Usually the small chip is inserted just under the skin on the animal's neck or upper back. It's a fairly painless procedure that takes only a minute to perform. The pet owner's information — name, address, phone number — is then entered into a nation-wide database through PetNet the company that operates the service. A hand-held scanner is used to scan the animal to locate the chip. If your pet is ever lost, a simple scan of the animal will provide all the information needed to get your pet back home. PetNet says its service helped reunite 10,000 Canadian pets with their rightful owners in 1999 alone.

Veterinarian Dr. Alison Sutton-Harmer says microchipping pets is an excellent way to track lost animals. She says, "when we find a chip, we cheer because we can call the person and they can come and get their animal within five minutes." PetNet distributes hand-held scanners to dog pounds, humane societies and animal control centres across Canada, so that all lost animals can be scanned when they are picked up. Microchipping is an excellent form of identifying pets because dog tags can be lost and tattoos can alter as a pet grows. The chip is always there, just below the skin ready to reveal the owner's name.

Having said this, the microchipping of pets is not failsafe. The hand-held scanners are available to be used for free at shelters and pounds, but they only work if someone bothers using them. Scanners can also malfunction or not be properly charged, which can lead to reading difficulties. The chips are also so tiny that they can shift under the skin and be difficult for the scanners to read. There have been many cases of microchipped dogs and cats being picked up by animal control officers, only to be sold to other owners, sent to research facilities, or put to death because no one bothered scanning them to check for a chip. Animal service operations or pounds will usually try to scan every animal that comes in, however like anything, there is room for error. Even microchipping is not foolproof. The shifting of the chips under the skin is fairly common and steel tables or other objects can sometimes cause interference with the scanners that read the chips.

Dr. Sutton-Harmer maintains that microchipping is still the best option for owners concerned about losing their pets. It's the responsibility of anyone in the business of caring for lost animals to make sure they are scanned properly. "We scan at least five times all around the animal before we say there is no chip. It would be a real shame if an animal was chipped and someone failed to find it." Pet owners should never rely solely on the chips when their pets go missing. Dog tags, rabies tags and writing your name in indelible ink on the inside of the collar will all help too. Check immediately and after a few days with all the local shelters and file a missing animal report. Pet owners must be proactive to find their pets and get them home safely.

CHARITY AND COMMUNITY GROUP FRAUD

The town bingo was a huge success selling out almost every week. Money was made on the door, cards and concession counter but after the prizes were handed out, the charity event barely broke even. The treasurer of the bingo said that the bottom line would likely improve as time went on. Still, it seemed even on the busiest nights, there was never a satisfactory amount of money raised to actually donate to the charitable foundation the bingo was set up to help. It was later discovered that the treasurer had been stealing from the bingo for years.

It's an unfortunate reality that sometimes volunteers who work for charitable and community groups steal from their organizations. Of course, the vast majority of people working for hockey clubs, historical societies, bowling leagues and other non-profit groups are honest, hardworking and dedicated. But enough volunteers have been caught taking money from the cashbox, that police are now warning community groups that volunteer fraud is a growing problem. In one documented case, a woman stole $120,000 from minor league hockey bingos, as no one was checking the bingo lottery reports she was submitting.

In another, a volunteer accountant was accused of stealing $80,000 from an historical group. There was also a case of a former politician stealing $72,000 from an athletic association. Sad but true cases of people put in charge of worthy causes, only to profit from it illegally.

Never allow just one person to be in charge of an organization's finances.

In Durham Region, an area east of Toronto, Ontario, authorities have taken an excellent approach to helping groups manage their finances and protect their organizations from theft. Durham's Police Department has developed guidelines entitled *Crime Prevention Tips for Not-For-Profit Organizations*, which could be used in communities across Canada. The police recommend never allowing just one person to be in charge of the money in your organization. Become suspicious if your group is in worse financial shape than last year, although your income and expenses haven't changed. Be concerned immediately if your club can't pay its bills and your treasurer can't explain the poor financial position you're in. Question your treasurer if he or she refuses to let anyone look at or work on the books. Don't be satisfied if the treasurer says things like "don't worry, we're in great shape." Beware of early warning signs, there may be a problem if other members are asked to sign blank cheques or blank lottery licence reports, or if cash deposits are being received late at the bank and are smaller or larger than they should be.

Fraud units advise that you should have job descriptions and spending limits for your decision makers. A budget should be struck at the start of the year or project and two people should have to sign important documents whenever possible. Limit the number of people allowed to take money; use cheques instead of cash. Separate duties so that the person receiving cash doesn't deposit it or that the person in charge of the bank account doesn't also write the cheques. It's safer to write a cheque to the supplier, rather than reimburse a member who has incurred an expense. Avoid using cash to pay bills but if you need a petty cash fund, keep it small and get receipts for everything. Finally, when money changes hands, record the amount and have the recipient sign for it.

Police say that the problem when investigating thefts from community groups is the lack of adequately maintained accounting records. An investigation may have to span several years and without proper records, it's difficult to determine how much money was actually stolen. Not-for-profit groups should use a basic accounting system that may be computer based or handwritten. It should be simple enough so that the books can be easily understood by the entire executive and can be passed from one treasurer to another as duties change. All groups should regularly submit to an independent audit to ensure all financial records are in order. Durham's Major Fraud Unit offers a sample set of bookkeeping records that have been prepared by a chartered accountant, so that community groups can see how to properly keep finance records in an easy to manage format. The fraud unit allows not-for-profit groups access to these sample records as a public service. Check if your local police department makes similar resources available.

Keep in mind when trying to bring about change in community-based organizations that the majority of all volunteers are people dedicated to the greater good of society. Never try to ram through changes that could be hurtful to members or executives who have been honest and forthright in their dealings trying to run not-for-profit groups. A good time to discuss the issue may be when starting a new group, or at the beginning of a new budget year. That way, guidelines can be placed on the table for everyone to discuss. It can help your organization run more smoothly and make it less likely to be defrauded. If you are concerned about a problem in your executive ranks, discuss it with other members and confront the person or persons in charge of finances. Deal with matters internally before they become messy public affairs, which may involve the police, court system and media.

CARPET CLEANERS

Joanne received a flyer for a carpet cleaning service advertising an offer to clean carpet in three rooms for a low price. She gave them a call and set up an appointment. When the cleaner got to her home, he explained that the low rate was for three small rooms and that her living room did not qualify for the advertised rate. The low rate was also for a basic cleaning job which was not recommended. Before she knew it, Joanne agreed to suggestions made by the cleaner. Her bill was four times more than what she had intended to pay.

There are many honest and ethical carpet cleaners who will do a good job cleaning your home for a fair price. There are also others who will use "bait and switch" tactics to try to get their foot in the door and then do everything possible to raise the price of the job. Many carpet cleaning services are operated by small businesses in a highly competitive marketplace, so it's common that some cleaners will use deceptive advertising and tactics to try to get work.

Consumers respond to advertised low prices such as "Any room for $12.99" or "Any Three Rooms for $49." However, low price is not necessarily the best way to pick a carpet cleaner. A higher price may mean that you are getting a professional job done by an experienced and established cleaner. An extremely low price could mean that the cleaner has little experience and cheap equipment. They may also cram more cleaning jobs into a day to try and make a profit, which means that they won't be able to spend as much time in your home. The cleaner may also say that there are different cleaning methods including single or dual purpose cleaning, and that the low rate is for a method which will not remove all the dirt from your carpet.

A bait and switch cleaner may use intimidation tactics or a high pressure sales pitch to get the homeowner to switch to a higher priced cleaning job. If the homeowner refuses and insists the cleaner do the work at the advertised price, the cleaner may recognize that they are not going to make much money on the job and do fast, poor quality work. You should never feel pressured when dealing with a carpet cleaner and if you do, this could be a signal that you are dealing with a shady operator. If a price is too low, don't expect a good quality job. A carpet cleaner is like any other business and must cover regular business expenditures such as vehicle and equipment expenses as well as soap, gas, insurance and other costs. So how could a business operate charging only $10 to clean a room?

Beware that in some cases, vacuum cleaner sales staffs have been known to operate under the guise of a carpet cleaner. They may come to your home offering a free carpet cleaning demonstration when they are in fact trying to sell you a high-priced vacuum. You can also rent carpet cleaning machines at grocery stores or rental centres. They do a good job at a fraction of the cost. I rented a professional machine for four hours from a rental centre and was able to clean my entire house. A word of caution though: a professional carpet cleaning unit is quite heavy and it's difficult to lug the machine up and down stairs and in and out of a vehicle.

> A carpet cleaner may use bait and switch or intimidation tactics to get the homeowner to upgrade to a higher priced cleaning job. Don't be pressured but if the price is too low, don't expect a quality job either.

If you are responding to an ad or a coupon, read the fine print so that you are certain you know what the advertised special includes. How much is it to do stairs? What about having furniture cleaned? Will the cleaner move your furniture and put it back in place when the job is done? Question their experience. Do they know the proper ways to clean different types of carpet and upholstery? Point out problem areas such as stain or spots beforehand. You can ask to have the price in writing before the job starts, so there are no hidden charges that will be added on during the cleaning process. Does the cleaner have a home base where you can reach them if there is a problem that crops up after they leave or do they just have an answering service which means they may decide not to phone you back? You may wish to check references or inquire at the Better Business Bureau to see if there are unresolved complaints against them.

If a cleaner pulls up in an unmarked vehicle and uses small portable equipment that you could rent yourself, that person may not be the best choice for the job. Ask your friends and family if they have had a good experience with a carpet cleaner and could recommend one. Once you get a good, reliable carpet cleaner, you may wish to use them in the future, instead of relying on coupons that you find in your mailbox.

ALERT

84

INFOMMERCIALS — Information or Advertising?

Tony was watching late night television when he took interest in an investment program. He recognized the host of the show and spent the next half hour watching it. Before long, there was an offer advertised for a 10-step program to help put you on the road to financial success. Tony took down the number, called and purchased the television offer. When he received the program weeks later, he was not impressed. He wanted to return it, but there was no money-back guarantee.

The product or services you buy through an infomercial may be completely legitimate but you should know that these shows are basically long commercials. The makers of a product will buy television time from networks, usually late at night when the air time is cheaper, to hawk their wares. The infomercials may look like regular television programming because they usually copy the look and feel of other popular TV shows. Infomercials also use well-known actors who may be past their prime on the acting circuit, but they will accept financial compensation in order to have their reputation associated with the services or merchandise being sold.

Keep in mind that an enthusiastic audience in an infomercial may be stacked with people being paid to clap and feign interest.

Often they are actually investors in the product which may also explain their enthusiasm. Infomercials sell a wide range of goods including hair replacement products, diet aids, smoking cures, appliances and get rich quick schemes. Usually there will be a warning at the beginning or end of the show stating that the program is a paid commercial broadcast. Throughout the infomercial there will be a phone number to call if you wish to buy the product, as this is the sole purpose of the show — to get you to buy something! When listening to infomercials, keep in mind that there is little journalistic integrity to these programs. Their product may do as they say, but you are not being advised by an impartial third party. The hosts you recognize from past television programs may believe in the product, but they are also being paid a large sum of money to endorse it.

> An enthusiastic audience in an infomercial may be stacked with people paid to clap and feign interest. Often they are investors in the product, which may explain their enthusiasm.

If you do decide to buy a product from an infomercial, find out as much as you can about the product and the company beforehand. Can you buy the product or one like it locally? What is so different about the product that it is available only through this company? What is the return policy if the product fails to live up to your expectations? Can you receive information about the product before you order it? If you go ahead with a purchase, do it on a credit card so you will have a paper trail of your order. You may also be able to cancel it through your credit card company, if there is a problem.

GOING OUT OF BUSINESS SALES

Miranda was interested in buying a Persian rug. She had been watching the newspapers for advertisements, to try to find a sale. When she read that a carpet and rug company was going out of business, she went to the store hoping to find a deal. She saw a rug that was originally $2,500 but that had been discounted to half-price. Feeling it was a purchase she couldn't pass up, she bought it. Six months later while reading the paper, she noticed that the same company was still operating and that they were still having their going out of business sale.

It may be true that you can find a bargain when a company, large or small, must close down and sell off its inventory. When the sale involves a well-known manufacturer whose bankruptcy may have even made the news, shoppers could very well find some *bona fide* bargains. Yet there are some unsavoury businesses that will use the illusion of a "going out of business sale" to generate interest, customers and profits. There have been cases of stores going out of business for *years*! Going out of business sales are more likely to be held in large cities, but inventory from these alleged sell-offs also end up in roving sales at hotels or flea markets.

Consumers love to think they are getting a bargain and a going out of business sale is often enough to light a fire under an eager shopper. Whether it's to sell rugs, coats or electronics, a store may have a never-ending going out of business sale, by constantly bringing in goods through their back door. The retailer's advertisements or in-store banners may read "all stock must go" or "it's a final inventory clear out," when in fact the computer or VCR will be replaced as soon as the naive customer walks out the door with their purchase. In Miranda's case, when she bought a rug that was marked down from $2,500 to half price, chances are the rug was only ever meant to be sold for about $1,200 in the first place. Stores have been charged for illegally marking up prices and then slashing them to make it appear that there are significant savings.

Another way that retailers try to get around laws or time restrictions regarding going out of business sales is to actually go out of business and then, immediately set up shop under another name and proceed to go out of business again! If you are interested in attending a going out of business sale, do your best to find out if the company is truly shutting down and selling off their merchandise. Ask the manager when the sale started and how long it will last. Find out how long the company was operating before the sale. Ask when the store plans to be completely out of business and if they are selling off inventory that is not on site that will replace items on the floor as they are sold. Check with a neighbouring store to double check what you have been told. They will know if the sale has been going on for a week or a year.

While you could find a bargain at a going out of business sale, don't be too trusting and believe that there will be incredible bargains. Check to see if what you are looking for is available elsewhere at a similar or better price. Also, what is the refund or return policy? The store may use the ruse of a going out of business sale to claim that the merchandise is not returnable or refundable. If you do buy an item from a company that is actually going out of business, any warranty or guarantees could also be void because of the nature of the sale. There are many cases of consumers getting what they think is an incredible deal, only to find out later they have bought defective merchandise. They are then unable to return it to the store and the manufacturer may refuse to repair or exchange it.

JEWELLERY FRAUD

Pamela had an exquisite 1.1 carat diamond ring that her husband bought her for an anniversary gift. She took the diamond to a local jewellery store and left it to be cleaned and appraised for insurance reasons. The jeweller returned the ring with the appraisal. Years later, when another store was offering a free appraisal service, she decided to have it appraised again. This jeweller told her that the ring was worth a fraction of what she thought. Pamela was aghast and said there must be some mistake. The jeweller informed her that the gemstone was not a real diamond at all. Pamela was left heartbroken and confused.

Diamond switching is an old scam practised by some unscrupulous jewellers. To the naked and untrained eye, it's virtually impossible to tell diamonds apart so it's difficult to know if the diamond ring you leave is the same one you'll get back. Jewellers have been charged with fraud, after taking high quality gems from jewellery and replacing them with inferior stones. The replacement stones may be real diamonds that have imperfections, or they may be fake diamonds made of a new synthetic material now available in Canada.

Moissanite has essentially the same qualities as a diamond but at a fraction of the price. The imitation gem can fool even seasoned jewellers into believing they're looking at a real diamond.

Instead of being mined out of an African hillside, moissanite is actually a crystal grown in a laboratory. This material can be excellent for someone who knows its true composition and doesn't mind the fact that it's not a true diamond. The fake jewellery industry generates millions of dollars in sales annually and some consumers are delighted to adorn themselves with moissanite, since most people wouldn't be able to tell the difference between it and real diamonds. A diamond worth $2,500 can be reproduced with moissanite for only about $250 and look the very same.

Gem Scan is Canada's largest independent jewellery appraisal laboratory and it does jewellery appraisals for major diamond retailers, as well as for consumers. The company uses a unique process which can help put a person's mind at ease while having diamonds cleaned or repaired. Gem Scan uses laser inscription technology to write microinscribed information on the outer surface of the diamond. Such information is not visible to the naked eye. The company says that this is the only way customers will have irrefutable proof that the diamond they drop off, is the same one they get back. Andrew Tatarsky, co-owner of Gem Scan, says "the lasering doesn't affect the clarity of the stone, and can be done on both set and unset stones. We can inscribe a social insurance number, a logo, a customer's name, the appraisal numbers or even a dedication on the outer perimeter of the diamond." The words or numbers can be seen through a ten power magnification microscope. Information about the lasered diamond is also entered in a Diamond Laser Registry database, in case the diamond is ever lost or stolen. The cost of the laser inscription starts at $75 for a maximum of 15 characters. More information about this service is available at www.gemscan.com or through their toll-free number, 1-877-868-6656.

> Laser inscription technology can microinscribe information onto the outer surface of the diamond. This information is not visible to the naked eye, but can provide irrefutable proof of the diamond's ownership.

Be cautious when getting fine jewellery appraised. Almost anyone can claim to be an appraiser and two appraisers may give vastly different opinions of a piece of jewellery's worth. There is no legislation in Canada governing appraisals and there are very few gemologists who have a total and complete understanding of the jewellery being assessed. You may have to pay to get an in-depth appraisal done on a piece of jewellery. Depending on the jewellery's value, this step will be well worth it. Have an expensive item appraised by two or more appraisers to see if their estimates are consistent. If you are concerned about leaving your diamond for cleaning, ask a reputable jeweller to clean the jewellery in front of you, so your precious diamond is in view at all times. If the jeweller won't do that, then go somewhere else.

DEALING WITH BUSINESS BANKRUPTCY

Tristan was renovating his kitchen and decided to get new oak cabinets. He visited a store that specialized in custom kitchens. He picked out a cupboard design and was told that it would take four to six weeks before the cabinets would be ready. He was asked for a deposit of $3,000, which he provided. After six weeks had passed, he called the company and was told there had been a slight delay, but that the cabinets would be ready soon. Two weeks later, he called again but no one answered. He drove to the store and saw that it was empty. The store had gone out of business.

Often a business can appear to be operating normally one day, and then close its doors the next. Little or no warning of a bankruptcy creates problems for consumers who have left deposits or goods with the company that has gone under. Consumers are often left feeling helpless, knowing that they not only lost hundreds or thousands of dollars, they will also not get the service or merchandise they were expecting.

If you can, try to find out how long a business has been in operation before leaving expensive merchandise or a large security deposit. Keep the amount of your deposit to 10%. If the business requires more than this, ask why it is necessary. The company may need to buy materials depending on the job at hand, but be leery if you are asked to leave a large amount of money or to pay the full amount upfront. When a company closes down in a hurry, several things could have happened. It may have declared bankruptcy, packed-up and moved elsewhere to operate under another name, or just disappeared with no intention of notifying anyone. Often the police are no help when a company closes up shop with a customer's money. While a customer could argue that the company knew it was about to close its doors while it was accepting deposits, the business could contend it was hoping the last deposit would help the company turn around its misfortunes, balance its books and stay in operation.

Keep your deposit to no more than 10%, and follow up on the progress of your job regularly. If the business goes bankrupt, you are classified as an unsecured creditor, and in most cases it will be extremely difficult to get your money back.

Make observations about the business. Does it look like a successful operation, or are there empty shelves or temporary signs? If you have left a deposit or expensive items to be repaired, drop by the store and call them often. Find out what's happening with your situation. Don't let them tell you "Don't call us, we'll call you." While it may be admirable to help the little guy by giving your business to a smaller company, beware of leaving deposits or property unless the business is well established. Following Tristan's ordeal, he said next time he would rather deal with a larger firm which may be less likely to go under, or be more likely to warn customers by having a going out of business sale. Contact the Better Business Bureau to see if there are any outstanding complaints against a company you plan to use. Word of mouth is always a good way to find out about a business, so canvass friends, family or co-workers if you are in the market for a particular good or service.

If a business does go under, find out how to get in touch with them. There will usually be a sign on the front door which will specify the Trustee in Bankruptcy handling the case. There also may be a former address, other locations of the same company, or a headquarters or main office for their operations. Ask neighbouring businesses if they know the circumstances as to why the business closed, or where they can be contacted. The landlord of the building may also be able to put you in touch with the business.

The federal office of the superintendent of bankruptcies oversees bankruptcies and insolvencies to ensure that they are conducted in a fair and orderly manner (see Alert 14 on bankruptcies). In the event of a bankruptcy, a trustee is appointed to liquidate or sell the company's assets. The assets will go to pay off the debt, which may include debts to creditors, investors and, if there is enough left over, customers. Depending on your situation, you may be able to retrieve your property. If you left a computer for repairs and the business went under, you are classified as a "property owner." You can fill out a property proof of claim form to prove that the computer is yours and get it back. Similarly, if you left your car for repairs, you can file a claim to get it back. In both cases, you will be required to pay for the repairs if they were already performed.

If you left a deposit with a business that goes bankrupt, you are classified as an "unsecured creditor," and in most cases it will be extremely difficult to get your money back. That is why it is so important to limit the amount of money you leave as a deposit. Speak to the trustee in bankruptcy about your situation and try to recoup your losses. Just keep in mind that there may be many before you in line to get the little that will be left when a business goes under.

DEALING WITH COLLECTION AGENCIES

Tyler was alarmed when he answered the phone one day and found he was being contacted by a collection agency. Due to family problems and other circumstances, he had admittedly ignored his financial responsibilities and had fallen behind on his loan payments. Now he was unsure of what to do and how to deal with the agency on the other end of the line.

While it is clearly in your best interests to pay your bills on time, predicaments can occur that cause a collection agency to enter your life. If this happens to you because you have defaulted on your financial obligations, don't panic — the agency just wants you to make good on your debts. Industry Canada's *Canadian Consumer Handbook,* states there are ways to deal with a collection agency to make the experience as painless as possible.

A collection agency is just a business that arranges for repayment of monies owed by a person or a company. If it is possible, try to settle the account and pay the money you owe immediately. If it is not, and often it isn't as this is the reason the collection agency is calling you, try to propose a schedule to repay your debt. Once your account is paid in full, you won't have to deal with the agency again. Explain your situation and offer an alternative method of restitution, either a lump sum or a series of monthly payments. Be civil and realize that the collection agency's involvement is nothing personal.

Industry Canada advises that you should never pay off debts by sending cash. Make payments in a way that you have something as proof of payment. A cancelled cheque or receipt will prevent arguments later. Once the account has been officially turned over to a collection agency, just deal with them. There is no need to contact the original business, unless there is an error in the account. Contacting the original business can create confusion. If there is a mistake or you dispute the amount owed, advise the collection agency and the creditor immediately and do your best to provide documents to back up your case. A collection agency has no problem with you per se, but how you deal with them also affects how they deal with you. Be sure not to miss payments or bounce cheques. If you do, it could result in court action, garnishee of your wages, or seizure of your assets, as well as a tarnished credit rating.

Industry Canada advises that rules regarding collection agencies vary from province to province. Generally a collection agency is forbidden from trying to collect a debt through garnishees or seizures without first notifying you in writing. An agency cannot proceed with court action unless you have been informed and they have the creditor's written permission. Collection agencies cannot make calls of a nature that a reasonable person would consider harassment. They cannot call you to collect a debt on a Sunday, statutory holiday or before 7:00 a.m. or after 10:00 p.m. They cannot give to any person false or misleading information that could damage you or your family, or demand payment of a debt without properly identifying themselves.

Some consumers may find themselves in the unfortunate situation of being contacted by a collection agency when they feel they don't owe anything to anyone. A collection agency cannot continue to demand payment from a person who claims not to owe a debt, unless the collector has tried every possible way to ensure the person does in fact owe the money. Collection agencies are not allowed to contact friends, employers, relatives or neighbours for information other than your telephone number or address. If you believe you are being unfairly treated by a collection agency, contact your provincial consumer ministry to find out what options are available to you.

WATCH OUT
FOR SNOW JOBS

Jeff was busy with his job and family and decided to hire a snow removal contractor for the winter. A man came to his door offering to clear his lane at a cut rate price if he signed up early. The contractor had a truck with a plow on the front, a business card and said that he had 15 years experience. Jeff signed a contract and paid in advance for snow removal services. When the first storm of the season came, Jeff expected that his driveway would be plowed clean, but it wasn't. He tried in vain to get in touch with the snowplow operator, but he never heard from him again.

When winter approaches many Canadians look for contractors to clear their driveways, parking lots and storefronts. Shovelling snow can be back breaking work and more and more people are willing to pay someone else to do it. Small and large businesses usually have to negotiate snow removal contracts with snowplow operators to ensure it will be business as usual when the inevitable snowstorm arrives. It may be possible to pay a neighbour down the street who has a plow or snow blower to clear your driveway, but not everyone has that convenience. In an urban area chances are you will end up dealing with a snow removal contractor you do not know first hand.

The majority of people involved in the snow removal business are honest professionals who offer legitimate services. However, problems can arise depending on the severity of the winter, the equipment the operator is using and whether or not the contractor overestimates or overextends their snow removal abilities. Whether you operate a business or just want snow removal for your residence, get all services, restrictions and obligations of the contractor in writing. Never rely on verbal contracts, as this could lead to problems later. Find out if there will be additional fees during and after severe snowstorms.

Word of mouth is usually a good way to find a snow removal contractor. If others have been satisfied with a contractor's work, chances are you will be too. If you are dealing with someone you don't know, be cautious. As Jeff found out, anyone can print up a business card and fake contracts and appear to have a legitimate business. Check with your local Better Business Bureau to see if the company is registered and has any unresolved complaints. Ask for references and check them! Find out if the contractor has a full-time snow removal business, or if it's a guy with another job who just tries to make a few extra bucks when it snows.

> Get all the services, restrictions and obligations of the snow removal company's agreement in writing, including whether there will be additional fees during or after severe snowstorms.

Don't prepay or give a large, upfront deposit to a snow removal contractor even if they insist that it's the only way to secure their services. It's best to make periodic payments; that way, you can be sure that they are doing a satisfactory job, before they get your money. Paying by instalment also prevents them from keeping your funds in the event that they don't keep their part of the bargain.

Get the contractor's refund policy in writing. If they don't clear your property in a timely fashion and you need to do it yourself or have someone else do it, you should be given a partial refund or at least a price reduction for future work.

PROTECTING YOURSELF AT GARAGE SALES

Lee was expecting a baby and was scouring garage sales for everything she would need when her new-born finally arrived. She bought a carriage, high chair and crib, along with other items at bargain prices. When she had her baby, she was prepared. One night she heard a cry from her child's room and found that her baby's head was stuck between the bars of the crib. The child was hysterical and Lee was distraught over what could have happened if she hadn't heard her baby's cries.

Every year, millions of Canadians take part in garage sales either by selling their used goods, or by looking for bargains for their own family. Yard sales are a great way to clean out the garage, attic or storage room and make a few dollars at the same time. However, you should be aware that many items being sold the second or third time around may have out-lived their usefulness and could pose a safety hazard for new owners. If you host the garage sale, you could also be held liable for any faulty products you sell.

Many items relating to babies and children are a major concern at garage sales. Carriages, baby gates, walkers, bouncers, play pens, strollers and old toys could be problems waiting to happen. Without the original paperwork and instructions on these items, you may not know their history or whether or not they have been the subject of safety recalls. As with many products relating to children, there are often improvements in cribs, bouncers and car seats as time goes by. Walkers with wheels are no longer sold in retail stores in Canada, as there have been too many cases of babies being hurt tumbling down stairs in them. Buying one at a garage sale could put your child in serious danger. Cribs made before 1986 may have bars placed further apart than they safely should be, allowing a child to stick his or her head through the bars and get hurt. You may think a car seat is a great deal at only $20, but if that car seat has previously been in an accident or has design flaws that have since been corrected in newer models, you may not know about it.

It's not just children's articles that could be a danger in yard sales. Items such as old helmets, used appliances and worn lamps may be more trouble than they're worth. Is a toaster really a great bargain at $5 if it has an electrical short that could burn your house down? Items such as lawn darts have been banned in Canada, but they still turn up occasionally in yard sales. Rather than being resold, they should be thrown in the garbage. All toys purchased at garage sales should be checked carefully for loose parts and sharp edges to make sure that they are safe for children.

If you have a garage sale, you should know that you can be held liable for the items you sell. For example, if you sold a faulty crib to a parent and a child was injured, you could be sued for damages. Anything you sell at a garage sale should be in a safe condition so that you will not be held liable if there is a problem. Most home insurance policies will provide adequate coverage if you decide to have an occasional garage sale to get rid of unwanted items. However, if you run yard sales as a regular money-making event, your home insurance policy may not cover you as this may be considered a business by many insurance companies. You might have to purchase additional insurance coverage, in case someone trips over a garden hose or gets cut on your old barbecue.

CASH REGISTER SCANNERS

Simonne shopped regularly at a large supermarket where checkout clerks used scanners to tally her food bill. She never gave it much thought as the clerk scanned her items through and bagged her groceries. One day she decided to check her receipt and was shocked to find four mistakes. In total, she had been overcharged more than $6.

Many stores now use electronic scanning devices to tally up sales. Whether it's milk, macaroni or meatballs, most products now come with a Universal Product Code, known as a UPC symbol. This symbol, also known as a bar code, contains pricing and other information about the product that is stored in a business's cash register and computer system. When the product is passed over a scanner, a beam of light decodes the various lines that make up the UPC symbol and sends the price to the cash register.

The problem? Research has shown that these scanners often charge consumers the wrong prices! Studies have shown that for every 100 scans, about three or four are wrong. On any trip to the grocery store, you could end up with a couple of mistakes on your bill. While the scanning technology is usually 100% accurate, it is human error that causes the mistakes. The price sticker on the can of beans may not be the same as the price that pops up on the register for various reasons. The store may have recently adjusted prices on the shelf and failed to do so in the computer. A manager can easily adjust pricing on the store's computer system but it could take hours for staff to make the necessary changes on hundreds or thousands of items.

The manual entry of prices is also not mistake-free. Some studies have shown that the error rate can be just as inaccurate when prices are entered manually by a cashier. Also, receipts from older machines list only prices, whereas newer models specify the item with the price, making it easier for consumers to identify pricing errors.

In 1996, Industry Canada's Competition Bureau conducted research on price accuracy in the Canadian marketplace and surveyed 162 businesses including grocery, drug and department stores. After more than 15,000 items were checked, the Bureau found that there was a combined average error rate of 6.3%. This included a 3.0% overcharge rate and a 3.3% undercharge rate — the frequency of overcharges and undercharges was fairly evenly split. Further study in 1999 and 2000 showed while some improvements have been made, mistakes with electronic scanners are still common across the country. The biggest overcharges are usually found in department stores and home improvement centres, usually because they sell bigger ticket items than in grocery stores.

Some grocery stores are now installing self-scanning technology so that consumers can scan, bag and pay for their groceries on their own. This move is designed to get rid of cashiers and save stores money, as the aisles are constructed so that one employee can oversee four self-scanning checkouts. This new technology also allows consumers to check prices for themselves, as they scan their purchases. Safeguards are also built in, such as video cameras and weighing mechanisms, so that consumers don't try to take goods without paying for them. Self-scanning aisles are already operational in some grocery and department stores in Ontario. This technology is still a long way off from being used in a widespread fashion across Canada, even though it is becoming more mainstream in the United States.

To protect yourself from being a scanner victim, become an attentive, vigilant shopper. Pricing errors are most common on sale items, so you should note sales and special discounts as you shop. Take flyers or newspaper ads with you to the cash register, in case there is a dispute. If you can, always watch the price on the cash register screen as the prices are being rung in. If you see a mistake, point it out to the cashier immediately. If you think there is an error, try to have it corrected before you pay as it's easier to correct items this way. Check your receipt when you get home and don't be timid about calling the store to point out errors. Some stores have policies that may reward you with coupons or free products for your troubles. Some stores which become aware of scanner errors even offer refunds of double the difference of the price mistake to try to keep customers happy.

Don't be afraid to call the store to point out pricing errors that you missed as your items were being rung through. Some stores will reward you with coupons, free products or double the difference in an effort to keep customers happy.

If you notice a pattern of scanning inaccuracies in a store, bring it to the attention of the store's manager. Recurring problems can be reported to your local Fair Business Practices Branch, found in the blue pages of your phone book under Industry Canada. Stores that don't make an effort to correct pricing errors can face criminal charges.

ALERT

92

GAMBLING

Greg had a good job but never seemed to save any money. He played lotteries, bet on football and baseball games and enjoyed going to the casino once a month. He never considered himself to be a serious gambler, but playing slot machines, sport pools and poker seemed to take up a lot of his time and a considerable amount of his income.

Problem gambling is a blight on society that is not discussed as openly as it should be. Governments at all levels profit from lotteries, bingos and casinos and no one in power wants to make waves and delve into the serious distress that gambling causes families and relationships. There are countless cases of individuals who have gambled away their life savings, including situations where a wife works two jobs to pay the mortgage, because her husband has gambled away his paycheque, or a husband who stays with the children because their mother is playing bingo five nights a week. There are people who sit in front of slot machines like zombies, wasting an entire week's pay in just a few hours. I knew of one man who checked his lottery numbers in the morning and would often cry when he didn't win.

To gamble for entertainment or a recreational activity is fine, provided you don't get carried away and spend large amounts of money. When gambling starts to control your life and your budget, it is an addiction that you must conquer if you are ever to have savings and a retirement plan. Whether it's race-track betting, scratch and win lottery tickets or video poker, too often gamblers believe a lottery win or huge gambling score will set them up for life. More likely is that they will gamble good money after bad, spending winnings along the way on gambling as well.

Experts have likened the emotional psychological crash after gambling to a cocaine addict coming down after a high. The introduction of video lottery terminals or VLTs is causing problems for many communities across Canada. Whether it's the Maritimes or Alberta, studies have shown that there are negative social consequences in areas that have VLTs. Many municipalities allow casinos to be built to generate taxes, but casinos also suck millions of dollars out of communities and leave behind ravaged lives. There is also great concern about the effects of gambling on Canada's young people who witness adults gambling to excess at VLTs, casinos, and through purchases of scratch and win tickets.

Because governments at all levels make profits from lotteries, bingos and casinos, no one in power wants to delve into the serious distress that gambling causes families and relationships.

Gambling is recognized as a serious addiction problem and you can get help if gambling is detrimental for you or a loved one. The compulsive gambler has an inability to control himself around gambling, regardless of what has happened in the past. Information from gambling counselling services warns there are danger signs that could indicate that gambling has become a problem. The following questions are from Gamblers Anonymous and are designed to help determine if you have a gambling addiction. If you answer yes to seven or more of the following questions, you should seek help.

1. Do you ever lose time from work or school due to gambling?
2. Has gambling ever made your home life unhappy?
3. Has gambling affected your reputation?
4. Have you ever felt remorse after gambling?

5. Did you ever gamble to get money to try and pay debts or solve other financial problems?
6. Has gambling caused a decrease in your ambition or efficiency?
7. After losing, did you feel that you must return as soon as possible and win back your losses?
8. After a win, did you have a strong urge to return and win more?
9. Have you gambled until your last dollar was gone?
10. Have you ever borrowed to finance your gambling?
11. Have you ever sold anything to finance your gambling?
12. Have you ever been reluctant to use "gambling money" for normal expenditures?
13. Has gambling made you careless of your welfare or that of your family?
14. Did you ever gamble longer than you had planned?
15. Have you ever gambled to escape worry trouble?
16. Have you ever committed or considered committing an illegal act to finance gambling?
17. Has gambling ever caused you to have difficulty sleeping?
18. Do arguments, disappointments or frustrations create within you an urge to gamble?
19. Did you ever have an urge to celebrate any good fortune by gambling for a few hours?
20. Have you ever considered self destruction or suicide as a result of your gambling?

Gambling counselling centres should be available in your area to offer help and advice. If you can't find one call your local elected official or municipal office. Once you enter counselling all information will be kept private and confidential.

SMALL CLAIMS COURT

Omar ran a small construction business and entered into a deal to build a garage for someone who had contacted him through the want ads. The person bought the materials and Omar spent the next three weeks building the garage. When it was done, he asked the person for payment. The person refused, saying that the construction of the garage was not satisfactory. When Omar told the man that he would sue to get the money owed to him, the man told him to go ahead. Hiring a lawyer and going to court would cost Omar more than what the job was worth. Omar was confused and angry about what to do.

Small Claims Court is a relatively inexpensive way to resolve disputes where the amount of money involved is less than $3,000 to $10,000, depending on the province. Small Claims Court offers a more informal atmosphere than regular court proceedings. Complainants can explain their side of the story to a judge to settle disputes concerning money and property. Cases can be filed in every area of the country but each Small Claims Court division falls under provincial jurisdiction.

Going to court will differ slightly in each province. For example, the Ontario Superior Court of Justice's *How to Make Small Claims Court Work for You* outlines general guidelines to help anyone going to Small Claims Court get a fair and impartial hearing. Ontario's guide can serve as a general overview for Small Claims Courts across Canada. There are limits on how much you can claim in damages and compensation and they change from time to time, so you check the maximum amount recoverable in court before proceeding with a case. In Ontario, you can sue for up to $10,000 not including interest and costs. Going to Small Claims Court requires some time and effort, but it is a simpler, inexpensive way to deal with a number of situations.

A plaintiff can go to Small Claims Court to seek money that is owed because of a loan that has not been repaid or to seek money that is owed for goods or services done by someone such as an electrician, dentist or contractor. Perhaps money is owed because of an N.S.F. cheque, or a tenant has failed to pay the rent. A person can also make a claim if she believes she has suffered a loss caused by another person such as property damage precipitated by careless service such as during a delivery or the dry cleaning process. A plaintiff may seek money if a service was not up to the standard agreed upon between the seller and buyer, such as a wedding catering service that grossly underestimated the food needed to serve invited guests. A person may go to court if a contract has not been carried out, if there has been damage to property caused by someone's else's negligence, or if there has been a personal injury caused by another party.

You may also go to Small Claims Court to seek the return of personal property that is in the possession of another person. It could be the lawn mower the neighbour borrowed and never returned, or a painting, set of tools or four wheeler. The person would have to prove without a doubt that the property is in fact theirs. A somewhat controversial new twist in Ontario is added by the *Parental Responsibility Act, 2000*, where a parent can be sued for damage done by a child under the age of 18 who intentionally takes, damages or destroys property. In most cases a person will represent themselves in court but you can have a lawyer or a law student assist you. It is also your right to file documents in French and request a judge who speaks French.

There are Small Claims Courts offices across Canada and you must file a claim where the problem occurred, where the party whom the claim is against lives or does business, or where the court is closest to where the defendant lives or does business. You will need to fill out claim forms and include information about the defendant in the case. You will have to have as much relevant information as possible regarding your claim, such as the cheque that bounced or the contract that was not honoured. If you are seeking interest, state this in your claim. The court claim will have to be served so the defendant is aware of what is transpiring. You may choose to serve the claim yourself, have someone else do it or have a lawyer arrange it. You must serve a claim within six months or it will have to be renewed by a judge.

If a claim is made against you, how you respond depends on your situation. You may decide that the claim is completely false and file a defense with the Small Claims Court office. You may agree that you do owe the money and to avoid going to court, you should pay the amount owed within 20 calendar days of receiving the claim. You may believe you only owe a portion of the money and you can file a defense stating only the part you feel you should have to pay. By settling with the person the amount you owe, the court case will only be for the amount that is still in dispute. You may also agree that you owe the money but that you can't afford to pay it right away. You must file a defense stating how much you owe and spell out your intentions on how you plan to pay it back. Alternatively you may feel that you don't owe that person money, but instead that he owes it to you! If you can, you should try to settle matters before they go to trial, and this will save you time and money.

If you end up in Small Claims Court and win, the person who owes you the money should pay it promptly. Of course this does not always happen. She may say she won't or can't pay and ignore the court order. You will then need to move ahead and ask the court to enforce an unpaid judgment which will involve either garnishment of wages or seizure of assets. For more information on going to Small Claims Court, contact the Small Claims Court or Provincial Court nearest you for self help guides and other information. You may also need to speak to a lawyer or experienced agent who understands Small Claims Court proceedings. Rest assured, you do have an avenue to recoup monies owed to you, if you are treated unfairly by a person or business.

CYBERSECURITY

Like many people, Sheila used the Internet to communicate with friends and family. She also enjoyed visiting chat rooms and discussing topics of the day. She started to communicate often with a chat room user named "George" and after a while, they exchanged e-mail addresses. George sent her a picture of himself and she was captivated by his attractive and harmless look. They decided to meet in a public place. Sheila sat in a coffee shop for over an hour, but George never showed up. There was a man there however, who stared at her and gave her the creeps.

The Internet is an exceptional invention that has changed our society forever. Originally it was created to allow government computers to communicate in case of war. It has become a world-wide network of personal computers that enables people to correspond, research or do business in cyberspace. It is unregulated and owned by no person, company or government. On the Internet, almost anything goes and while there are tremendous benefits to using this exciting technology, there are also certain safety parameters that users should adhere to.

First and foremost, parents should be aware of how their children are using the Internet, as pornography and hate crime materials are easily accessible with the click of a mouse button. There are certain software programs that can filter out offensive material and the history feature on most Internet browsers allows you to view sites that have been visited by anyone using the computer. Parents should know exactly what their children are doing on-line and if they are participating in chat rooms. Like any activity, it's best not to spend endless hours on one thing. Monitor your child's Internet usage and keep the computer in an accessible family room, rather than a child's locked bedroom.

You or your children should never give out personal information on-line. Talking in a chat room may be happening in cyberspace, but if you give out your name, address or phone number, this constitutes contact with someone in the real world. A person saying that she is a 14-year-old girl in cyberspace could actually be a 52-year-old male pervert. There have been many documented cases of this situation happening. In the example, Sheila expected to meet "George," a handsome man. Just because someone sends you a photo on the Internet doesn't mean that it's really them. It's never a good idea to send your picture to someone you don't know. Once a photo is digitally sent on the Internet, it could end up anywhere in the world! It could also be used in ways you wouldn't appreciate or find appropriate.

Create code names for yourself and your children who use the Internet. Be polite and courteous when communicating with others on-line, the same way you would in person. Being disrespectful and abusive on the Internet, known as "flaming," is bad "netiquette." Be aware that the Internet is being used to send junk e-mail and fraudulent material. Many of us have a tendency to believe what we see in black and white. When you read something on the Internet, it could have just been written by one person in his basement and may not be based on fact. Web sites can be made to look like professional organizations, when they're not. This is a problem for investors who research on-line and who believe that they are getting independent, trustworthy information, when they may be reading erroneous, red herring material. Let common sense prevail on-line and if you ever are concerned that you are receiving harassing, threatening or hateful messages, contact the police. They can advise you on how to best deal with the situation.

MOVING TROUBLES

Gilles and Sylvie were moving from their apartment into a condominium. They picked a mover from the yellow pages and received an estimate as to how much it would cost for the cross-city move. However, once their goods were loaded onto the moving truck, the movers said that they had miscalculated how much stuff the couple had. They demanded double the negotiated moving price. When Gilles and Sylvie refused, the movers left with their goods and said that they would be kept in storage until they paid their bill in full. Despite their protests, they ended up paying the extra money to get their household goods back.

Moving can be a stressful time and every year, hundreds of thousands of Canadians count on moving companies to get their belongings safely from their old address to their new one. Each year, there are also thousands of complaints from consumers concerning movers who have overcharged them, lost furniture and damaged their property. What happened to Gilles and Sylvie is a common complaint and a scam used by movers to get extra money from clients. Moving companies may low-ball a customer to get a moving contract. But once the furniture is loaded onto the truck, they will say they underestimated the amount of furniture and time needed to complete the move.

Once the furniture is in the truck, the customer's goods are held hostage as the unscrupulous mover tries to extort money from the client. There are countless horror stories of movers who charge hidden fees for padding or unnecessary packing materials and of movers who have damaged or lost their clients' property and make no effort to reimburse them.

Many of the problems that arise with a move happen because movers are unregulated across Canada and consumers are usually left to fight back against dishonest companies on their own. Complications also arise when people are moving from province to province, where laws may differ and consumers could be left thousands of kilometres away, at a new address without their belongings. A dissatisfied client may seek to go to court, which can be time-consuming and costly. If your belongings are locked up in storage, you may not be able to wait the months it could take to hear your case. This is why many people simply break down and pay the additional charges so they can get their goods back.

When hiring a moving company, get at least three estimates and determine how the estimate is made, based on weight, time and distance. Find out if your goods are automatically insured, or if you need to pay extra or pursue other protection.

Government agencies and consumer protection groups now recognize that some disreputable movers have been abusing the public for a long time and getting away with it. Changes to consumer protection legislation are being discussed across Canada to better protect the public from dishonest operators. Auto mechanics must give estimates in writing and stick to them, unless they receive permission from customers first for additional repairs or charges. Movers should face a similar criterion. All prices, terms and services should be agreed to before the moving job commences and any goods are packed and loaded. There should never be an increase in the bill of more than 10% and consumers should not have to pay for charges that were not properly disclosed. Regardless of fine print in contracts, moving companies should not be able to use contractual language as an excuse to lose or damage goods since the timely delivery of intact articles is what the consumer is paying for. However, these new directives are not yet in place in many parts of the country so you must pick a mover carefully to avoid disputes.

When hiring a moving company, try to get at least three written estimates. Depending on the mover, the estimate could be determined on weight, time spent on the move and the distance involved. Find out if your goods will automatically be insured while in the movers' care. Do you need to purchase additional insurance from the mover? Will your home insurance policy cover your goods if they are damaged during a move?

If you do your own packing, make sure you do a thorough job of trying to protect your goods. Many complaints arise after goods are unpacked and found broken. The mover can say it's your fault for the way you packaged the items. If the mover is doing the packing, make sure you know upfront how much it is going to cost, as custom packing can be expensive.

Most importantly, know whom you are dealing with! If you know someone who has moved recently, ask him or her who they used and if it was a positive experience. Find out how long the mover has been in business, and if there are unresolved complaints against them with the Better Business Bureau. If your move is work related, you may be able to get advice through your company, and assistance in finding a reputable mover. Be aware that you may be eligible for tax breaks if your move is work related. You may consider going with a large reputable firm when choosing a mover. An independent mover may appear to have a lower price, but if that company tries to pull some of the tactics discussed in this Alert, you may end up paying a lot more in the end. A reputable mover is also more likely to have a dispute process in place, if a problem does arise.

LOST LUGGAGE

Angelo took a flight to Los Angeles from Vancouver to meet an old friend and do some sightseeing. In his luggage, he packed a portable computer and a digital camera. When he arrived, his luggage was missing. He was told it would be located, but it was never found. Angelo assumed he would be compensated for his $3,000 computer and $800 camera. He was shocked when the airline offered him only $400 in compensation.

Nothing quite ruins a trip like lost luggage. But what many travellers fail to realize is that they will be paid only the bare minimum if their bags go missing. While many missing suitcases turn up after a day or two, if yours ends up on the conveyor belt of no return, don't expect to receive what your suitcase and contents are actually worth. Often the compensation offered by airline, train and bus companies barely covers the cost of the suitcase.

Somewhere on the plane, train or bus ticket, the company will usually spell out their lost luggage policy. It may have a dollar limit of $250 per lost bag or it may reimburse passengers based on the suitcase's weight. For instance, some airlines will pay $20 per kilogram in compensation, to a maximum of 20 kilograms. Transportation services have different policies regarding lost luggage and it's up to you to know ahead of time how much you'll be covered for if it's lost. You may be able to buy additional insurance, if you are carrying or shipping expensive items.

Knowing that an airline is unlikely to offer adequate compensation means that you should take precautions when you travel. Don't check a suitcase containing expensive items such as jewellery, personal digital assistants or cell phones. All of these compact expensive items should go on-board with you, in a carry-on bag. Also, never check a suitcase containing something you consider an absolute necessity. Medication, glasses or contact lenses, an important business speech or clothing for a wedding needed shortly after your arrival is better off close at hand than in the belly of an airport terminal. While theft by baggage handlers is unlikely, it does happen. Some airlines now offer suitcase wrapping services to ensure that luggage won't be opened during transit.

> Medication, glasses or contact lenses, an important business speech or clothing for a wedding needed shortly after your arrival is better off close at hand than in the belly of an airport terminal.

Depending on the carrier, if your luggage is misplaced for 12 hours, a day or a week, you may be compensated. You may be reimbursed for clothes, toiletries and other items that you had to buy while waiting for your suitcase to arrive. Check before spending money to make sure you will get it back and keep receipts. Transportation companies set compensation limitations to avoid fraudulent claims by travellers, but they don't want to anger or lose future customers. If you are not satisfied with the compensation you get for a lost or late bag, it can pay to complain. A letter, on company letterhead if you have it, explaining how your luggage was lost and the trouble that it caused you can sometimes, but not always, cause an airline to reward you with free air miles, a break on a future trip or an upgrade to first class.

EXTENDED WARRANTIES — Are They Worth It?

When Julie was buying a new television set, the salesperson told her that she should pay extra and get an extended warranty. He claimed it would give her piece of mind and that if anything ever went wrong with the television, she would be protected. The TV was priced at $500 and she went ahead and bought a three-year extended warranty at an additional cost of $80. Afterward, she wondered if it was the wise thing to do.

Many new appliances and products are being pitched with an extended warranty offer. A warranty may mean additional protection for some consumers, but more often than not, it's just an easy way for the retailer to make additional money on the sale. Extended warranties can be tremendous cash cows for businesses. When you buy an extended warranty, you are betting that the product will fail, whereas the retailer is betting it won't. Extended warranties can be expensive, some as much as 20% of the price of the product. When you buy a brand-new VCR for $300, do you really want to spend another $60 in case something goes wrong with it?

Retailers are also in the driver's seat knowing the average life of the products they make. If the equipment you buy does break down, it can often be fixed at a cheaper cost than the price of the extended warranty. *Consumer Reports* magazine, a respected consumer protection publication, did research into extended warranty offers to see if they are worth getting. Paul Reynolds, with *Consumer Reports*, says, "the first year of an extended warranty or service plan mostly duplicates what's in the factory warranty. And the extras you do get with the plan, like routine maintenance, usually aren't needed." Researchers found that the extra coverage is rarely worth buying and the odds that most equipment will need repairs in the first five years is less than one in four. Depending on the product, you also may want to replace it rather than fix it.

Of course, only you know if an extended warranty might make sense for your situation. My daughter spends a lot of time on the phone and for Christmas we bought her a modern $40 hands-free phone, the kind you can wear around your neck with a headset. The store offered a $10 three-year extended warranty. The phone would be replaced free of charge if anything were to happen to it. With all the fine wires in the small phone and knowing how my teenager was likely to bang it around while using it, I thought the $10 might be a good investment. I was glad I did as six months after I bought it, it quit working and we had it replaced. Who knows if we may have to replace it again?

Researchers at *Consumer Reports* did find that an extended warranty might be a worthwhile investment on projection televisions and digital camcorders because both are expensive to fix. A new car just off the lot will usually come with a three-year warranty, so buying additional coverage may not be necessary. Beware of extended warranties on used cars as they are often expensive and offer extremely limited protection. Read the fine print to be sure of exactly what kind of coverage you're getting. Weigh the risks for yourself when considering extended warranties and don't be talked into buying one by smooth talking sales staff.

MAILING LIST MULTIPLICATION

Renee lives a good life and enjoys giving money to charity when she can afford to. She does get frustrated though because it seems whenever she helps one cause, she is then bombarded by others. In fact, after donating to one charity she received more than 50 letters from other charities over the next year — all seeking money! Renee wishes she could do more, but she can't give to all the charities requesting funds and throwing out the letters makes her feel guilty.

Many Canadians do not realize that the buying and selling of names and addresses in this country is a big business that generates tens of millions of dollars. That's why when people like Renee donate money to a cause that fights heart disease, she may then be contacted by other health-related charities representing lung disease, cancer, diabetes and so on. People donating money to a charity that deals with pets, for example, may find that they are then contacted by other animal-related charities that hope they will also be considered for a donation.

Direct mail marketers operate by sending solicitations to millions of individuals hoping that some people won't simply throw them out. Of course many people do, so those who actually respond with a donation are considered hot property or a "hot name." Individual companies, charities and even governments are in the business of renting and selling names. Names are also traded with telephone solicitors, who use "hot names" to narrow down whom they believe will be most likely to make a donation.

The selling of names in this country is legal, but consumers can also request to have their names removed from mailing and telephone solicitation lists. The agency that oversees direct mail marketing in this country is the Canadian Marketing Association (CMA). It is a self-regulating body whose membership includes Canada's major financial institutions, publishers, catalogues, advertising agencies and charities. In 1997, the association had more than 650 corporate members, accounting for more than 80% of the annual $11.2 billion spent in direct response marketing sales in Canada. Member organizations must adhere to a *Code of Ethics and Standards of Practice* and the association professes to be interested in helping consumers who do not wish to be bothered by unwanted advertising.

Consumers who do not want their names bought and sold can take steps to stop it. John Gustavson, the President of the CMA, says consumers can halt the trading, exchanging and renting of their name. "Simply tell the charity that you are making a donation to that you do not want your name given to any other group," he says. You can also stop the annoying letters and calls by asking that your name be removed from most lists by writing, faxing or e-mailing the Canadian Marketing Association (contact information at end of Alert). Consumers should request the CMA's Do Not Mail/Do Not Call service. Gustavson says that "this will get rid of 80% of the addressed advertising to your home."

The members of the association must honour your request not to be bothered by mailing and phone solicitation campaigns. The service is free. Groups that are not members of the association such as local carpet cleaners and local charities are not included in the service. Every three months, individuals who have registered with the service will have their names sent to association members who are obligated to remove the names from marketing lists. Consumers who request to have their names removed should see a reduction in addressed advertising mail and telephone solicitations within three months. The consumer's name will remain on the deletion list for a period of three years. After this time, you may have to request the service again.

This service will not stop delivery of flyers and other unaddressed advertising mail. Subscribing to the Do Not Mail/Do Not Call service could also prevent other companies such as catalogue and coupon businesses from mailing you items. If you move to a new address, you may want to register your new address with the service. Consumers can also limit their mail volume by informing their favourite mail order company that they wish to be kept on an "in house" list. This way, they can receive their desired mailings but their names will not be bought or sold to other marketers.

Contacting the Canadian Marketing Association and asking for the Do Not Mail/Do Not Call service will result in an 80% reduction in addressed mail within three months.

To request the Do Not Mail/Do Not Call service, write to The Canadian Marketing Association, One Concorde Gate, Suite 607, Don Mills, Ontario, M3C 3N6. You can also check their Web site at www.the-cma.org or fax them at 416-441-4062. All requests should include the full name (plus any spelling variations you find on mail solicitations) of all members of the home who wish to be registered for the service. Include your full address, postal code and telephone number with area code.

UV PROTECTIVE SUNGLASSES

Mary was never one to spend a lot of money on sunglasses and when she did buy a pair, she usually made her decision based on style. If she bought sunglasses for her children, she usually paid the bare minimum — cheap glasses with dark lenses. She thought as long as the lenses were dark in colour, they must offer protection against the sun's damaging rays.

It's a misconception that all dark sunglasses offer protection against the sun's ultraviolet rays. In fact, eye care professionals say that you're better off wearing no sunglasses, than wearing ones with dark lenses that don't offer UV protection. Dr. Josh Josephson, Chairman of Josephson Opticians, says that dark lenses without UV filters can cause the pupil to widen and let in even more damaging sunlight. "The tint itself has no UV protective factor at all. There is an ultraviolet component that is added to plastic to make it UV protective," explains Dr. Josephson.

Everyone is susceptible to the sun's harmful rays and over-exposure to sunlight can lead to a wide variety of medical conditions. The most common is the early onset of cataracts, a clouding of the lens which makes it difficult to see clearly. UV rays may be a causative factor in macular degeneration, a retinal disease that could lead to early loss of vision. Other experts say that keratitis, the inflammation of the cornea and pterygium and an abnormal growth of tissue on the white part of the eye, can also be attributed to excessive ultraviolet radiation. Years of exposure to sunlight could also lead to skin cancer around the eye. Some studies have shown that people living in tropical areas with more intense sunlight can have vision problems earlier than those in less sunny climates.

You should wear sunglasses that conform to the shape of your face and never assume that sunglasses offer UV protection unless they clearly say they do. There will usually be a sticker on the lens that clearly states the amount of UV protection. There are both long (UVA) and short (UVB) wavelengths of ultraviolet radiation. "When buying sunglasses, you want to make sure that they are fully UV protective. That means blocking all light below 400 nanometers and some glasses will say that on the label. If it just says UV protection, then it's too general and it may not be fully protective," Dr. Josephson says. It's the number 400 that you should be looking for. The label on the glasses should indicate that they offer 100% UV protection or protection to 400 nanometers. Anything less will not provide complete protection. Also, never stare at the sun as it takes only 10 to 15 seconds for the sun's intense light to burn your retina, the seeing layer of the eye.

Overexposure to sunlight can cause a variety of medical conditions including cataracts, macular degeneration, and keratitis. Sunglasses which offer full UV protection are the best way to protect your eyes.

If you are buying sunglasses in discount stores or from street vendors be sure to check for proof of UV protection. Young children are the most vulnerable to UV radiation. Parents may be tempted to buy cheap sunglasses for their children, knowing that they may only wear them a couple of times at the beach before losing them. But a child's eye actually lets in more light, so the sun can potentially do more damage. "Their eyes are at greater risk of ultraviolet exposure as compared to a mature adult eye," Dr. Josephson says. Parents should make sure that sunglasses for their children offer full UV protection and they should also encourage their children to wear them.

Sunglasses also help protect the eyes from highly reflective surfaces such as water and snow. You don't have to spend a lot of money to get good eye wear. You can purchase relatively inexpensive sunglasses that still offer full UV protection. But check the label! If it doesn't promise that the glasses are 100% UV protective, they probably aren't.

TATTOO REMOVAL

When Tony was a teenager, he decided on impulse to get a tattoo. He went into a tattoo parlour, picked a design off the wall and ended up with a large dragon etched on his arm. Not long after having the tattoo, he regretted his decision. The dragon that he thought looked cool as a teen became a symbol he didn't want as he got older. Tony wasn't sure how to get rid of the tattoo, or if he even could.

Tattooing has been around for thousands of years and was originally used as a form of identification. Tattoos are back in vogue and many people are proud of the art they have on their bodies. However, there are others who for various reasons regret getting permanent lifelong tattoos. Dr. Frank Beninger is a Toronto plastic surgeon who specializes in tattoo removal. He says his clients have tattoos removed for many different reasons. "Some are younger people who have homemade tattoos that were done when they were teenagers and they now regret it. Others have had their spouse, boyfriend or girlfriend's name as a tattoo and the relationship ends, so they no longer want it," says Beninger. "A tattoo can sometimes interfere with jobs or family. A tattooed parent may be concerned that they're setting a bad example or they just don't like it anymore. A cute teddy bear when you're twenty may not look so cute when you're forty or fifty."

Government-funded health care will usually not pay for tattoo removal, unless there are exceptional circumstances such as a cult symbol or religious tattoo that must be removed because it's affecting a person's mental health. For the most part, you will have to pay to have your tattoo removed and it's not cheap. A tattoo that cost $200 to get, may cost more than $1,000 to remove. The expense to remove a tattoo will depend on how elaborate it is, its size and colour. Dr. Beninger uses laser treatments to get rid of tattoos. The laser shatters the pigment of the tattoo and after several treatments, the tattoo may fade to a point where it is *almost* no longer noticeable.

> If you are considering a tattoo, look at it as being permanent. Some can be removed but they will usually leave behind permanent scarring or obvious blemishes on the skin.

If you have a tattoo or are thinking of getting one, be aware that not all tattoos can be completely removed. They will usually leave behind permanent scarring or obvious blemishes on the surface of the skin and some colours are more complex to eliminate than others. "Yellows, reds and oranges are the most difficult colours to remove," says Beninger. "Not all tattoos can be fully removed and not all of them can be removed without leaving some scarring or change in the skin." As well as lasers, tattoos can be removed through dermabrasion — the scraping of the skin, or by using skin grafts — actually cutting out the tattoo and using skin grafts or stitching together the wound.

Don't acquire a tattoo thinking that you can just get rid of it later. Dr. Beninger says "look at a tattoo as being permanent. However, if you're going to get one and think you might get it removed later, black is easier to remove than some other colours. You should just really think it over before getting one in the first place." The people who seem to suffer from "tattoo regret" are those who got a tattoo without planning ahead. If you want a tattoo, consider all your options, the colours, placement and size. Be as sure as you can that the art you are choosing is something you will still want on your body in future decades. While attitudes regarding tattooing have changed, many people still associate tattoos with gangs and lower levels of society, which is not necessarily the case. Still, why let a tattoo on your arm limit your job prospects?

Be extremely careful when choosing a tattoo artist, as tattooing is potentially dangerous. If the tattooist does not follow strict sterile procedures, the viruses that cause hepatitis and AIDS can be transmitted through the needles used to inject the dyes into the skin. Along with the tattoo craze came another fad — temporary or fake tattoos. If you're unsure if you want a permanent tattoo, start with a temporary tattoo to help you decide if a lasting tattoo is really for you.

CHOOSING A DAYCARE CENTRE

Heather had stayed home with her new baby Erika for eight months but because of her family's financial situation, she and her husband Dennis decided it was best that she return to work. The couple knew they would need a safe, caring place to leave their precious child but had no idea where to start looking for daycare. A nanny was too expensive for their budget and they were unsure if they should use a daycare centre or leave their baby with someone watching children in their own home. Heather and Dennis were confused, anxious and worried about what to do.

While many parents would like to stay at home with their child or children, most have no other option but to use some form of daycare. It's estimated that 85% of Canadian mothers end up back at work within a year of their child's birth. While the federal government has extended parental leave to one full year as of January 1, 2001, many parents will still need someone to care for their children when they return to the workforce. In some families, grandparents or relatives may be able to offer child care; however in most situations, families do not have this option, which can cause parents stress, worry and guilt.

Taking the time and effort to find the right child care provider will pay off by giving you peace of mind and allowing your child to be cared for in a loving, healthy and emotionally stable environment. Children are deeply affected by their early experiences and the daycare provider who watches over your children in your absence will have a significant impact on their lives.

Cheri Szereszewski runs CGS Early Childhood Consulting, a childhood consulting business which helps parents decide what kind of child care would be best suited for their families. "Each family has to decide what is right for them. If you decide daycare is necessary, then you should do your utmost to find ways to build quality time with your child at other times of the week," says Szereszewski. "You may wish to set aside blocks of time when no one does anything but spend time together as a family. It could be mealtime, bedtime or whenever."

She advises parents to consider more than just cost, when choosing child care. "I really believe when it comes to child care, this is one area you don't want to skimp on, because you are entrusting the most precious thing in the world to someone else. I don't think child care is something where you want to risk saving a few dollars here and there." There are tax breaks and tax credits for parents who use daycare and there may be subsidized daycare spots available in your area, depending on your income level. Generally speaking daycare for an infant to a two-and-a-half year old toddler will cost $175 a week, while two-and-a-half years and older will cost $150 a week.

The first thing you have to do is determine what days and hours you work, and if you have a partner, his or her schedule as well. You will want to find daycare near your workplace or home. There are three main child care options — a nanny, a daycare centre or child care provided in a private home. A nanny is the most expensive route to go but a nanny may also be able to do some house-cleaning, meal preparation and laundry while the baby is napping. "If a nanny takes over some of the household chores, this can free you up when you get home to spend quality time with your child rather than having to start doing housework," says Szereszewski. A nanny may also allow you greater flexibility in your work hours as daycare centres and private home care providers generally have set hours. Be aware that there is a huge waiting list for baby spots at many daycare centres and in some areas, couples actually put their names on waiting lists before they are even expecting a child! Infant care is also the most expensive because the caregiver/child ratio is much lower.

Szereszewski believes that infants and toddlers are best cared for in a home environment. "Good quality home childcare can provide a really positive, nurturing start for a child as it's very much like being at home," says Szereszewski. While there are many unregulated home daycare providers, Szereszewski says it's important to choose a provider from a *licenced home child care agency.* This ensures that provincial ministry standards are being met as licenced providers receive training and may be monitored by impromptu visits to ensure children are being well cared for. This system benefits the licenced operator as well, as he or she has someone to call for help or advice. In a licenced home care situation, there are also on-going requirements including criminal reference checks on daycare providers. Reference checks are done on anyone who works with children and while it won't necessarily screen out everyone with a less than appropriate background, it does eliminate a lot of potential problems. In addition, should your child care provider be unavailable due to illness or vacation, the agency arranges for back-up care for your child. This is important because if your provider is unavailable, one parent has to stay home from work, which can be a problem both financially and emotionally for parents.

> Keep in mind that many daycare centres keep strict hours of operation and that they want children picked up on time! To enforce their business hours, some daycares charge a dollar for every minute that parents are late.

In a home child care setting, there are also much smaller ratios so it's more likely a child will get individual attention. In a daycare centre, activities are more scheduled to the average, meaning children generally eat and take naps at around the same time. "For infants, a home environment is more suitable, but once a child hits 18 months to two-and-a-half years old, social interaction becomes quite critical, so that can be a good time to enroll a child in a daycare centre," advises Szereszewski.

If you are interested in having someone care for your child in your home or in theirs, you will want to know as much as you can about that person. Who are they? Why have they decided to care for children? Is it because they are staying home with their own children and desire extra income? What is their experience? Ask the caregiver for references — and check them. Put together a written agreement describing the days, hours of work and payment schedule. Include details such as who is responsible for snacks and include emergency contact numbers if the child is hurt or becomes ill.

Some daycare centres are licensed to look after children six weeks and older, while others look after children two-and-a-half years and up. In each province, the office responsible for daycare licensing (check the blue pages under daycare) can tell you the daycare centres in your area. After you make a list of the ones you want to visit, set up an appointment with the director or supervisor. "I would not visit at naptime, but at a time when it would be an active playtime for the children. This way you can get a really good picture of what happens in a typical day," advises Szereszewski.

Make observations about the daycare centre such as what is the atmosphere like? Is it relaxed? Is it clean? Are the bathrooms neat and tidy? Are the children involved in activities or are they running around with no focus? Are there books to read? Are there creative ideas to challenge the children? "Make sure all areas of development such as social, creative, sensory, cognitive, language, fine motor skills, and gross motor skills are being developed," says Szereszewski.

Observe the staff. "Are they sitting up on chairs overseeing children or are they getting right down to their level, eye-to-eye, involved and interacting with the children. This is very important," Szereszewski says. Caregivers should be interested, energetic and genuinely enjoying and responding to the children. Ask about philosophy of discipline. What will they do if one child hits another? What if your child doesn't want to eat? What if your child doesn't want to nap at naptime? Also insure that the centre is licenced by a government body and that staff is fully trained and qualified. Province to province training requirements vary from college degrees to six month training programs.

A daycare centre will usually have hours starting from 7:00 to 8:00 am and close between 5:30 and 6:00 pm. Typical daycare centres will offer year round, full daycare services for children of all ages and some may offer onsite kindergarten classes. Keep in mind that daycare centres keep strict hours of operation and that they want *children picked up on time!* To enforce their business hours, some daycares charge a dollar for every minute that parents are late. Szereszewski says, "it gets expensive to have staff stay after hours to care for one, two or three children, so they really want to discourage people from being late." However, don't always be in a rush when dropping off and picking up your child. Leave a few minutes to either speak to staff or to see for yourself how your child acts in the daycare setting.

Many parents fear that their child could be the victim of physical or sexual abuse. While the vast majority of all daycare centres are loving caring places, parents must be aware that abuse could occur. If your child is unusually fearful of going to child care, has unexplained bruises or other signs of physical abuse, or talks about inappropriate actions on the part of adults or other children, you may want to consider making other child care arrangements. If you are worried that your child or any child in a child care setting is being abused, report it to the Children's Aid Society.

Szereszewski's child care consulting business suggests some excellent questions you should ask when searching for child care. By asking the following questions, you should be able to find a comfortable and caring environment that will benefit your entire family.

Play

- What activities with infants or toddlers do you enjoy the most?
- What learning activities do you do with young children?
- How would you plan a day with my child(ren)? (Encourage the caregiver to give details.)

- When you take my child(ren) out, where would you go? What would you do?
- How much TV do you think is good for children? What kinds of shows are appropriate for infants or toddlers?

Safety and Health

- One of my biggest fears is ...(my child falls off a swing, chokes, stops breathing, etc.). What would you do if this happened?
- How could you prevent it from happening?
- Under what circumstances would you call me at work?
- What would you do if my child became ill suddenly or were injured?
- What kind of first aid training do you have?

Nutrition and Sleep

- How would you introduce my toddler to new foods?
- What would you serve my toddler for lunch?
- What would you do if my child(ren) refuses to eat?
- How do you settle a child who refuses to sleep? What if nothing works?
- How do you give a child a bottle?
- How do you deal with a child who cries continuously for a half-hour after his parents leave?
- What would you do if a child put his bowl on his head? Eats with his fingers? Throws food? Hits you?
- What methods of discipline do you find work best with an infant or toddler?
- What kinds of behaviour do you set limits on?
- Think of other children you have cared for. What behaviour irritated you most? How did you deal with it?
- How do you handle a child who whines? Bites? Has temper tantrums?

Personal Suitability

- What do you like most about child care?
- What child care situations have you worked with? What did you like best about these situations? Least? How did you deal with it?

- What are your reasons for leaving your present job? (Compare answers with the caregiver's references.)
- What are your interests and hobbies?
- What are your expectations of parents?

Details of the Job
- Do you have any questions?
- May I have the names of two parents whose children you have cared for as references?
- What are your salary expectations?
- Are you flexible about hours? Changes in day (with notice)?

If considering a home care situation, survey all areas that your child would have access to and observe the "child-proofing" that has been done. For example, are there safety caps on electrical plugs or cords that your child could get caught in? Are knives stored safely out of reach or in a locked cupboard? Be sure to ask about methods of discipline and how they would handle situations where a child is not sharing, or is physical with another child, etc.

Take the time to find the right child care provider for your family and lifestyle. The resulting peace of mind will benefit everyone and allow you to be productive, knowing your child is happy and safe.

CONTACTS

Contact information generously provided by Industry Canada.

GOVERNMENT OFFICES / 314
BETTER BUSINESS BUREAUS / 316
YOUR AUTOMOBILE / 318

Manufacturers' Head Offices / 318

Automobile Protection Association (APA) / 319
The APA is a non-profit auto industry watchdog working for improved legislation, industry sales practices and automobile safety.

Dispute Resolution

Canadian Motor Vehicle Arbitration Plan (CAMVAP) / 319
CAMVAP resolves disputes between consumers and vehicle manufacturers. Issues are put before a third party (arbitrator) for resolution. More information is available on its Web site: www.camvap.ca.

Marketplace Standards & Services Branch, Consumer Services Bureau (Ontario) / 320
This office handles car repair complaints and reviews them for contravention of the *Ontario Motor Vehicle Repair Act*.

Alberta Motor Vehicle Industry Council (AMVIC) / 320

Ontario Motor Vehicle Industry Council (OMVIC) / 320
OMVIC is a not-for-profit, self-managed industry counsel, delegated to administer the *Motor Vehicle Dealers Act*. OMVIC regulates/registers dealers and salespersons and handles consumer complaints, dealership inspections and investigations.

Insurance Corporation of British Columbia (ICBC) / 320
ICBC offers dispute resolution between itself and its clients.

Consumer and Non-Governmental Groups

Automobile Protection Association / 321
This is a consumer watchdog of the automobile industry.

Automobile Journalists Association of Canada / 321
Journalists provide reviews of automobiles.

overview of the typical steps involved in buying a house through a real estate agent. The Real Estate Council of Alberta (RECA) is responsible for the regulation of the real estate industry in the province.

YOUR MONEY / 327

Helpful Numbers / 327

Canadian Banking Ombudsman / 328

Your Bank's Ombudsman / 328

Self and Government Regulation of Banks

Canadian Bankers Association (CBA) / 329
The CBA develops industry standards and provides a forum for dialogue between the banks and the public.

Office of the Superintendent of Financial Institutions (OSFI) / 329
OSFI is the primary regulator of federal financial institutions and pension plans.

Trust Companies, Credit Unions, Co-operatives and Caisses Populaires / 329
If you cannot resolve your problems with your financial institution, contact one of the government regulations listed here.

Securities
Before purchasing securities you may want to seek out information and advice. Four sources — from consumer groups to industry associations — that answer securities questions are set out below.

Canadian Shareowners Association (CSA) / 331
The CSA is an independent non-profit organization whose mandate is to educate Canadians on successful investing. It currently has approximately 10,000 members ($89 annual membership) and ten regional chapters have been formed in cities across Canada. It also produces and distributes the *Canadian Shareowner* magazine on a bi-monthly basis ($68/year subscription).

The Investor Learning Centre of Canada (ILC) / 331
The ILC is a not-for-profit organization dedicated to providing non-promotional investment materials.

Investment Fund Institute of Canada (IFIC) / 331
The IFIC is the national association of the Investment Funds Industry. Its responsibilities include broadening the public

awareness and understanding of mutual funds and the overall investment funds industry.

The Canadian Association of Financial Planners (CAFP) / 331
The CAFP can explain the role of a financial planner and give advice on choosing an appropriate planner.

Securities Commisions / 331

Insurance. See Your Health.

YOUR HEALTH / 333

Health Canada

Headquarters / 333

Regional Offices / 333

Provinical Departments and Ministries of Health / 333

Canadian Food Inspection Agency / 334

Consumer and Non-Governmental Groups

The Canadian Hard of Hearing Association (CHHA) / 334
CHHA is a non-profit, self-help, bilingual consumer organization run by and for persons who are hard of hearing. CHHA creates public awareness and seeks standards for technical devices such as hearing aids.

Carrefour Adaption Quebec / 335
Multiples services spécialisés: conseils techniques, guides d'achat, soutien juridique.

Office des personnes handicapées du Quebec / 335
Multiples services spécialisés: conseils techniques, guides d'achat, soutien juridique.

Dietitians of Canada / 335

National Institute of Nutrition (NIN) / 335
The NIN is a national non-profit organization serving as a credible source and objective authority on issues related to nutrition and strengthening nutrition research and education in Canada.

Insurance / 335
If you are unable to solve your problem with your insurance agent or broker, contact your nearest Insurance Bureau of Canada (IBC) consumer inquiry centre or your provincial/territorial office.

CONSUMER GROUPS / 336

Canadian Toy Testing Council (CTTC) / 336
The Council promotes the design, production, and distribution of toys that meet the expectations of children and parents for function, durability, and play value. The Council annually publishes the *Toy Report* which contains testing results of over 1,600 toys.

Consumers' Association of Canada (CAC) / 336
The CAC is an independent, non-profit, volunteer organization committed to defending the rights of consumers. It protects consumers in the marketplace by lobbying government, business, and industry for standards and legislation.

Consumers Council of Canada (CCC) / 337
The CCC is a not-for-profit organization that aims to improve the marketplace for consumers through active cooperation with business, government, and special interest groups. The Board of Directors includes well-known national and international experts in the fields of consumer advocacy, policy development, and research.

One Voice — Seniors Network / 337
One Voice is a national, not-for-profit, voluntary, charitable organization promoting the enhancement of the status and independence of older Canadians. One Voice advocates policies and programs to improve the well-being of Canadian seniors and encourages and enables their full and active participation in decisions affecting their lives.

Public Interest Advocacy Centre (PIAC) / 337
PIAC is a registered charitable organization providing legal advice, representation, and specialized research on a non-profit basis to groups and individuals voicing public concern, and who would otherwise not have access to such services. The Centre has developed a reputation for providing effective advocacy in telecommunications, cable broadcasting, energy, transportation and privacy. Nine member organizations: Alberta Council on Aging, Canadian Pensioners Concerned, Consumers Fight Back Associations, Dying with Dignity, Manitoba Society of Seniors, One Voice — Seniors Network, Ontario Coalition of Senior Citizen Organizations, PEI Council of the Disabled, and Rural Dignity of Canada.

Quebec Consumer Protection Organizations / 337

ADDRESSES

GOVERNMENT OFFICES

Industry Canada

Office of Consumer Affairs
235 Queen Street, 9th Floor East
Ottawa, Ontario K1A 0H5
Fax: (613) 952-6927
Web site: consumerconnection.
ic.gc.ca

Industry Canada

Competition Bureau
50 Victoria Street
Hull, Quebec K1A 0C9
Tel: (819) 997-4282
Toll free: 1-800-348-5358
TDD: 1-800-642-3844
Fax: (819) 997-0324
Fax-on-demand: (819) 997-2869
Web site: competition.ic.gc.ca
(English); concurrence.ic.gc.ca
(French)
E-mail: compbureau@ic.gc.ca

British Columbia

Ministry of Attorney General
Community Justice Branch
Consumer Services Division
Consumer Services Head Office
5th floor, 1019 Wharf Street
Victoria, British Columbia
V8V 1X4
Tel: (250) 387-3045
Fax: (250) 953-3533

P.O. Box 9297 Station Prov Govt
Victoria, British Columbia
V8W 9J8
Tel: (250) 387-3045
Fax: (250) 953-3533

Investigations/Trade Practices:
(250) 387-5433 Motor Dealer
Licensing
(250) 387-1271 Cemetery &
Funeral Services
(250) 387-1627 Debt Collection
Investigations/Trade Practices:

4211 Kingsway, Suite 402
Burnaby, British Columbia
V5H 1Z6
Tel: (604) 660-3570
Investigations/Trade Practices
(604) 660-3540 Travel/Direct
Sellers
Fax: (604) 660-3521

100 Cranbrook Street North
Cranbrook, British Columbia
V1C 3P9
Tel: (250) 426-1497
Fax: (250) 426-1561

235 1st Avenue
Kamloops, British Columbia
V2C 3J4
Tel: (250) 828-4667
Fax: (250) 371-3822

1726 Dolphin Avenue
Kelowna, British Columbia
V1Y 9R9
Tel: (250) 717-2019
Fax: (250) 717-2021

1044 – 5th Avenue
Prince George, British Columbia
V2L 5M2
Tel: (250) 565-6030
Fax: (250) 565-6180
Web site: www.lcs.gov.bc.ca/cob/
cob.htm

Alberta

Alberta Government Services
Consumer Services Division
10155 – 102 Street, Floor 13
Edmonton, Alberta T5J 4L4
Tel: (780) 427-4088
Toll-free in Alberta 1-877-427-4088
Fax: (780) 422-9106
Web site: www.gov.ab.ca/gs

7015 Macleod Trail South
Room 301
Calgary, Alberta T2H 2K6
Tel: (403) 297-5700
Fax: (403) 297-6138

Saskatchewan

Consumer Protection Branch
Saskatchewan Department of
Justice
1871 Smith Street
Regina, Saskatchewan S4P 3V7
Tel: (306) 787-5550
1-888-374-4636 (in-province
use only)
Fax: (306) 787-9779

Manitoba

Consumers Bureau
Manitoba Consumer and
Corporate Affairs
302 – 258 Portage Avenue
Winnipeg, Manitoba R3C 0B6
Tel: (204) 945-38001-800-782-0067
Fax: (204) 945-0728
E-mail: consumersbureau@cca.
gov.mb.ca

Ontario

Ministry of Consumer and
Commercial Relations
General Inquiries Unit
250 Yonge Street, 35th floor
Toronto, Ontario M5B 2N5
Tel: (416) 326-8555
1-800-268-1142
Web site: www.ccr.gov.on.ca

Quebec

Office de la protection du
consommateur
400 Jean-Lesage Boulevard,
Room 450
Quebec, Québec G1K 8W4
Tel: (418) 643-1484
Fax: (418) 643-8686
Web site: www.opc.gouv.qc.ca

New Brunswick

Consumer Affairs Branch
Department of Justice
670 King Street, P.O. Box 6000
Fredericton, New Brunswick
E3B 5H1
Tel: (506) 453-2659
Fax: (506) 444-4494
Web site: www.gov.nb.ca/justice/
E-mail: al@gov.nb.ca

Nova Scotia

Nova Scotia Department of
Business and Consumer Services
P.O. Box 2502
Halifax, Nova Scotia B3J 3N5
Tel: 1-800-670-4357 or
(902) 424-5200
Fax: (902) 424-0720
Web site: www.gov.ns.ca/snsmr/
consumer/

Prince Edward Island

Consumer, Corporate and
Insurance Services
Department of Community
Services and Attorney General
95 Rochford Street, 4th Floor
P.O. Box 2000
Charlottetown, Prince Edward
Island C1A 7N8
Tel: (902) 368-4580
Toll free: 1-800-658-1799
Fax: (902) 368-5283
Web site: www.gov.pe.ca

Newfoundland and Labrador

Trade Practices & Licencing
Division
Department of Government
Services & Lands
2nd Floor
Confederation Building West
P.O. Box 8700
St. John's, Newfoundland
A1B 4J6
Tel: (709) 729-2600
Fax: (709) 729-3205

Government Service & Lands
McCurdy Complex
P.O. Box 222
Gander, Newfoundland
A1V 2N9
Tel: (709) 256-1019
Fax: (709) 256-1438

Government Service Centre
P.O. Box 2006
Corner Brook, Newfoundland
A2H 6J8
Tel: (709) 637-2445
Fax: (709) 637-2905

Yukon Territories

Department of Justice
Consumer Services Branch
P.O. Box 2703
Whitehorse, Yukon Y1A 2C6
Tel: (867) 667-5111
Fax: (867) 667-3609
E-mail: consumers@gov.yk.ca

The Andrew Philipson
Law Centre
2130 – 2nd Avenue
Whitehorse, Yukon Y1A 5C3
Tel: (867) 667-5111

Northwest Territories

Consumer Services
Community Operations
Programs
Municipal and Community
Affairs
Government of the Northwest
Territories
500 5201 – 50th Avenue
Yellowknife, Northwest Territories
X1A 3S9
Tel: (867) 873-7125
Fax: (867) 920-6343
Web site: www.maca.gov.nt.ca
E-mail: mgagnon@maca.gov.nt.ca

BETTER BUSINESS BUREAUS

Suite 350
7330 Fisher Street SE
Calgary, Alberta
T2H 2H8
Tel: (403) 531-8686
Fax: (403) 531-8697
Web site: www.bbb.org

British Columbia

BBB of Mainland British
Columbia
788 Beatty Street
Suite 404
Vancouver, British Columbia
V6B 2M1
Tel: (604) 682-2711
Fax: (604) 681-1544
Web site: www.bbbmbc.com
E-mail: www.bbbmbc.com

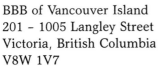

BBB of Vancouver Island
201 – 1005 Langley Street
Victoria, British Columbia
V8W 1V7
Tel: (250) 386-6348
Fax: (250) 386-2367
Web site: www.bbbvanisland.org/

Alberta

BBB of Southern Alberta
7330 Fisher Street SE
Suite 350
Calgary, Alberta T2H 2H8
Tel: (403) 531-8780
Fax: (403) 640-2514
Web site: www.southern
albertabbb.ab.ca
E-mail: bbbmail@cadvision.com

BBB Central & Northern Alberta
9707 110th Street, Suite 514
Edmonton, Alberta T5K 2L9
Tel: (780) 482-2341
Fax: (780) 482-1150
Web site: www.edmonton.bbb.org

Saskatchewan

BBB of Saskatchewan
2080 Broad Street
Suite 302
Regina, Saskatchewan S4P 1Y3
Tel: (306) 352-7601
Fax: (306)565-6236
Web site: www.saskatchewan.
bbb.org

Manitoba

BBB of Winnipeg & Manitoba
365 Hargrave Street
Room 301
Winnipeg, Manitoba R3B 2K3
Tel: (204) 989-9010
Fax: (204) 989-9016
Web site: www.manitoba.bbb.org

Ontario

BBB of Metropolitan Toronto
7777 Peel Street, Suite 210
Vaughn, Ontario L4K 1V7
Tel: (905) 761-0115
Web site: www.toronto.bbb.org

BBB of Mid-Western Ontario
35 Charles Street, East
Kitchener, Ontario N2G 4L5
Tel: (519) 579-3080
Fax: (519) 570-0072
Web site: www.bbbkitchener.on.ca/

BBB of Ottawa and Hull
The Varette Building
130 Albert Street
Suite 603
Ottawa, Ontario K1P 5G4
Tel: (613) 237-4856
Fax: (613) 237-4878
Web site: www.ottawa.bbb.org

BBB of South Central Ontario
100 King Street, East
Hamilton, Ontario I8N 1A8
Tel: (905) 526-1112
Fax: (905) 526-1225
Web site: www.hamilton.bbb.org

BBB Western Ontario
200 Queens Avenue
Suite 616
P.O. Box 2153
London, Ontario N6A 4E3
Tel: (519) 673-3222
Fax: (519) 673-5966
Web site: www.bbblondon.on.ca

BBB of Windsor & District
800 Ouellette Avenue
Windsor, Ontario N9A 5K6
Tel: (519) 258-7222
Fax: (519) 258-5905
Web site: www.wincom.net/wbbb/

Quebec

BBB of Montreal
2055 Peel Street, Suite 460
Montreal, Quebec H3A 1V4
Tel: (514) 286-9281
Fax: (514) 286-2658
Web site: www.montreal.bbb.org

Nova Scotia

BBB of Nova Scotia
1888 Brunswick Street, Suite 601
Halifax, Nova Scotia B3J 3J8
Tel: (902) 422-6581
Fax: (902) 429-6457
Web site: www.bbbns.com/

Newfoundland

BBB of Newfoundland and
Labrador
P.O. Box 360, Topsail Road
St. John's, Newfoundland
A1E 2B6
Tel: (709) 364-2222, 9:00–4:30
Fax: (709) 364-2255
Web site: www.newfoundland.
bbb.org

YOUR AUTOMOBILE

Manufacturers' Head Offices

Audi North America

3800 Hamlin Road
Auburn Hills, Michigan
48326 USA
Tel: 1-248-340-5000
Fax: 1-248-340-5140
Web site: www.audi.com

Chrysler

Chrysler Canada Customer
Service
P.O. Box 1621
Windsor, Ontario N9A 4H6
Toll free: 1-800-465-2001 (English)
Toll free: 1-800-387-9983 (French)
Web site: www.chryslercanada.ca

Ford

Ford Customer Assistance Centre
P.O. Box 2000
Oakville, Ontario L6J 5E4
Toll free: 1-800-565-3673
Web site: www.ford.ca

General Motors of Canada

Customer Service
1908 Colonel Sam Drive
Oshawa, Ontario L1H 8P7
Toll free: 1-800-263-3777 (English)
Toll free: 1-800-263-785(French)
1-800-263-3830 (TDD users)
Web site: www.gmcanada.com

Honda

Customer Service
715 Milner Avenue
Scarborough, Ontario M1B 2K8
Tel: (416) 299-3400
Web site: www.honda.com

Isuzu

Saturn-Saab-Isuzu Customer
Communications
1908 Colonel Sam Drive
Oshawa, Ontario L1H 8P7
Toll free: 1-800-263-1999
Web site: www.gmcanada.com

Mazda

Customer Service
305 Milner Avenue, Suite 400
Scarborough, Ontario M1V 2V2
Toll free: 1-800-263-4680
Web site: www.mazda.ca

Mercedes-Benz Canada Inc.

Customer Service
849 Eglinton Avenue East
Toronto, Ontario M4G 2L5
Tel: (416) 425-3550
Fax: (416) 423-5027
Web site: www.mercedes-benz.ca
E-mail: CAC@mercedes-benz.ca

Nissan
Satisfaction Centre
5290 Orbitor Drive
Mississauga, Ontario L4W 4Z5
Toll free: 1-800-387-0122
Web site: www.nissancanada.com

Saab
Saturn-Saab-Isuzu Customer
Communications
1908 Colonel Sam Drive
Oshawa, Ontario L1H 8P7
Toll free: 1-800-263-1999

Saturn
Saturn-Saab-Isuzu Customer
Communications
1908 Colonel Sam Drive
Oshawa, Ontario L1H 8P7
Toll free: 1-800-263-1999
Web site: www.gmcanada.com

Subaru
Customer Service
5990 Falbourne Street
Mississauga, Ontario L5R 3S7
Toll free: 1-800-876-4293
Web site: www.subaru.ca

Suzuki
American Suzuki Motor
Corporation
Automotive Customer Service
Head Quarters
Brea, California 92821 USA
Toll free: 1-800-650-4445
Web site: www.suzukiauto.com

Toyota
Customer Service
1 Toyota Place
Scarborough, Ontario M1H 1H9
Tel: (416) 438-8175 (Toronto)
Toll free: 1-800-263-7640
Fax: (416) 431-8035
Web site: www.toyota.ca

Volkswagon of North America
Customer Service
3800 Hamlin Road
Auburn Hills, Michigan
48326 USA
Toll free: 1-800-822-8987
Web site: www.vw.com

Volvo Cars of North America
Customer Service
7 Volvo Drive, P. O. Box 914
Rockleigh, New Jersey
07647 USA
Toll free: 1-800-458-1552
Web site: www.volvocars.com

*Automobile Protection
Association (APA)*
2 Carlton Street, Suite 1319
Toronto, Ontario M5B 1J3
Tel: (416) 204-1444
Fax: (416) 204-1985
Web site: www.apa.ca

292 St. Joseph Boulevard West
Montreal, Quebec H2V 2N7
Tel: (514) 272-5555
E-mail: apa1@cam.org

Dispute Resolution

*Canadian Motor Vehicle
Arbitration Plan (CAMVAP)*

British Columbia
Better Business Bureau of
Mainland BC
788 Beatty Street, Suite 404
Vancouver, British Columbia
V6B 2M1
Tel: (604) 682-6280 (Vancouver)
(604) 386-6347 (Victoria)
Toll free: 1-800-207-0685
Fax: (604) 681-1544
E-mail: bbbmail@bbbmbc.com

Yukon
Department of Justice
Consumer Services Branch
P.O. Box 2703
Whitehorse, Yukon Y1A 2C6
Tel: (867) 667-5111
Fax: (867) 667-3609
E-mail: consumers@gov.yk.ca

Alberta & Northwest Territories
Alberta Arbitration &
Mediation Services Inc.
110 Law Centre
University of Alberta
Edmonton, Alberta T6G 2H5
Tel: (780) 439-9359 (Edmonton)
Toll free: 1-800-207-0685
Fax: (780) 433-902

Saskatchewan
Better Business Bureau of
Saskatchewan Inc.
2080 Broad Street, Suite 302
Regina, Saskatchewan S4P 1Y3
Tel: (306) 352-7602 (Regina)
Toll free: 1-800-207-0685
Fax: (306) 565-6236

Manitoba
Better Business Bureau of
Winnipeg & Manitoba Inc.
365 Hargrave Street, Room 301
Winnipeg, Manitoba R3B 2K5
Tel: (204) 947-0637 (Winnipeg)
Toll free: 1-800-207-0685
Fax: (204) 943-1489

Ontario
O&P Services Inc.
595 Bay Street, Suite 300
Toronto, Ontario M5G 2C2
Tel: (416) 596-882 (Toronto)
Toll free: 1-800-207-0685
Fax: (416) 596-789

Atlantic Canada
Better Business Bureau of
Nova Scotia
1888 Brunswick Street, Suite 601
Halifax, Nova Scotia B3J 3J8
Tel: (902) 422-2230 (Halifax)
Toll free: 1-800-207-0685
Fax: 902-429-6457

Marketplace Standards & Services Branch, Consumer Services Bureau (Ontario)
Ministry of Consumer &
Industrial Relations
250 Yonge Street, 35th Floor
Toronto, Ontario M5B 2N5
Tel: 416-326-8600
Toll free: 1-800-268-1142

Alberta Motor Vehicle Industry Council (AMVIC)
Suite 303, 9945 – 50 Street
Edmonton, Alberta T6A 0L4
Tel.: (780) 446-1140
Toll free: 1-877-313-3833
Fax (780) 462-0633
Web site: www.amvic.org

Ontario Motor Vehicle Industry Council (OMVIC)
Suite 110, 36 York Mills Rd
North York, Ontario M2P2E9
Tel: (416) 326-8590
Toll free: 1-800-943-6002
Fax: 416-226-3208

Insurance Corporation of British Columbia (ICBC)
151 West Esplanade
North Vancouver, British
Columbia V7M 3H9
Tel: (604) 661-2800
Toll free: 1-800-663-3051
Fax: 604-661-2896

Consumer and Non-Governmental Groups

Automobile Protection Association

292 St. Joseph Boulevard West
Montreal, Quebec H2V 2N7
Tel: (514) 272-5555
Fax: (514)273-0797
Web site: www.apa.ca

2 Carleton Street, Suite 1319
Toronto, Ontario M5B 1J3
Tel: (416) 204-144
Fax: (416) 204-1985
Web site: www.apa.ca
Email: apa1@cam.org

Automobile Journalists Association of Canada

90 Burnhamthorpe Road West
Suite 1400
Mississauga, Ontario L5B 3C3
Tel: (416) 762-5388
Toll free: 1-800-361-1516
Web site: www.ajac.org

Automobile Associations

Canadian Automobile Association (CAA)
National Office
1145 Hunt Club Road, Suite 200
Ottawa, Ontario K1V 0Y3
Tel: (613) 247-0117 (Ottawa)
Fax: (613) 247-0118
Web site: www.caa.ca

British Columbia Automobile Association (BCAA)
4567 Canada Way
Burnaby, British Columbia
V5G 4T1
Tel: (604) 268-5000
Fax: (604) 268-5564

Alberta Motor Association (AMA)
10310 – 39th Avenue
Edmonton, Alberta T6T 6R7
Tel: (780) 430-5555
Toll free: 1-800-642-3810
Web site: www.ama.ab.ca/home.htm

Québec Canadian Automobile Association (CAA Quebec)
CAA Building
1180 Drummond Street
Montreal, Qubec H3G 2R7
Tel: (514) 861-5111
Fax: (514) 861-9896

New Brunswick
Canadian Automobile Association Maritimes
737 Rothesay Avenue
Saint John, New Brunswick
E2H 2H6
Tel: (506) 634-1400
Fax: (506) 653-9500

Government Offices

Transport Canada, Road Safety

2780 Sheffield Road
Ottawa, Ontario K1A 0N5
Tel: 1-800-333-0510
Web site: www.tc.gc.ca/road-safety/rsindx_e.htm (English);
www.tc.gc.ca/roadsafety/rsindx_f.htm (French)

Natural Resources Canada
Energy Efficiency Branch
580 Booth Street
Ottawa, Ontario K1A 0Z4
Tel: 613-995-0947
Fax: 613-943-8279
Web site: www.nrcan.gc.ca/

YOUR HOME

Canada Mortgage and Housing Corporation (CMHC)

National Office
700 Montreal Road
Ottawa, Ontario K1A 0P7
Tel: (613) 748-2000
Fax: (613) 748-2098
Web site: www.cmhc-schl.gc.ca

British Columbia and Yukon Business Centre
2600 Granville Street, Suite 400
Vancouver, British Columbia
V6H 3V7
Tel: (604) 731-5733
Fax: (604) 737-4139

Prairies and Northwest Territories Business Centre
708 11th Avenue Southwest
Suite 500
Calgary, Alberta T2R 0E4
Tel: (403) 515-3000
Fax: (403) 515-2130

Ontario Business Centre
100 Sheppard Avenue East
Suite 500
Toronto, Ontario M2N 6Z1
Tel: (416) 221-2642
Fax: (416) 218-3310

Quebec Business Centre
Place du Canada, 11th Floor
Montreal, Quebec H3B 2N2
Tel: (514) 283-4464
Fax: (514) 283-7595

Atlantic Business Centre
7001 Mumford Road, Halifax
Shopping Centre
Suite 300, Tower 1
Halifax, Nova Scotia B3L 2H8
Tel: (902) 426-3630
Fax: (902) 426-9991

Provincial Ministries of Departments of Housing

British Columbia
Ministry of Municipal Affairs
and Housing
P.O. Box 9491 Station Prov. Govt.
Victoria, British Columbia
V8W 9N7
Tel: (604) 387-7088
Fax: (604) 387-5120

Northwest Territories
Northwest Territories Housing
Corporation
Box 2100
Yellowknife, Northwest
Territories X1A 2P6
Tel: (867) 873-7898
Fax: (867) 669-7010

Yukon
Yukon Housing Corporation
410H – Jarvis Street
Whitehorse, Yukon Y1A 2H5
Tel: (867) 667-5759
Fax: (867) 667-3664
E-mail: cloverin@gov.yk.ca

Alberta
Seniors Housing
Alberta Community Development
16th floor, 10155 – 102 Street
Edmonton, Alberta T5J 4L4
Tel.: (780) 427-4190 (Edmonton)
(403) 297-4190 (Calgary)
Info. line: 1-800-642-3853

Saskatchewan
Saskatchewan Housing Division
Municipal Government
1855 Victoria Avenue
Regina, Saskatchewan S4P 3V7
Tel: (306) 787-4177
Toll free: 1-800-667-7567

Manitoba

Residential Tenancies Branch
302 – 25 Edmonton Street
Winnipeg, Manitoba R3C 3Y4
Tel: (204) 945-2476
Fax: (204) 945-6273

Ontario

Ministry of Municipal Affairs
and Housing
777 Bay Street, 17th Floor
Toronto, Ontario M5G 2E5
Tel: (416) 585-7000
Fax: (416) 585-6400
Web site: www.mah.gov.on.ca/
english.asp

Quebec

Ministère des Affaires
municipales, Quebec
20, Pierre-Olivier-Chauveau Street
Quebec City, Quebec G1R 4J3
Tel: (418) 691-2015
Web site: www.mam.gouv.qc.ca

Société d'habitation du Quebec
Direction des communications
1054, Louis-Alexandre-
Taschereau Street
Aile Conroy, 2nd floor
Quebec City, Quebec G1R 5E7
Tel: (418) 643-7676
Fax: (418) 643-4560
Toll free: 1-800-463-4315
Web site: www.shq.gouv.qc.ca

New Brunswick

Department of Municipalities,
Culture and Housing
P.O. Box 6000
Third Floor, Marysville Place
Fredericton, New Brunswick
E3B 5H1
Tel: (506) 453-2690
Fax: (506) 457-4991
Web site: www.gov.nb.ca/mch

Office of Chief Rentalsman
Department of Justice
P.O. Box 6000
Fredericton, New Brunswick
E3B 5H1
Tel: (506) 453-2682
Fax: (506) 444-4494

Nova Scotia

Department of Housing and
Municipal Affairs
P.O. Box 216
Halifax, Nova Scotia B3J 2M
Tel: (902) 424-4141
Fax: (902)424-0531
Web site: www.gov.ns.ca/snsmr/

Prince Edward Island

Residential Rental Property
Division
Island Regulatory and Appeals
Commission
134 Kent Street, P.O. Box 577
Charlottetown, Prince Edward
Island C1A 7L1
Tel: (902) 892-3501
Fax: (902)566-4076

Newfoundland

Newfoundland and Labrador
Housing Corporation
Department of Municipal and
Provincial Affairs
P.O. Box 220
St. John's, Newfoundland
A1C 5J2
Tel: (709) 724-3000
Fax: (709) 724-3250
Web site: www.nlhc.nf.ca/

New Home Warranty Programs

National Home Warranty
Edmonton: 1-800-472-9784
Calgary: 1-888-776-7707
Vancouver: 1-888-243-8807

Alberta New Home Warranty Program
201, 208 – 57th Avenue SW
Calgary, Alberta T2H 2K8
Tel: (403) 253-3636
(780) 484-0572 (Edmonton)
Toll free: 1-800-352-8240
Fax: (403) 253-5062
Web site: www.anhwp.com

Ontario New Home Warranty Program
5160 Yonge Street
6th Floor
North York, Ontario M2N 6L9
Tel: (416) 229-9200
Toll free: 1-800-668-0124
Fax: (416) 299-3800
Web site: www.newhome.on.ca

Atlantic Home Warranty Program
15 Oland Crescent
Halifax, Nova Scotia B3S 1C6
Tel: (902) 450-9000
Fax: (902) 450-5454
Toll free: 1-800-320-9880
Web site: www.ahwp.org

New Home Warranty Program of Saskatchewan
4 – 3012 Louise Street East
Saskatoon, Saskatchewan S7J 3L8
Tel: (306) 373-7833
Fax: (306) 373-7977

Guarantee plan for new residential buildings
La Régie du bâtiment du Quebec
545 Boulevard Crémazie East
Montreal, Quebec H2M 2V2
Web site: www.rbq.gouv.qc.ca/plan-de-garantie/anglais/index-an.html

Office of Energy Efficiency, Natural Resources Canada
580 Booth Street
Ottawa, Ontario
K1A 0Z4
Tel: (613) 995-0947
Fax: (613) 943-8279
Web site: www.nrcan.gc.ca

Ontario Energy Marketers Association
P. O. Box 490
Dutton, Ontario N0L 1J0
Toll free: 1-888-263-3742

Provinical Utility Corporations and Commissions

British Columbia
B.C. Hydro Customer Services
6911 Southpoint Drive
13th Floor
Burnaby, British Columbia
V3N 4X8
Tel: (604) 528-1600
Toll free: 1-800-663-0431

P. O. Box 9501
Vancouver, BC V6B 4N1
Tel: 1-800-663-0431
Energy Information Line
(604) 540-8883
Hydrofax (fax automated sys)
1-800-663-0431 (menu item #4)
Web site: www.bchydro.bc.ca

British Columbia Utilities
Commission
900 Howe Street, 6th Floor
Box 250
Vancouver, British Columbia
V6Z 2N3
Tel: (604) 660-4700
Toll free: 1-800-663-1385
Fax: (604) 660-1102

Alberta

Alberta Customer Service
TransAlta Utilities Corporation
TransAlta Corporation
P.O. Box 1550, Station M
Calgary, Alberta T2P 4P7
Customer Service: 1-800-667-2345
Energy Matters telephone
advisory service: 1-800-267-5300
Web site: www.transalta.com

Alberta Energy and Utilities Board
640 – 5th Avenue SW
Calgary, Alberta T2P 3G4
Tel: (403) 297-8311
Fax: (403) 297-7336
Web site: www.eub.gov.ab.ca

Saskatchewan

SaskPower
Customer Services
2025 Victoria Avenue
Regina, Saskatchewan S4P 0S1
Tel: (306) 566-2727
Toll free: 1-888-757-6937
For Emergencies and Power
Outages: 24-hours: 310-2220

SaskTel
Corporate Affairs
7th Floor
2121 Saskatchewan Drive
Regina, Saskatchewan S4P 3Y2
Tel: (306) 777-2067
Calling and Service Information
1-800-727-5835
1-800-667-8211 (Main)

SaskEnergy
1945 Hamilton Street
Regina, Saskatchewan S4P 2C7
Tel: (306) 777-9200
24 Hour Natural Gas
Emergency Services
Tel: (306) 777-9222

Manitoba

Manitoba Hydro
P.O. Box 815, 820 Taylor Avenue
Winnipeg, Manitoba R3C 2P4
Tel: (204) 474-3233
Fax: (204) 475-2452
Web site: www.hydro.mb.ca

Public Utilities Board
2nd Floor – 280 Smith Street
Winnipeg, Manitoba R3C 1K2
Tel: (204) 945-2638
Fax: (204) 945-2643
E-mail: publicutilities@cca.gov.
mb.ca

Ontario

Ontario Hydro
Customer Solutions
Central Ontario Office
301 Mulock Drive
Newmarket, Ontario L3Y 4X9
Tel: (905) 895-8605
Toll free: 1-888-664-9376
Fax: 905-895-0631
Web site: www.hydro.on.ca

Ontario Energy Board
Suite 2601, 2300 Yonge Street
P.O. Box 2319
Toronto, Ontario M4P 1E4
Tel: (416) 481-1967
Fax: (416) 440-7665

Quebec

Hydro-Quebec
800 place Victoria
2nd floor, suite 255
C.P. 001 Tour de la Bourse
Montreal, Quebec H4Z 1A2
Tel: (514) 289-2211
Fax: (514) 289-7168
Toll free: 1-800-363-3844
Web site: www.hydro.qc.ca

Régie de l'énergie
800 place Victoria
2nd floor, Suite 255
C.P. 001 Tour de la Bourse
Montreal, Quebec H4Z 1A2
Tel: (514) 873-2452
Toll free: 1-888-873-2452
Fax: (514) 873-2070
Web site: www.regie-energie.qc.ca

New Brunswick

New Brunswick Power
Box 2000, 515 King Street
Fredericton, New Brunswick
E3B 4X1
Tel: (506) 458-4444
Toll free: 1-800-663-6272
Fax: (506) 458-4706

Board of Commissioners of
Public Utilities
110 Charlotte Street, Box 5001
Saint John, New Brunswick
E2L 4Y9
Tel: (506) 658-2504

Nova Scotia

Nova Scotia Power
P.O. Box 910
Halifax, Nova Scotia B3J 2W5
Tel: (902) 428-6230
Toll free: 1-800-428-6230
Web site: www.nspower.ca

Utility and Review Board
P.O. Box 1692, 3rd Floor
1601 Lower Water Street
Postal Unit M
Halifax, Nova Scotia B3J 3S3
Tel: (902) 424-4448
Fax: (902) 424-3919

Prince Edward Island

Maritime Electric
P.O. Box 1328, 180 Kent Street
Charlottetown, Prince Edward
Island C1A 7N2
Tel: (902) 629-3799
Toll free: 1-800-670-1012
Fax: (902) 629-3630
Web site: www.maritimeelectric.
com

Island Regulatory and Appeals
Commission
13 Kent Street, Suite 501
P.O. Box 577
Charlottetown, Prince Edward
Island C1A 7L1
Tel: (902) 892-3501
Toll free: 1-800-501-6268
Fax: (902) 566-4076

Newfoundland

Newfoundland Power
P.O. Box 8910
St. John's, Newfoundland
A1B 3P6
Tel: (709) 737-5600
Fax: (709) 737-2903
Web site: www.nfpower.nf.ca

Newfoundland Public
Utilities Board
P.O. Box 21040
St. John's, Newfoundland
A1A 5B2
Tel: (709) 726-8600
Fax: (709) 729-2508

Northwest Territories

Northwest Territories Public
Utility Board
#203 – 62 Woodland Drive
Hay River, Northwest Territories
X0E 1G1
Tel: (867) 874-3944
Fax: (867) 874-3639
E-mail: pubhrv@cancom.net

Yukon
Yukon Utilities Board
P.O. Box 6070
#19 – 111 First Avenue
Whitehorse, Yukon Y1A 3N4
Tel: (867) 667-5058
Fax: (867) 667-5059
E-mail: yub@yknet.yk.ca

Professional Groups

Canadian Association of
Home Inspectors
National Headquarters
P.O. Box 507, 49 Reddick Road
Brighton, Ontario K0K 1H0
Tel: (613) 475-5699
Fax: (613) 475-1595

British Columbia: 1-800-610-5665

Alberta: 1-800-351-9993

Saskatchewan: (306) 751-0115

Ontario: (416) 256-0960

Toll free: 1-888-744-0244

Quebec: (514) 234-2104

Atlantic: (506) 862-8555

Canadian Real Estate
Association (CREA)
344 Slater Street, Suite 1600
Ottawa, Ontario K1R 7Y3
Tel: (613) 237-7111
Fax: (613) 234-2567

Saskatchewan Real Estate
Commission
231 Robin Crescent
Saskatoon, Saskatchewan
S7L 6M8
Tel: (306) 373-3350
Fax: (306) 373-5377

Real Estate Council of
Alberta (RECA)
2424 – 4 Street, S.W., Suite 340
Calgary, Alberta T2S 2T4
Tel: (403) 228-2954
Fax: (403) 228-3065
Toll free: 1-888-425-2754
Web site: www.reca.ab.ca
E-mail: recainfo@reca.ab.ca

YOUR MONEY

Helpful Numbers

Amex Bank of Canada
1-800-668-2639

Banca Commerciale Italiana
of Canada
1-800-263-5431

Bank of Montreal
(416) 927-6000
InfoService: 1-800-555-3000

The Bank of Nova Scotia
Scotiabank Information Line:
(416) 866-6161
(call to find out the number of
your local vice-president's office)

CIBC
Customer Care Centre:
(416) 980-2255
Toll free: 1-800-465-2255

Canadian Western Bank
1-888-874-8574

Citibank
1-800-387-9292

Hongkong Bank of Canada
Complaints & Enquiries Officer:
(613) 990-6011
Toll free: 1-800-343-1180

Laurentian Bank of Canada
(514) 522-6306
LBC-Assistance: 1-800-252-1846

National Bank of Canada
TelNat: 1-888-835-6281

Royal Bank of Canada
Solutions Centre:1-800-769-2540
(English); 1-800-769-2541 (French)

Toronto Dominion Bank
TD Access: 1-800-983-2265

Ombudsman

Canadian Banking Ombudsman

4950 Yonge Street
Suite 1602
North York, Ontario M2N 6K1
Tel: (416) 287-2877
Toll free: 1-888-451-4519
Fax: (416) 225-4722,
1-888-422-2865
E-mail: mail@bankingombudsman.
com

Your Bank's Ombudsman

AMEX Bank of Canada
101 McNabb Street
Markham, Ontario L3R 4H8
Tel: (905) 474-8233
Fax: (905) 479-2062

Bank of Montreal
Bank of Montreal Tower
55 Bloor Street West
8th Floor
Toronto, Ontario M4W 3N5
Tel: 1-800-371-2541
Fax: 1-800-766-8029

The Bank of Nova Scotia
Scotia Plaza
4 King Street West
Toronto, Ontario M5H 1H1
Tel: (416) 933-3299
Toll free: 1-800-785-8772
Fax: (416) 933-3276

CIBC
CIBC Ombudsman
P.O. Box 342, Commerce Court
Toronto, Ontario M5L 1G2
Tel: (416) 861-3313
Toll free: 1-800-308-6859
Fax: (416) 980-3754
Toll free: 1-800-308-6861

Canadian Western Bank
Suite 152
Royal Bank Building
10117 Jasper Avenue
Edmonton, Alberta T5J 1W8
Tel: 1-888-874-8574
Fax: (780) 428-9499

Citibank Canada
Citibank Place
123 Front Street West
Suite 1900
Toronto, Ontario M5J 2M3
Tel: 1-888-245-1112
Fax: (416) 947-4123

Hongkong Bank of Canada
Suite 500
885 West Georgia Street
Vancouver, British Columbia
V6C 3E9
Tel: 1-800-343-1180
Fax: (604) 641-2945

ING Direct
111 Gordon Baker Road
Suite 900
Toronto, Ontario M2H 3R1
Tel: 416-758-5241
Fax: (416) 758-5215

Laurentian Bank of Canada
130 Adelaide Street West
Suite 200
Toronto, Ontario M5H 3P5
Tel: 1-800-473-4782
Fax: (416) 865-5695

National Bank of Canada
P.O. Box 275
Montreal, Quebec H2Y 3G7

Small Business
Tel: (514) 394-6441
Fax: (514) 394-8012
Personal Banking
Tel: 1-888-300-900
Fax: 1-800-260-8003

Royal Bank of Canada
P.O. Box 1, Royal Bank Plaza
Toronto, Ontario M5J 2J5
Tel: (416) 974-4591
Toll free: 1-800-769-2542
Fax: (416) 974-6922

Toronto Dominion Bank
P.O. Box 1
Toronto Dominion Centre
Toronto, Ontario M5K 1A2
Tel: 1-888-361-0319
Fax: (416) 983-3460

Self and Government Regulation of Banks

Canadian Bankers Association (CBA)

Suite 3000
Commerce Court West
199 Bay Street, P. O. Box 348
Toronto, Ontario M5L 1G2
Tel: (416) 362-6092
Fax: (416) 362-7705
Toll free: 1-800-263-0231
Web site: www.cba.ca

Office of the Superintendent of Financial Institutions (OSFI)

National Headquarters
255 Albert Street
Ottawa, Ontario K1A 0H2
Tel: (613) 990-7788 (Ottawa)
Toll free: 1-800-385-8647

Trust Companies, Credit Unions, Co-operatives and Caisses Populaires

Canada Trust
National Customer Service Centre
1-800-668-8888

British Columbia
The Financial Institutions Commission (FICOM)
Suite 1900, 1050 W. Pender Street
Vancouver, British Columbia
V6E 3S7
Tel: (604) 660-2947
Fax: (604) 660-3170
Web site: www.fic.gov.bc.ca/cudic/#top

Deputy Superintendent of Credit Unions and Trust Companies
Ministry of Finance and Corporate Relations
1900 – 1050 West Pender Street
Vancouver, British Columbia
V6E 3S7
Tel: (604) 660-0138
Fax: (604) 660-3170

Northwest Territories
Security Registry
Department of Justice
5th Floor Court House
4903 – 49th Street
Yellowknife, Northwest Territories
X1A 2L9
Tel: (867) 920-3318
Fax: (867) 873-0243

Alberta
Alberta Treasury
Financial Institutions Division
Credit Unions
Room 402, 9515 – 107 Street
Edmonton, Alberta T8K 2C3
Tel: (780) 427-5064 ext. 222
Fax: (780) 422-2175

Credit Counselling Services
of Alberta
10011 – 109 Street, #804
Edmonton, Alberta T5J 3S8
Tel: (780) 423-5265

Credit Counselling Services
of Alberta
602 – 11th Avenue SW, #225
Calgary, Alberta T2R 1J8
Tel: (403) 265-2201
Toll free: 1-888-294-0076
Web site: www.creditcounselling.
com

Saskatchewan
Superintendent of Insurance,
Registrar of Credit Unions
Department of Justice
1871 Smith Street
Regina, Saskatchewan S4P 3V7
Tel: 1-888-374-4636
Toll free: (306) 787-5550
(Saskatchewan)
Fax: (306) 787-9779

Manitoba
Department of Consumer and
Corporate Affairs
315 – 258 Portage Avenue
Winnipeg, Manitoba R3C 0B6
Tel: (204) 945-2771
Fax: (204) 945-0728

Ontario
Credit Union and
Co-operative Branch
30th Floor
250 Yonge Street
Toronto, Ontario M5B 2N7
Tel: (416) 326-9300 (English)
(416) 326-9991 (French)
Fax: (416) 326-9313

Quebec
Inspecteur général des
institutions financières
Direction des services
administratifs
800, place D'Youville, 9e etage
Quebec, Quebec G1R 4Y5
Tel: (418) 528-9072
Web site: www.igif.gouv.qc.ca/
general/iplan.htm

Inspecteur général des
institutions financières
800, place d'Youville, 9e etage
Quebec, Quebec G1R 4Y5
Tel: (418) 528-9072

New Brunswick
Department of Justice
Credit Union, Co-operatives &
Trust Companies Branch
Centennial Building, Room G-70
P.O. Box 6000, 670 King Street
Fredericton, New Brunswick
E3B 5H1
Tel: (506) 453-2315
Fax: (506) 453-7474

Nova Scotia
Department of Business and
Consumer Services
9th Floor South
1505 Barrington Street
P.O. Box 2271
Halifax, Nova Scotia B3J 3C8
Tel: 1-800-670-4357 or
(902) 424-5200
Fax: (902) 424-0720

Prince Edward Island
Department of Community
Services and Attorney General
P.O. Box 2000, 4th Floor
Shaw Building
95 Rochford Street
Charlottetown, Prince Edward
Island C1A 7N8
Tel: (902) 368-4550
Fax: (902) 368-5283

Newfoundland
Commercial and Corporate
Affairs
Department of Government
Services and Lands Registrar of
Credit Unions and Chair of the
Credit Union Deposit Guarantee
Corporation Commercial and
Corporate Affairs Department of
Government Services and Lands
Confederation Building West
P.O. Box 8700
St. John's, Newfoundland
A1B 4J6
Tel: (709) 729-2571
Fax: (709) 729-4151

Securities

*Canadian Shareowners
Association (CSA)*

Suite 1317, 2 Carlton Street
Toronto, Ontario M5B 1J3
Tel: (416) 595-9600, ext. 0
Fax: (416) 595-0400
Web site: www.shareowner.ca

*The Investor Learning Centre
of Canada (ILC)*

Resource Centre
121 King Street West, Main Floor
Toronto, Ontario M5H 3T9
Tel: (416) 364-6666

*Investment Fund Institute of
Canada (IFIC)*

151 Yonge Street
5th Floor
Toronto, Ontario
M5C 2W7
Tel: 416-363-2158
Fax: 416-861-9937
Web site: www.mutfunds.com

*The Canadian Association of
Financial Planners (CAFP)*

439 University Avenue
Suite 1710
Toronto, Ontario
M5G 1Y8
Tel: (416) 593-6592
Toll free: 1-800-346-2237
Fax: (416) 593-8459
Web site: www.cafp.org

Securities Commisions

**British Columbia Securities
Commission**
Suite 200
865 Hornby Street
Vancouver, British Columbia
V6Z 2H4
Tel: (604) 899-6500
Toll free: 1-800-373-6393
Fax: (604) 899-6506
Web site: www.bcsc.bc.ca
E-mail: inquiries@bscs.bc.ca

**Alberta Securities
Commission**
19th Floor, Telus Plaza
North Tower
10025 Jasper Avenue
Edmonton, Alberta
T5J 3Z5
Tel: (780) 427-5201

Alberta Securities Commission
4th Floor, Alberta Stock Exchange Tower
300 – 5 Avenue South West
Calgary, Alberta T2P 3C4
Tel: (403) 297-6454

Saskatchewan Securities Commission
800 – 1920 Broad Street
Regina, Saskatchewan S4P 3V7
Tel: (306) 787-5645
Fax: (306) 787-5899

Manitoba Securities Commission
1128 – 405 Broadway Avenue
Winnipeg, Manitoba R3C 3L6
Tel: (204) 945-2548
Fax: (204) 945-0330

Ontario Securities Commission
Suite 800
Box 5520 Queen Street West
Toronto, Ontario M5H 3S8
Reception: (416) 597-0681
Inquiries: (416) 593-8314
Publications: (416) 593-8117
Fax: (416) 593-8122
Web site: www.osc.gov.on.ca
E-mail: inquiries@osc.gov.on.ca

Quebec Commission des valeurs mobilières du Quebec
800, Place Victoria
Tour de la Bourse
17th Floor
Montreal, Quebec H4Z 1G3
Tel: (514) 873-5326
Toll free: 1-800-361-5072
Web site: www.cvmq.com

New Brunswick Securities Commission
Department of Justice
P.O. Box 5001
Saint John, New Brunswick
E2L 4Y9
Tel: (506) 658-3060
Fax: (506) 658-3059

Nova Scotia Securities Commission
2nd Floor, Joseph Howe Building
1690 Hollis Street, P.O. Box 458
Halifax, Nova Scotia B3J 2P8
Tel: (902) 424-7768
Fax: (902) 424-4625

Prince Edward Island
Securities Section of Community Services and Attorney General
95 Rochford Street, P.O. Box 2000
Charlottetown, Prince Edward Island C1A 7N8
Tel: (902) 368-4550
Fax: (902) 368-5283

Newfoundland Securities Division
Department of Government Services and Lands
P.O. Box 8700
Confederation Building
Second Floor, West Block
St John's, Newfoundland A1B 4J6
Tel: (709) 729-4189
Fax: (709) 729-6187

Northwest Territories Securities Registry
Department of Justice
5th Floor Court House
4903 – 49th Street
Yellowknife, Northwest Territories X1A 2L9
Tel: (867) 920-3318
Fax: (867) 873-0243

YOUR HEALTH

Health Canada

Headquarters

General Enquiries
Address Locator 19128
Ottawa, Canada K1A 0K9
Tel: (613) 957-2991
Fax: (613) 941-5366
E-mail: info@www.hc-sc.gc.ca
Health Promotion Online:
www.hc-sc.gc.ca

Division of Aging and Seniors
Health Canada
Jeanne Mance Building, 8th Floor
Tunney's Pasture, A.L. #1908A1
Ottawa, Ontario K1A 1B4
Tel: (613) 952-7606
Fax: (613) 957-7627
Web site: www.hc-sc.gc.ca/
seniors-aines/index.htm

Regional Offices

British Columbia
Suite 405, Winch Building
757 West Hastings Street
Vancouver, British Columbia
V6C 1A1
Tel: (604) 666-2083
Fax: (604) 666-2258

Alberta
Suite 710, Canada Place
9700 Jasper Avenue
Edmonton, Alberta T5J 4C3
Tel: (780) 495-2651
Fax: (780) 495-3285

Manitoba
391 York Avenue, Suite 425
Winnipeg, Manitoba R3C 0P4
Tel: (204) 983-2508
Fax: (204) 983-3972

Ontario
25 St. Clair Avenue East
4th Floor
Toronto, Ontario M4T 1M2
Tel: (416) 973-4389
Fax: (416) 973-1423

Québec
200, Sainte-Foy
Quebec City, Quebec G1R 4X6
Tel: (418) 643-2673

Nova Scotia
Suite 702, Ralston Building
1557 Hollis Street
Halifax, Nova Scotia B3J 3V4
Tel: (902) 426-2038
Fax: (902) 426-3768

Prince Edward Island
Health Information Resource
Centre
1 Rochford Street, P.O. Box 2000
Charlottetown, Prince Edward
Island C1A 7N8
Tel: (902) 368-6526
Toll free: 1-800-241-6970

Provinical Departments and Ministries of Health

Northwest Territories
Department of Health and
Social Services
Box 1320
Yellowknife, Northwest Territories
X1A 2L9
Tel: (867) 920-6173
Fax: (867) 873-0266

British Columbia
Ministry of Health INFOline
Tel: (250) 952-1742
Toll free: 1-800-465-4911
Web site: www.hlth.gov.bc.ca

Office For Seniors
1st Floor – 1515 Blanshard Street
Victoria, British Columbia
V8W 3C8
Tel: (250) 952-1238
Fax: (250) 952-1159
E-mail: seniors@bcsco2.gov.bc.ca
Web site: www.hlth.gov.bc.ca/seniors

Alberta

10025 Jasper Avenue
Edmonton, Alberta T5J 1S6
Tel: (780) 427-1432
Fax: (780) 422-0102

727 – 7th Avenue S.W.
Main Floor
Calgary, Alberta T2P 0Z5
Tel: (403) 297-6411
Dial: 310-0000 anywhere else
in Alberta
E-mail: ahinform@health.gov.ab.ca
Web site: www.health.gov.ab.ca

Saskatchewan

Saskatchewan Health
3475 Albert Street
Regina, Saskatchewan S4S 6X6
Tel: (306) 787-3013
Fax: (306) 787-3823
Toll free: 1-800-667-7766
Web site: www.health.gov.sk.ca/

Ontario

INFOline
Toronto (416) 314-5518
Toll free: 1-800-268-1154
TTY 1-800-387-5559
E-mail: infomoh@gov.on.ca
Web site: www.gov.on.ca/health

Quebec

1075, Sainte-Foy
Quebec City, Quebec G1S 2M1
Tel: (418) 643-3380

New Brunswick

Department of Health and
Community Services
P.O. Box 5100, Carlton Place
7th Floor
Fredericton, New Brunswick
E3B 5G8
Tel: (506) 453-2536
General Inquiries: 1-888-762-8600
Fax: (506) 444-4697
Web site: www.gov.nb.ca/hcs
Seniors – General Inquiries
1-888-762-8600 (English)
1-888-762-8700 (French)
After Hours Emergency
Social Services
Fredericton: (506) 453-2145
Other areas: 1-800-442-9799

Nova Scotia

Nova Scotia Department of Health
1690 Hollis Street, P.O. Box 488
Halifax, Nova Scotia B3J 2R8
Toll free: 1-800-387-6665
TTY/TDD: 1-800-670-8888
Web site: www.gov.ns.ca/health

Canadian Food Inspection Agency

59 Camelot Drive
Nepean, Ontario K1A 0Y9
Tel: (613) 225-2342
Food Complaint Telephone Line:
1-800-701-2737
Fax: (613) 228-6634
Web site: www.cfia-acia.agr.ca

Consumer and Non-Governmental Groups

The Canadian Hard of Hearing Association (CHHA)

2435 Holly Lane, Suite 205
Ottawa, Ontario K1V 7P2

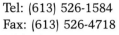

Tel: (613) 526-1584
Fax: (613) 526-4718
Web site: www.cyberus.ca/
~chhanational

Carrefour Adaption Quebec

360, du Pont, B.P. 1000
Quebec, Quebec G1K 6M6
Tel: (418) 522-1251
Fax: (418) 522-1252

*Office des personnes
handicapées du Quebec*

600, Fullum Street, Local 506
Montreal, Quebec H2K 3L6
Tel: (514) 873-3905
Toll free: 1-800-873-3905
Fax: (514) 873-4299

Dietitians of Canada

480 University Ave, Suite 604
Toronto, Ontario M5G 1V2
Tel: (416) 596-0857
Fax: (416) 596-0603
Web site: www.dietitians.ca

*National Institute of
Nutrition (NIN)*

265 Carling Avenue, Suite 302
Ottawa, Ontario K1S 2E1
Tel: (613) 235-3355
Fax: (613) 235-7032
Web site: www.nin.ca

Insurance

Insurance Bureau of Canada Head Office

151 Yonge Street, Suite 1800
Toronto, Ontario M5C 2W7
Tel: (416) 362-2031
Toll free: 1-800-387-2880
Fax: (416) 361-5952
Web site: www.ibc.ca

Life/Disability Insurance

Canadian Life & Health
Insurance Association Inc.
1 Queen Street East
Suite 1700
Toronto, Ontario M5C 2X9
Tel: 1-800-268-8099 or
(416) 777-2221
Fax: (416) 777-1895
Web site: www.clhia.ca

British Columbia and Yukon

409 Granville Street
Suite 550
Vancouver, British Columbia
V6C 1W9
Tel: (604) 684-3635. Beyond (604)
area, request call back
Fax: (604) 684-6235

Superintendent of Insurance
P.O. Box 2703
The Andrew Philipson Law
Centre
2130 – 2nd Avenue
Whitehorse, Yukon Y1A 2C6
Tel: (867) 667-5111
Fax: (867) 667-3609
E-mail: consumers@gov.yk.ca

Alberta

10080 Jasper Avenue
Suite 801
Edmonton, Alberta T5J 1V9
Tel: (780) 423-2212
Toll free: 1-800-232-7275
Fax: (780) 423-4796

Alberta Insurance Council
Suite 901
Toronto Dominion Tower
Edmonton Centre
Edmonton, Alberta T5J 2Z1
Tel: (780) 421-4148
Toll free: 1-800-461-3367

Saskatchewan, Manitoba, Northwest Territories

10080 Jasper Avenue
Suite 801
Edmonton, Alberta T5J 1V9
Tel: (780) 423-2212
Toll free: 1-800-377-6378
Fax: (780) 423-4796

For complaints against insurance companies:
Superintendent of Insurance
Consumer Protection Branch
Department of Justice
1871 Smith Street
Regina, Saskatchewan S4P 3V7
Tel: 1-888-374-4636
Toll free: (Saskatchewan) or
(306) 787-5550
Fax: (306) 787-9779

For complaints against agents/ brokers:
Saskatchewan General
Insurance Council
310 – 2631 28th Avenue
Regina, Saskatchewan S4S 6X3
Tel: (306) 347-0862
Fax: (306) 569-3018

Ontario

151 Yonge Street
Suite 1800
Toronto, Ontario M5C 2W7
Tel: (416) 362-9528
Toll free: 1-800-387-2880
Fax: (416) 362-2602

155 Queen Street
Suite 1208
Ottawa, Ontario K1P 6L1
Tel: (613) 236-5043
Fax: (613) 236-5208

Quebec

500 Sherbrooke Street West
Bureau 600
Montreal, Quebec H3A 3C6
Tel: (514) 288-1563
Toll free: 1-800-361-5131
Fax: (514) 288-0753

Prince Edward Island

Superintendent of Insurance
Department of Community
Services & Attorney General
95 Rochford Street, 4th Floor
P.O. Box 2000
Charlottetown, Prince Edward
Island C1A 7N8
Tel: (902) 368-4564
Fax: (902 368-5283

Atlantic Provinces

1969 Upper Water Street
Suite 1706
Halifax, Nova Scotia B3J 3R7
Tel: (902) 429-2730
Toll free: 1-800-565-7189
Fax: (902) 420-0157

CONSUMER GROUPS

Canadian Toy Testing Council (CTTC)

22 Antares Drive, Suite 102
Nepean, Ontario K2E 7Z6
Tel.: (613) 228-3155
Fax: (613) 228-3242
Web site: www.toy-testing.org

Consumers' Association of Canada (CAC)

307-267 O'Connor Street
Ottawa, Ontario K2P 1V3
Tel: (613) 238-2533
Fax: (613) 563-2254
E-mail: cacnational@sprint.ca
(General Information)

cacmembership@yahoo.com
(Membership)
cacliteracy@yahoo.com
(Consumer Literacy Program)
cacfoundation@yahoo.com
(CAC Foundation)

*Consumers Council of
Canada (CCC)*

14845 – 6 Yonge Street
Suite 149
Aurora, Ontario L4G 6H8
Tel: (905) 713-2740
Fax: (905) 713-2739
Web site: www.geocities.com/
WallStreet/ Floor/3105/
E-mail: cc@tvo.org

One Voice — Seniors Network

One Voice
350 Sparks Street, Suite 1005
Ottawa, Ontario K1R 7S8
Tel: (613) 238-7624
Fax: (613) 235-4497

*Public Interest Advocacy
Centre (PIAC)*

1 Nicholas Street, Suite 1204
Ottawa, Ontario K1N 7B7
Tel: (613) 562-4002
Fax: (613) 562-0007
Web site: www.piac.ca/
E-mail: piac@web.net

Quebec Consumer Protection Organizations

Association des consommateurs du Québec (ACQ)
3120 Masson Street, Suite 101
Montreal, Quebec H1Y X8
Tel: (514) 376-8517
Fax: (514) 376-1029

Coalition des association de consommateurs du Québec (CACQ)
4017 Notre-Dame West, Suite 102
Montreal, Quebec H4C 1R3
Tel: (514) 932-5577
Fax: (514)932-2602
E-mail: acefsom@consommateur.
qc.ca

Fédération des associations coopératives d'économie familiale (FACEF)
815 Laurier Avenue East
Montreal, Quebec H2J 1G2
Tel: (514) 271-7004
Fax: (514) 271-1036
E-mail: facef@cam.org

Action Réseau Consommateur (ARC)
1215 de la Visitation Street
Suite 103
Montreal, Quebec H2L 3B5
Tel: (514) 521-6820
Fax: (514) 521-0736
E-mail: action@total.net

Action-Alimentation, Carrefour d'éducation populaire
2356 Centre Street
Montreal, Quebec H3K 1J7
Tel: (514) 596-4444
Fax: (514) 596-4443

Abitibi-Téémiscamingue ACEF (FACEF)
3Gamble Street East, Suite 202
Rouyn-Noranda, Quebec J9X 3B7
Tel: (819) 764-3302
Fax: (819) 762-0543

Amiante-Beauce-Etchemins ACEF
37 Notre-Dame Street South
Thetford-Mines, Quebec G6G 1J1
Tel: (418) 338-4755
Fax: (418) 335-0850

Basses-Laurentides ACEF
42 Turgeon Street
Sainte Therese, Quebec
Tel: (514) 430-2228
Fax: (514) 435-7184

Bois-Francs ACEF
59 Monfrette Street
Suite 230
Victoriaville, Quebec G6P 1J8
Tel: (819) 752-5855
Fax: (819) 758-8270

Montréal East ACEF
2226, boul. Henri-Bourassa est
Suite 100
Montréal, Québec H2B 1T3
Tel.: (514) 384-2013
Fax: (514) 384-8911

Estrie ACEF (ARC)
187 Laurier Street
Suite 202
Sherbrooke, Quebec J1H 4Z4
Tel: (819) 563-8144
Fax: (819) 563-8235

Granby ACEF (ARC)
500 Guy Street
Granby, Quebec J2G 7J8
Tel: (514) 375-1443
Fax: (514) 372-1269

Grand-Portage ACEF (FCAEF)
553 Lafontaine Street
Riviere-du-Loup, Quebec
G5R 3C5
Tel: (418) 867-8545
Fax: (418) 862-6096

Haut Saint-Laurent ACEF
28 St-Paul Street
Suite 111
Valleyfield, Quebec J6S 4A8
Tel: (514) 371-3470
Fax: (514) 371-3425

Île-Jésus ACEF (FACEF)
111 des Laurentides Boulevard
Suite 101
Laval, Quebec H7G 2T2
Tel: (514) 662-9428

Lanaudière ACEF (FACEF)
200 de Salaberry Street, Suite 124
Joliette, Quebec J6E 4G1
Tel: (514) 756-1333
Fax: (514) 759-8749

Lévis-Lauzon ACEF (FACEF)
(South Shore of Quebec)
33 Carrier Street
Levis, Quebec G6V 5N5
Tel: (418) 835-6633
Fax: (418) 835-5818

Mauricie ACEF (FACEF)
27 Bureau Street
Trois-Rivières, Quebec G9A 2M7
Tel: (819) 378-7888
Fax: (819) 376-6351

Montreal North ACEF (FACEF)
7500 Chateaubriand Street
Montreal, Quebec H2R 2M1
Tel: (514) 277-7959
Fax: (514) 277-7730

Outaouais ACEF
109 Wright Street
Hull, Quebec J8X 2G7
Tel: (819) 770-4911
Fax: (819) 771-1769

Péninsule ACEF
158 Soucy Street, Suite 211
Matane, Quebec G4W 2E3
Tel: (418) 562-7645

Quebec ACEF
570 du Roi Street
Quebec City, Quebec G1K 2X2
Tel: (418) 522-1568
Fax: (418) 522-7023

Rimouski-Neigette & Mitis ACEF
12 Sainte-Marie Street, Suite 202
P.O. Box 504
Rimouski, Quebec G5K 2X2
Tel: (418) 723-0744
Fax: (418) 723-7972

South Shore ACEF (ARC)
18 Montcalm
Longueuil, Quebec J4J 2K6
Tel: (514) 677-6394
Fax: (514) 677-0101

Montréal South-West ACEF
4017 Notre-Dame Street West,
Suite 102
Montreal, Quebec H4C 1R3
Tel: (514) 932-5577
Fax: (514) 932-2602

Association des consomma-teurs pour la qualité dans la construction (ACQC)
2226 Henri-Bourassa Blvd.
Suite 100
Montreal, Quebec H2B 1T3
Tel: (514) 384-2013
Fax: (514) 384-8911

Association pour la protection des Automobilistes (APA)
292 St-Joseph Blvd. West
Montreal, Quebec H2B 1T3
Tel: (514) 272-5555
Fax: (514) 273-0797
Public line: (514) 272-5555

Association pour la protection des épargnants et des investisseurs du Québec (APEIQ)
737 Versailles Street
Montreal, Quebec H3C 1Z5
Tel: (514) 932-8921
Fax: (514) 932-9366

Association pour la protection des intérêts des consommateurs de la Côte-Nord (APIC)
86 de Puyjalon Street
Baie-Comeau, Quebec G5C 1N2
Tel: (418) 589-7324
Fax: (418) 589-7088

BBB of Montreal Inc.
2055 Peel Street
Suite 460
Montreal, Quebec H3A 1V4
Tel: (514) 286-1236
Fax: (514) 286-2568

Consumer Information Office
Laval University
Maurice-Pollack Pavillion
Suite 2208
Sainte-Foy, Quebec G1K 7P4
Tel: (418) 656-3548

Carrefour d'entraide Drummond Inc.
405 des Écoles Street
Drummondville, Quebec J2B 1J3
Tel: (819) 477-8105
Fax: (819) 477-7012

Centre d'information et de recherche en consommation de Charlevoix Ouest (CIRCCO)
3 Clarence-Gagnon Street
P.O. Box 183B
Baie-St-Paul, Quebec G0A 1B0
Tel: (418) 435-2884
Fax: (418) 435-5488

Centre populaire de Roberval
106 Marcoux Avenue
Roberval, Quebec G8H 1E7
Tel: (418) 275-4222
Fax: (418) 275-0099

Centre de recherche et d'information en consommation (CRIC)
3 des Pins Street
P.O. Box 204
Port-Cartier, Quebec G5B 2A5
Tel: (418) 766-3203
Fax: (418) 766-3312
E-mail: cricpc@bbsi.net

Groupe de recherche en animation et planification économique (GRAPE)
2235 de la Paix Street
Quebec City, Quebec G1L 3S8
Tel: (418) 522-7356
Fax: (418) 522-0845
**Please call before faxing any document.

Option Consommateurs
2120 Sherbrooke Street East
Suite 604
Montreal, Quebec H2K 1C3
Tel: (514) 598-7288
Fax: (514) 598-8511

Service d'aide aux consommateurs (SAC)
453 5th Street
Suite 1
Shawinigan, Quebec G9N 1E4
Public line: (819) 537-1414
Toll-free: 1-800-567-8552
Fax: (819) 537-5259

Service budgétaire et communautaire de Chicoutimi
2422 Roussel Street
Chicoutimi-Nord, Quebec G7G 1X6
Tel: (418) 549-7597
Fax: (418) 549-1325

Service budgétaire et communautaire de Jonquiere
3971 du Vieux Pont
P.O. Box 42
Jonquiere, Quebec G7X 7V8
Tel: (418) 542-8904
Fax: (418) 542-1424

Service budgétaire et communautaire d'Alma Inc.
415 Collard Street West
P.O. Box 594
Alma, Quebec G8B 5W1
Tel: (418) 668-2148

Service budgétaire populaire Dynamique
1230 Wallberg Boulevard
Suite 304
Dolbeau, Quebec G8L 1H2
Tel: (418) 276-1211

Service budgétaire populaire de l'Estrie Inc.
6 Wellington Street South
Suite 302
Sherbrooke, Quebec J1H 5C7
Tel: (819) 563-0535

Service budgétaire populaire de la MRC d'Asbestos
312 Morin Boulevard
Asbestos, Quebec J1T 3B9
Tel: (819) 879-4173

Service budgétaire populaire de St-Félicien Inc.
1211 Notre-Dame Street
Saint-Felicien, Quebec G8K 1Z9
Tel: (418) 679-4646
Fax: (418) 679-5902

CREDITS

Alert 14: Declaring Bankruptcy — a Last Resort (page 47)
Information collected and used with permission from Pat
Robinson Inc., Trustee in Bankruptcy, www.patrobinson.com
Alert 20: Buying a New Vehicle (page 67)
Alert 21: Buying Nearly New (page 70)
Information collected and used with permission from
articles published by Dennis DesRosiers.
Alert 57: Matchmaking — Magic or Misery? (page 177)
Information collected and used with permission from
Peter Crocker, *A Consumer's Guide to Dating and
Introduction Services in Ontario.*
Alert 74: Effective Complaining (page 226)
Sample letter on page 228 reproduced with the permission
of Industry Canada.
Alert 93: Small Claims Court (page 281)
The information on small claims court procedures is used
with permission from the Ministry of the Attorney
General of Ontario.
Contacts (pages 309-340)
Information reproduced with the permission of Industry
Canada.

INDEX

ABOUT THE AUTHOR

Pat Foran began work as a reporter in 1985 at Kitchener's CKCO and later joined ATV (Atlantic Television) in New Brunswick. In 1990 he was hired by CFTO in Toronto where, as a front line reporter, he filed the top stories of the day and also reported on national issues for *CTV National News*. He has interviewed the famous and infamous, including the likes of Wayne Gretzky, Sarah, the Duchess of York, prime ministers and premiers.

In 1998, Pat's career took a new direction when he was asked to create a unique segment to deal with consumer issues. Since then, Pat's *Consumer Alert* has become a popular component of *CFTO News*. His stories air on the number one rated newscast in Ontario and are also shown across the country on CTV's 24-hour network, *Newsnet*. Pat also brings his consumer expertise to a national audience as a regular guest on CTV's popular morning show *Canada AM*.

Recognized as one of Canada's leading consumer advocates, Pat is regularly asked to speak publicly on consumer and safety issues. He receives countless emails and faxes from loyal viewers thanking him for the information he provides.

He lives in Ajax, Ontario, with his wife and three daughters.

For additional information, check out the Web site at www.patforan.com.

How Much Is Enough?

0-07-088064-6
paperback
$24.99

**Allowances, Dollars
and Sense**

0-07-560929-0
paperback
$21.99

PERSONAL FINANCE
MADE EASY

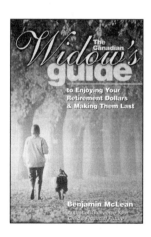

**The Canadian Guide to
Will and Estate Planning**

0-07-551740-X
paperback
$24.99

To Have and to Hold

0-07-087590-1
paperback
$24.99

**The Canadian Widow's
Guide to Enjoying Your
Retirement Dollars and
Making Them Last**

0-07-087399-2
paperback
$24.99